UNDEAD ENDS

UNDEAD ENDS

Stories of Apocalypse

S. TRIMBLE

RUTGERS UNIVERSITY PRESS
New Brunswick, Camden, and Newark, New Jersey, and London

Library of Congress Cataloging-in-Publication Data

Names: Trimble, S. (Sarah), author.
Title: Undead ends : stories of apocalypse / S. Trimble.
Description: New Brunswick : Rutgers University Press, 2019.
Identifiers: LCCN 2018035884 | ISBN 9780813593654 (cloth) | ISBN 9780813593647 (pbk.)
Subjects: LCSH: Apocalyptic films—United States—History and criticism. | Apocalyptic films—Great Britain—History and criticism. | Apocalypse in motion pictures. | BISAC: LITERARY CRITICISM / Caribbean & Latin American. | SOCIAL SCIENCE / Black Studies (Global). | SOCIAL SCIENCE / Feminism & Feminist Theory.
Classification: LCC PN1995.9.A64 T77 2019 | DDC 791.43/616—dc23
LC record available at https://lccn.loc.gov/2018035884

A British Cataloging-in-Publication record for this book is available from the British Library.

∞ The paper used in this publication meets the requirements of the American National Standard for Information Sciences—Permanence of Paper for Printed Library Materials, ANSI Z39.48-1992.

www.rutgersuniversitypress.org

Manufactured in the United States of America

For my family

CONTENTS

PREFACE

A friend once asked me why this book begins with *The Road*. We were writing together and I was wrestling with a draft of my first chapter, so she invited me to walk and talk. The problem with *The Road*, I tried to explain, is that it works hard not to notice how haunted it is. I have to bring in another story to crack it open. But while Toni Morrison's *Beloved* helps me get at the ghosts *The Road* can't admit, reading the two together prompts methodological questions that, at the time, I was struggling to think through. And that brought my friend to a question of her own: Why is it important for you to start with this film? The answer took months to arrive. Finally I realized that of all the characters in the films I explore, the unnamed boy in *The Road* is the one whose predicament feels most familiar to me. He's caught between parental perspectives that locate hope and horror in different places, which means he's negotiating two very different ways of seeing The End. And that's something I understand. So I start with *The Road* because if I have an avatar in this book, it's him. Before we get to his story, then, here's one of mine.

As 1999 drew to a close, I was finishing high school and my dad was preparing for Y2K. In anticipation of disruptions to our digitized, networked society, the nooks and crannies of our wide white bungalow were stuffed with bulk goods. Closets held boxes of mac and cheese, canned tuna, bottled water, acetaminophen. Plastic fifty-five-gallon drums of gasoline were stacked behind an aluminum shed in the corner of our backyard. Gold and silver bars were on hand, too, though I preferred not to know where they were stashed. They made me uneasy, as if their presence alone conjured cutthroats and marauders. The blue barrels of gasoline had a similar effect on my mom, who laid awake at night imagining explosions ripping through the dark. But these things represented security to my dad. If our computerized world went on the fritz when the clocks ticked into a new century, we'd have a little store of food, water, fuel, and currency to get us through the disorder. And when the dust settled—when the frailty of the global economy and the impotence of big government had been exposed—we might even be free to pursue a simpler way of life.

My mom wasn't so keen on any of this. Where my dad saw a fresh start emerging from the ruined world, a chance to reinvent himself even, my mom saw the dystopian underbelly of this fantasy. She didn't share my dad's belief that the end was nigh. But if widespread collapse ever did occur, she was pretty sure she knew what would happen: men with guns would reclaim the world. A feminist and a film buff, her view of The End was refracted through the hopelessness of *On the Beach* (1959), the sexual violence of *Mad Max* (1979), the woman who becomes dinner in *A Boy and His Dog* (1975). So while my dad saw Y2K as potentially clearing the way for a renewed sense of personal and familial autonomy, my mom was asking some complicated questions. If able-bodied men are the model survivors, what does that mean for the rest of us? What will we do with our supplies if our neighbors don't have any? And more starkly: Do we really want to stick around if everything goes to shit?

For a long time I resisted putting my parents at the beginning of this book. A survivalist and a feminist gearing up for Y2K sounds like the beginning of a (probably bad) joke. But these are the competing ways of seeing The End that I've inherited. One imagines apocalypse as the condition of possibility for personal and social renewal. The other sees it as deepening the vulnerability of those who are already precarious. I lived with these perspectives when end-times talk was everywhere, from Christian prophecy to conspiracy theory to the science fiction noir of *Strange Days* (1995) and *12 Monkeys* (1995). Looking back, I realize my family has helped me see the humanness of the characters I consider in this book—even, and maybe especially, the ones whose worldviews I find troubling. The unnamed man in *The Road* might be driven by what I call a logic of chosenness, a sense of himself and his kid as more worthy of survival than everyone else they meet, but that doesn't make him a bad man. He's terrified. And the story he tells himself, the one that turns his child into a little god, is the only thing keeping that terror at bay. Similarly, his wife, the woman who kills herself and dreams of taking her child with her, isn't unhinged so much as she's stuck. She can't get on board with her husband's story but struggles to invent another one. So she calls it quits because, well, does she really want to stick around when everything's gone to shit?

None of this was on my radar in 1999. I just knew that I was—and am—enthralled by cinematic depictions of The End. I always see more than one story unfolding in these films. And only when I became curious about this as a graduate student did I realize my family might have something to do with it. This led me to investigate visions of apocalypse that archive the fantasies and nightmares that animate, specifically, the white patriarchal family form: the futures in which white families invest, the pasts we forget, the horrors we disavow, the monsters we make. That "we," in this instance, signals my place in this imaginary. I'm a white person who grew up in a white family on a mostly white suburban street. I was raised on a media landscape dominated by stories in which I could roughly recognize my own family. But I was also a queer kid who didn't do gender in the expected ways—a misfit who usually looked askance at the heroes and futures offered up by the films that fascinated me. Over time, then, I've become attuned to the hidden costs of white kinship structures and white family stories. *The Road* tries to sidestep those costs. So I start there because it pushed me to feel around for the cracks and question marks in a story that felt weirdly familiar. It's an awfully grim tale, yes, but it's the one that brought this project home to me.

Undead Ends is more about invention than critique. The introduction outlines how I see myself as both critic and storyteller, poking at the limits of the filmic imaginary to push the story past it. I play with adaptations, discarded endings, genre conventions, and casting choices to imagine new worlds in which more of us might feel more at home. Because the "we" I invoke throughout this book isn't the same as the one I used above—the one that speaks of white people and the stories we tell. The "we" I conjure here seeks to make room for the many of us who, in different ways for different reasons and to different degrees, live with the costs of the world as it is. It's for those of us who are surviving otherwise and imagining something else.

UNDEAD ENDS

INTRODUCTION
Storytelling and Survival

In the rippling plains of Kansas, about thirty miles from Salina, luxury condos plunge fifteen stories into the earth. Until 1965 this former silo housed an Atlas missile. Now it's the first phase of the Survival Condo Project: private apartments in which as many as seventy people can live off-grid for five years in the wake of disaster. An elevator glides into the earth, opening along the way onto condo doors with biometric locking systems. And behind those doors is up to eighteen hundred square feet—three million dollars' worth—of bunker living space: three bedrooms, two bathrooms, stainless steel appliances, a Jacuzzi tub. "Simulated view" windows show the big Kansas sky above, a wind turbine turning in the distance. The apparatus around these living spaces includes a hydroponic food program, diesel generators, and "military-grade security." Near the armory, there's "a bare-walled room with a toilet" where misbehaving residents can be sent for "'an adult time-out.'"[1] Maybe this little room is forgotten by those who buy into the project. Maybe they focus on the pool, the movie theater, the Astroturf dog park. But the image stays with me . . . makes me wonder who'd be sent for a time-out, under what circumstances, for how long, and on whose orders. The devil, they say, is in the details.

When it comes to visions of survival, some of us see danger where others see security; some of us locate terror right where others are pinning their hopes for the future. In this book I wonder about how we imagine survival, even as that "we" strains in different directions. *Undead Ends* considers visions of apocalypse as sites of interpretive struggle. What, exactly, is ending? Who dreams of starting over in the ruins? Who gets recruited into rebuilding projects, and at what cost? And what about those of us who are seen as unrecruitable, unfit for a new beginning? I explore these questions by thinking with some of the world-ending scenarios that exploded into American and British cinemas in the first decades of the twenty-first century. While the active pursuit of off-grid survival isn't exactly mainstream (yet?), popular film offers a well-funded, widely distributed archive of imaginings of The End. Most of the films I consider—*The Road* (U.S. 2009), *I Am Legend*

(U.S. 2007), *28 Days Later* (U.K. 2002) and *28 Weeks Later* (U.K. 2007), and *Children of Men* (U.K. 2006)—all saw significant global distribution and box office success, with *Legend* standing out as a proper blockbuster. And while *Beasts of the Southern Wild* (U.S. 2012) had only a limited theatrical release, it was a darling of the festival circuit and received four Academy Award nominations. These are films that millions of people discussed, reviewed, and argued about. Some of us might identify with one or more of the protagonists they offer—the dying white father in *The Road*, the pregnant black refugee in *Children*—and some of us might see ourselves, too, in the scenes of panic, lockdown, and quarantine that haunt those protagonists' worlds. These films are teeming with sight lines, which means that none of them is telling a single, stable story.

What we see and fail to see in ruined worlds is informed by a late capitalist moment in which speculating on devastated landscapes—mastering their meaning—can be a profitable exercise. Part of the context in which this book was written is that combination of economic deregulation, government restructuring, and globalization usually called neoliberalism. As thinkers from David Harvey to Naomi Klein to Stuart Hall have shown, neoliberalism promises freedom but makes disaster. And it needs the disasters it makes. Harvey (2007) understands it as a process of "creative destruction," of dismantling institutions and narratives that aim at a more democratic society and replacing them, piece by piece, with a vision of freedom as economic opportunity. And Stuart Hall, Doreen Massey, and Michael Rustin (2013) have outlined how, when this unleashing of the market generates financial crisis as it did in 2007–2008, the crisis paradoxically becomes justification for a further reshaping of state and society on the model of the market. This is the rhythm of what Naomi Klein (2007) calls "disaster capitalism." But since neoliberalism creates and then capitalizes on disaster, its advocates need to control the narratives that circulate about sites of ruin. Because from the bankrupt streets of Detroit to ashen Grenfell Tower in London, ruins might expose the violence undergirding the neoliberal notion of freedom as free markets.

Neoliberalism reproduces itself, in spite of the mounting failures of its economic policies, by telling emotionally persuasive stories about disaster and survival. These stories invite us to forget the violence that generates ruined landscapes and see them, instead, as freedom-in-the-making; as new frontiers ripe for reinvestment. Recasting aftermath as opportunity, neoliberal storytelling scripts its subjects as enterprising, scrappy—poised to capitalize on fresh new zones of competition because we think and act and feel and fashion ourselves in ways that befit survival. Because we make good choices. In the face of spreading precariousness, we're offered the (seemingly) comforting illusion that our survival is in our own hands; and, moreover, that our persistence is disconnected from the fact that others are struggling against very steep odds. Judith Butler describes neoliberal rationality as pivoting on the "fantasy of the individual capable of undertaking entrepreneurial self-making under conditions of accelerating precarity, if not destitution." And according to this fantasy, "we are each responsible only for ourselves, and certainly not for others" (2015, 16, 14). Like the well-heeled survivalists who've bought into that bunker in Kansas, good neoliberal subjects earn their security through preparedness and gumption. They owe nothing to those who must—or choose to—stay on the surface, riding out the storm.

In *Undead Ends,* I argue that contemporary apocalypse films offer an occasion to intervene in neoliberal storytelling. At the heart of this claim is the conviction that stories make and remake worlds. My approach is indebted to black feminist and postcolonial thinkers for whom stories are both technologies of survival and sites of political struggle. I'm especially inspired by Sylvia Wynter, whose work on the "invention of Man" shapes much of this book (2003, 263). For Wynter, Man is a figure that emerges from Western ways of narrating humanness that began to take shape with the epistemological upheavals of the Renaissance—when the stories Europeans told about themselves and their place in the cosmos underwent fundamental shifts. As the Christian tale of humanness gave way first to a vision of the human as rational (Man1) and then to a "biocentric" vision of the human as a living organism imperiled by natural scarcity (Man2), the figure of Man took shape in relation to Others imagined as exploitable and/or killable (2003, 267). So this new story of humanness—a story that derives from a particular perspective but passes itself off as universal—established the colonial coordinates of an emergent capitalism. All of this prompts Wynter to put forward what, in a 2006 interview, she calls a "heresy": "that capitalism itself is a function of the reproduction of 'Man'" (Thomas 2006, 29–30). In other words, as part of a larger quarrel with the more economically deterministic forms of Marxism, Wynter proposes that global capitalism is underpinned and regenerated by an origin story that tells us what it means to be human.[2] This insight prompts me to approach neoliberal storytelling via its protagonist: Man2 is the figure that Wynter calls *homo oeconomicus,* or "optimally economic Man" (2003, 314). Economic Man defines good humanness in terms of economic productivity and security: jobholder, breadwinner, masterer of natural scarcity. And because this figure has been centuries in the making, it exposes the long colonial roots of a worldview premised on relentless accumulation.

By focusing on economic Man, a figure that both animates and exceeds the neoliberal "now," I emphasize the changeability of neoliberal storytelling. I'm methodologically inspired by cultural theorist Stuart Hall, whose work shows how stories are thick with linkages—chains of meaning—that open onto other times and storylines. For Hall, the ideological thrust of any given representation is a question of articulation: it derives from the contingent links that form between ideas and, in turn, between those linked ideas and the subjects for whom they make sense. Hall's theory of articulation offers an understanding of neoliberal ideology as composed of many moving parts—as having joints where, for example, a bit of nineteenth-century American frontier ideology meets a piece of 1980s family values discourse; or where a critique of the British welfare state hinges on a moral panic about youth subcultures, which finds expression, too, in the rhetoric of a civilizing mission. Such links, Hall argues, are "nonnecessary" (2016, 122). This means both that neoliberalism is a mutable set of ideas and that its joints might, under narrative pressure, bend in unexpected directions. They might even be rearticulated to tell a surprising story.[3] So in this book I attend to how popular visions of apocalypse negotiate Man's endgame. I'm alert to how some films enact an eleventh-hour revival of economic Man just when he seems to be on the verge of extinction. *The Road*, for instance, splits its scavenger protagonist away from his cannibalistic Others, affirming Man's goodness despite the fact that his ways of practicing humanness have become obsolete. But even *The Road* is haunted by the possibility of radical rearticulations: story-places that might unveil its vision of The End of the world as, more precisely, the end of Man's world.[4]

Imagining the end of Man's world—an imagining often organized by the trope of the Last Man—can unlock the revolutionary narratives that spring from what Wynter calls "demonic grounds."[5] Encrypted in every telling of Man's story, Wynter argues, are foreclosed narrative "slots" that index alien worldviews (1990, 364). These slots are inhabited by those whose perspectives on the world unsettle a dominant narrative that casts them as Man's Others—those who are "demonic" in a dual sense: both theologically damned and mathematically unpredictable. For Wynter, demonic grounds are the story-places inhabited by women of color; narrative slots where a worldview shaped by experiences of sustained marginalization might infiltrate the story of Man, twisting it in unexpected directions. So *Undead Ends* tracks the gravitational pull of demonic grounds within stories of apocalypse. Often I focus directly on black women characters in the films I explore, but I attend, too, to the young people and white women—particularly mothers—who exist in the vicinity of these storytelling disturbances. This isn't about identity as much as it's about the "grammars" that order Man's world, informing what kinds of stories can be told and what kinds of subjects—and futures—can emerge.[6] Black women, white mothers, and children are typically relegated to the narrative margins of apocalypse films. They're characters whose ways of looking, knowing, acting, and feeling usually complicate the worldview mapped out by the Last Man—the figure that, as I elaborate in the section on genre below, orients audiences to an undone world. As a trope, the Last Man tends to hew close to the figure of economic Man, often deriving his authority from patriarchal white masculinity and its colonial coding as benevolent, capable, father-knows-best. Like Major Henry West, the rogue military man in *28 Days Later* who promises to secure women for his soldiers, the patriarchal survivalist needs Others to begin the world again. So he seeks to manage them by recruiting them into a familiar story that authorizes a familiar set of imperatives: claim territory, annihilate threats, hoard resources, and gain access to reproductive labor. But tropes change as genres evolve. And *28 Days* is a case in point. The white patriarch, Henry West, becomes a source of horror. And the other character in the film who functions as a kind of Last Man—Jim, the first survivor we meet—is actually, in the end, "closer to a Final Girl" (Mafe 2018, 30).[7]

As apocalypse films trouble the trope of the Last Man, they also tend to become emotionally unruly so that terror, despair, love, and hope spring up in unexpected places. So I read affectively, looking and listening for feelings that encode ambivalence about the end of Man's world—feelings that index radical, sometimes impossible desires that open the story up to rearticulation. In this my approach is indebted to postcolonial and psychoanalytic thinker Dina Georgis, for whom every story is haunted by feelings it can't admit. For Georgis—and for me—we narrate to survive, inventing stories that make it possible to go on living in the wake of hurt, despair, and dispossession. Sometimes we cling to even the most costly of these tales, guarding them against revision because of the security and consolation they provide. But when we see a story from the perspective of those who bear its costs, we might begin to discern the narrative presence of what Georgis describes as "queer affect." Queer affect "haunts and disquiets and refuses endings" (2013, 11). It registers unsettlement with the tale we've been offered, attuning us to our ambivalence about the security it affords so that we might risk unraveling the story, along with the self it holds together, enough to revise both. By attending to the Others who navigate postapocalyptic worlds, I notice how queer affect loosens Man's grip on the filmic imaginary. And in the process it agitates for the telling of what Georgis calls a "better story."

I think many of us are ambivalent about pop culture visions of The End. We're intrigued by the ways they imagine the catastrophic consequences of processes we recognize—and drawn to the possibility of critique that such imagining affords. But old forms of violence resurface in postapocalyptic worlds. So sometimes—often—these cinematic stories seem oriented toward familiar futures in which, to borrow a line from Audre Lorde, "we were never meant to survive."[8] Maybe I'm taking liberties with Lorde's "we," mobilizing a black lesbian feminist voice as a white nonbinary queer writing a book that's preoccupied, at least in part, with the white family stories that still dominate popular film in the United States and Britain. But the stories white people tell about families and futures are a key site where descriptions of the human as Man are reproduced. So these stories are part of the terrain of struggle identified by Wynter—a narrative terrain on which to destabilize Man and work toward imaginaries that foster, as she puts it, "the well-being, and therefore the full cognitive and behavioral autonomy of the human species itself/ourselves" (2003, 260). This is the messy, multivalent "we" I have in mind throughout this book. It reaches for the many of us who are cast by Man's story as deviantly human, though recognizing that we're differently enmeshed in the world made by this tale. The stakes of telling a better story might not be the same for me as they are for you. You might not always feel at home in the "we" I'm conjuring here. I don't always feel at home in it either. But the crafting of a contestable, alterable, as yet unimagined "we" is exactly what's at stake in visions of The End.

STORY, OR, REBIRTH

At the end of this book is a human called Hushpuppy—a genderqueer black girl who lives with her sick dad on an island that's sinking into the Gulf of Mexico. Benh Zeitlin's *Beasts of the Southern Wild* (U.S. 2012) isn't an apocalypse film in the usual sense. It's about a community of outsiders surviving the destructiveness of an unsustainable modern world. On Isle de Charles Doucet—or, to its residents, The Bathtub—the violence of economic dispossession and climate change takes the form of rising waters, a gathering storm. And in this context, Hushpuppy tells us, "I'm recording my story for the scientists in the future. In a million years, when kids go to school, they gonna know: once there was a Hushpuppy, and she lived with her daddy in The Bathtub." So this book is headed toward a child with a story to tell—a kid who, in the midst of disaster, conjures a future in which her life story will be a source of insight. I imagine Hushpuppy's scientists as engaged in what Wynter, following Aimé Césaire, calls a Science of the Word. Wynter agitates for ways of making knowledge that begin with the stories we tell and work out, from there, to our biological lives and the material worlds we navigate. In other words, I see Hushpuppy as anticipating a science adequate to the entanglements of world and story. That's where *Undead Ends* is going. So I begin with the world-making force of storytelling.

Story, Georgis writes, is "the principle of freedom" (2013, 2). Our stories shape our sense of who and what we are by knitting us into the histories through which we came to be here, now. In turn, we have the capacity to expand and rewrite our stories—to live them otherwise so that new, if forever-receding endings come into view. Putting it differently, story is the mechanism of rebirth. This is an insight shared among Georgis, Wynter, and Hannah Arendt. This section puts the latter two into conversation to explore how storytelling both underpins the world as it is and conjures new possible worlds at every turn. Admittedly, though Arendt and Wynter are both interdisciplinary thinkers with shared interests—humanness, freedom, terror, story—they also make strange bedfellows. Arendt's thinking about blackness, especially in the context of revolution and revolt, is often myopic. As David Scott points out, Arendt's "complete elision" of the Haitian Revolution in 1963's *On Revolution* is disappointing, especially given that one of her concerns in that book is the role of remembrance in preserving the revolutionary spirit (2004, 217). But, as Scott also observes in his critical and appreciative discussion, "if in all the conventionally recognizable ways Arendt was a Eurocentric, this is not all that she was" (219). In some ways what follows is an exercise in, to borrow Butler's description, "push[ing] against Hannah Arendt even as I draw upon her resources" (2015, 75). I'm indebted to those, including Butler, who have explored the limits of Arendt's ideas about race, gender, and embodiment.[9] Keeping these insights in mind, I consider how Arendt arrives at what she calls the principle of natality and how this idea complicates the public/private distinction that structures—and often constrains—her thinking. I propose that natality points to a feedback loop in which new (life) stories potentially mutate the dominant story that shapes the world into which we're born. So while neoliberal ideology secures its subjects by offering persuasive, seemingly coherent stories about freedom and survival, storytelling is also the Achilles' heel of ideological thinking. Tropes take on a life of their own. Meanings mutate. Readers read. And story, Georgis, Wynter, and Arendt all agree, is the basis of a conception of freedom that has nothing to do with free markets.

Wynter and Arendt offer complementary accounts of the human in which freedom is grounded in our storytelling activities. For Wynter, humans are born into the world as biological, flesh-and-blood organisms and then reborn into origin stories, narratives projected behind us to stabilize the "we" we say we are. The origin story provides what Wynter calls a "master code of symbolic life/death" that indicates which ways of being in the world are viable and, conversely, which ones are deadly (2003, 272). Feelings that estrange us from the story of "we" seem like they threaten our very survival, but the fact that "we" emerge through story means the terms of belonging are changeable. Arendt, too, is attentive to the alterability of our shared world, a quality she links to the rhythm of intergenerational time—to what she describes as the "onslaught with which each new generation must insert itself" into a preexisting common world (1958, 191). Like Wynter, Arendt sees our arrival into the world as a two-stage process in which the "naked fact" of birth is followed by rebirth into a collective (177). Even as newcomers are recruited into an existing narrative, Arendt argues that we generate new stories by inserting ourselves into what she calls "the space of appearance," a relational scene modeled on her understanding of the ancient Greek polis as "the organization of the people as it arises out of acting and speaking together" (198). What we say and do in this public context, she argues, coalesces into the "stuff" of a unique life story that can only be told by others. So we insert ourselves into an "already existing web of human relationships," disclosing something of our uniqueness to those around us so that the story we live unfolds into and alongside the life stories of others (184). The plurality of humans composing this "web" means the reverberations incited by our activities are unpredictable. This is why our actions are free—free, even, of our own intentions and desires. It's also why, as Butler puts it, freedom for Arendt should be "understood not as an individual act but as a plural action" (2015, 112). Even in times when the formal political scene has atrophied, a web of life stories and storytellers preserves the possibility of politics—and of revolutionizing our sense of "we."[10]

For both Wynter and Arendt, this understanding of human freedom as activated by story is also why the figure of Man is politically dangerous. Wynter's work shows that Man's story suppresses a key insight: humans author stories of humanness. Economic Man is the protagonist of a story that tells us how to live well, the truth of which seems to be, in Wynter's terms, "extrahumanly" guaranteed (2003, 271). So Wynter's account of the inventions of Man reveals not only the colonial inheritance of neoliberal storytelling, but also its theological underpinnings. Both Man1 (political Man) and Man2 (economic Man) emerged as reformulations of medieval Europe's conception of the human as Christian. Wynter sees the Christian story of humanness as structured by the postulation of a "significant ill" and a correlated "plan of salvation"—narrative coordinates that carry over into the inventions of Man that follow (265).[11] In short, though economic Man arises from the first purely secular definition of the human as a biological organism, he's narrated as constrained by the law of natural scarcity (rather than original sin) and seeking redemption through accumulation (rather than piety). And where the Christian story of true humanness was anchored by God, the story of economic Man is no less "extrahumanly" anchored, Wynter says, because we "project our collective authorship of our contemporary order onto the imagined agency of Evolution and Natural Selection and, by extrapolation, onto the 'Invisible Hand' of the 'Free Market'" (317). Man2 is a product of the rise of the biological sciences in the eighteenth century, "naturally selected" by superior genetic makeup for survival and success. And this means his Others—"the Poor, the jobless, the homeless, the 'underdeveloped'"—are, in Wynter's terms, "dysselected by Evolution until proven otherwise" (317, 267). Wynter further argues that this new master code is mapped onto what W.E.B. Du Bois called the Color Line. If Man is the apex of a hierarchy of humanness, then "the figure of the Negro," Wynter observes, is its subhuman "nadir" (301). So Man's story casts many of us as abnormally human, but it's particularly costly to black subjects who are, Wynter writes, "narratively condemned" by its logic (1994, 70). The reproduction of the story of Man is a matter of life and death—for some of us more than others—and the story is told in such a way that we fail to recognize our agency in its telling.

Arendt, too, is alert to the political costs of a worldview that casts the human as Man. In her investigation of totalitarianism, the figure of Man emerges when politics-destroying terror erupts into the world. In spite of the fact that Arendt persistently uses "man" as the universal subject in her writing, her insights concerning the distinction between Man in the singular and men in the plural strain against the assumptions embedded in this practice. Politics is possible, for Arendt, because of the human condition of plurality; because "men, not Man, live on the earth and inhabit the world" (1958, 7). And terror destroys the political scene by absorbing this plurality into "One Man of gigantic dimensions" (1951, 466). Animated by Man, not men, the totalitarian worldview that Arendt sought to understand was organized by a law of movement—the progressive unfolding of Nature or History—through which the unfit are culled and the world becomes more perfect.[12] And what was novel about totalitarian rule, for Arendt, was that it bypassed the distinction between lawful and lawless government and claimed what Wynter might call "extrahuman" authorization: the direct application of the law of Nature or of History to "mankind without bothering with the behaviour of men" (462). From this point of view, new beginnings are threatening interruptions to the developmental or "processual" time of Man.[13] Terror is the totalitarian solution, then, to the problem that "with each new birth, a new beginning is born into the world, a new world has potentially come into being" (465). Arendt's account offers another angle on the implications of Wynter's assertion that Man is the current answer given to "the question of who and what we are" (2003, 317). Man is a description of *what* we are that constructs some of us as fundamentally unlike the others: subhuman, dysselected. And, for Arendt, *who* each of us is takes shape in narrative, in a story told by others who glimpse something of the uniqueness we reveal in our words and deeds. So the suppression of our relational possibilities is, at the same time, a suppression of our storytelling capacities. This is how Man stifles stories that might remake the world.

In light of these life and death stakes, Wynter proposes another redescription of the human, this time as *homo narrans*: a species of storytellers. She presents a new myth of origins grounded in Blombos Cave in South Africa, where a 2008 excavation unearthed an ochre-processing workshop that included hundred-thousand-year-old tools and ingredients used in the making of paints. This is the earliest evidence of humans practicing "the *symbolic transformation of biological identity*" (Wynter and McKittrick 2015, 67, emphasis original). The discovery at Blombos interrupts Man's Darwinian narrative by drawing attention to what Wynter formulates as the hybridity of humanness, or the fact that we're biological beings who narratively reinvent ourselves. "In my own terms," she explains,

> the human is *homo narrans*. This means that as a species, our *hybrid* origins only emerged in the wake of what I have come to define over the last decade as the Third Event. The First and Second Events are the origin of the universe and the explosion of all forms of biological life, respectively. I identify the Third Event in Fanonian-adapted terms as the origin of the human as a hybrid-auto-instituting-languaging-storytelling species: *bios/mythoi*. The Third Event is defined by the singularity of the *co-evolution* of the human brain *with* . . . the emergent faculties of language, storytelling. (Wynter and McKittrick 2015, 25, emphases original)[14]

The Third Event points to the role of initiation in human societies: in ways that change across time and cultures, the newly born are recruited into a "we" through the story a group tells about what it is and where it came from. And this story's master code serves as a "behavior-motivating/-demotivating" schema, encouraging us to conduct ourselves in ways that affirm the group's worldview and, conversely, discouraging deviant life trajectories (Wynter 2003, 279). Against the violence of Man's narrative and the master code it supports, Wynter redescribes the human as a biological form of life that tells stories about what it is, a process that opens us up to transformation. The hybridity of humanness means that we can reimagine what it means to "be" human; that, in fact, "*humanness* is no longer a *noun. Being human is a praxis*" (Wynter and McKittrick 2015, 23, emphasis original). A reimagining of the human as *homo narrans* means, in short, that we can narrate and practice humanness differently, generating an expansive understanding of what we are that makes more room for new arrivals to show who they are.[15]

In the world according to Hannah Arendt, we are, each of us, miraculous in our newness. Since "nobody is ever the same as anyone else who ever lived, lives, or will live," our story of humanness—our group story—is endlessly open to the revisions incited by "the constant influx of newcomers who are born into the world as strangers" (1958, 8, 9). Arendt doesn't discuss reproduction and children, really, but her thinking about natality suggests an unsentimental view of young people as threateningly-promisingly alien. "With word and deed," she writes, "we insert ourselves into the human world, and this insertion is like a second birth, in which we confirm and take upon ourselves the naked fact of our original physical appearance" (176–177). We appear naked and new, and, over time, we offer something of our newness to a world shared with others. Built into the concept of natality, then, is an interval between birth and rebirth that maps onto Arendt's problematic separation of the private realm from the public. As Butler observes, Arendt's schema in *The Human Condition* (1958) generates a fantastical division of embodied life: "If there is a body in the public sphere, it is presumptively masculine and unsupported, presumptively free to create, but not itself created. And the body in the private sphere is female, ageing, foreign, or childish, and always prepolitical" (2015, 75). The principle of natality both arises from and confounds this distinction. Our capacity to act, to unleash new beginnings in a shared world, is "ontologically rooted" in the fact that we are, ourselves, beginners; in the fact that we're born (Arendt 1958, 247). Every time we act in the public space of appearance, we cite and activate the potentialities inherent in our arrival into the world as strangers. This yokes the space of appearance to the private sphere as its condition of possibility, illuminating the otherwise paradoxical position that, as Butler writes, "Arendt maintains that politics requires the space of appearance, [but] she also claims that space brings politics about" (2015, 73). Simmering beneath the surface of Arendt's seemingly rigid schema is an insight that indexes political action to an extrapolitical space-time—an insight that holds open the possibility of politics even when the space of appearance, dominated by Man, disappears.

Arendt's thinking about natality points, implicitly, to the family as a site where those "who are born into the world as strangers"—strange arrivals—begin to shape their life stories (Arendt 1958, 9). This is why the family and the gender roles it teaches are, to return to Wynter, the first step in our initiation into Man's origin story. Reading the two thinkers together illuminates how initiation seeks to manage the unpredictability inherent in the fact that we are, in Arendt's terms, "*ini-*

tium, newcomers and beginners by virtue of birth" (1958, 177). The master code that valorizes economic Man establishes a "magma of role allocations" that tell us what it means to be good men and women (Wynter and McKittrick 2015, 38). What Katherine McKittrick calls Man's "story-lie" gives rise to figures like "the taxpayer," "the savvy investor," and "the virtuous breadwinner" whose complement, the equally virtuous housewife of the postwar period, still ghosts the entrepreneurial feminine subject (Wynter and McKittrick 2015, 19). But many of us deviate from these gendered scripts. As I elaborate in the next section, mothers, in particular, are points of trouble and intensity in a genre that stages—and often defers—the end of Man's world. In chapter 1 I consider a ghostly maternal figure, a white woman whose actions haunt her husband's story of survival. And in chapter 4 I focus on an expectant black woman, a refugee who activates what McKittrick calls "respatializations" that disturb the geographic patterns of Man's world (2006, xix). Mothers remind us that while we're all miraculously new, we're also accretions of origins that always potentially exceed the origin story into which we've been recruited. Our bodies are made up of what Sara Ahmed describes as sedimented "histories of arrival," which are also "histories of labor" (2006, 38, 49): an inheritance in which reproductive and maternal labor unspools into the long and often difficult histories that inform where, when, and under what conditions women give birth to new humans. So in the films I explore, mothers usher into the story pasts that expose the terrible costs of Man's world and gesture, too, to alternative imaginaries. They harbor monsters and impossible desires; they kill themselves when survival isn't enough; they survive when they've been left for dead. They inscribe question marks and lines of flight into patriarchal fantasies of survival.[16]

This means the young people in these films are strange arrivals trailing long, deep, and often unresolved histories. They inherit the questioning, deviant trajectories suggested by maternal figures who are often sidelined in postapocalyptic tales—an inheritance that engenders what Ahmed might call a "slantwise" perspective on (the end of) Man's world (2006, 107). The slantwise, for Ahmed, is a "queer orientation," a way of seeing that "allow[s] other objects to come into view" (107). And this queerness is as much about time as space. So some visions of apocalypse might locate hope for a recognizable future in the figure of the child, an ideological coupling that Lee Edelman pinpoints with the term "reproductive futurism" (2004, 4). For Edelman, we're unable to imagine a future without conjuring a symbolic child, a limit he expresses by asking, rhetorically, what kind of subject would "stand *against* reproduction, *against* futurity, and so against *life*? Who *would* destroy the Child?" (16, emphases original). But not all real, actual children are seen as fit to bear this symbolic load. And Edelman's opposing of the Child to the queer—"the place of the social order's death drive" (3)—can obscure, well, the queerness of children. So in this book I emphasize the queer temporalities associated with young people to illuminate the multiple futures these stories make possible. Inspired by queer theorists who attend to backwardness, delay, and other interruptions to the time of reproductive futurism—or what Jack Halberstam calls "family time" (2005, 5)—I notice the kinks in time wrought by strange arrivals who evade the imperatives of social reproduction, sending new stories rippling out into the world.[17] Kathryn Bond Stockton, for example, imagines the queer child and others who are "broadly strange" as inhabiting a time of delay, a space-time of suspension in which it's possible to grow sideways rather than up (2009, 3). Growing sideways opens up the possibility of making unexpected connections, of a life story unfolding slantwise to our origin story and, perhaps, inducing in it revisions and mutations. This possibility derives from the interval built into the principle of natality: the space-time between the "naked fact" of arrival and our self-directed appearance in a shared world (Arendt 1958, 177). It's a space-time of contestation in which what we do with our inheritance is an open question—and one in which our life stories might twist in unexpected directions.

Undead Ends is full of young people navigating such intervals. Six-year-old Hushpuppy is trying to figure out what kind of "little piece" she is in the context of a "big, big universe." And the question of what a future without both her dad and The Bathtub could look like unfurls, across "a million years," into the question of what scientists in the future might do with her story. As I show in my discussion of *Beasts,* these questions about futures are also questions about pasts; about how an absent mother, colonial legacies, and geological time all press on Hushpuppy's present. The boy in *The Road* and the kids in *28 Weeks Later* are also struggling to breathe life into futures they can live with—and their stories, too, are shaped by efforts to come to grips with what their mothers have done. One chose suicide over survival. And one returned unexpectedly, having survived something she shouldn't. Together, mothers and their offspring usher in ghosts that whisper of the "strange and queer truths" the prevailing stories can't admit (Georgis 2013, 11). In the process, they illuminate the limits of the story we tell ourselves and incite us, perhaps, to inquire into the cost of surviving *this* way.

GENRE, OR, UNVEILING

A wide shot captures a man wandering through a desolate, hushed city street. Vehicles are still, often overturned; trash and sometimes cash blows in the wind; sagging buildings stare out of gaping window frames. And if we're far enough into the postapocalyptic future, nature has begun to reclaim the city, green tendrils reaching through cracks in the concrete. Richard Slotkin understands genre as "the development of a powerful association between particular kinds of setting and particular story-forms" (1992, 232). Going back to the Book of Revelation, in which the razing of Babylon makes way for the arrival of a new Jerusalem, the dead city is at the heart of apocalyptic storytelling. The sole survivor scene invites viewers to linger with the deadness; to take in the magnitude of the undoing and orient ourselves, emotionally, in the aftermath. And we usually take our cue from a Last Man. He might be stalking his prey through the wild grasses of Times Square, or staring around, bewildered, at the stillness of Piccadilly Circus. Like *I Am Legend*'s Robert Neville, whose wristwatch alerts him to an impending Manhattan sunset before we understand why this matters, he's the one who knows all the rules have changed. Or, like Jim in *28 Days Later*, who wakes from a coma to find himself alone in a London hospital, he's about to find out. It's through the Last Man that we discover where, when, and how the broken city is dangerous ground. His story of postapocalyptic survival unfolds as a remapping of urban space shaped by two questions: What happened here? And what *could* happen here?[18]

Behind the sole survivor, the empty streetscape attests to another iconic scene—one that belongs to the film's narrative background, whether or not we see it in flashback: the scene of swarming, panicked civilians. Borders close, bridges blow. Riot gear. Quarantine. Our Last Man is haunted by the scene of lockdown and the losses it represents. His relationship to other survivors—and to the possible futures kindling between them—begins to take shape in the story he tells himself about the dead. If he adopts a narrative of chosenness, understanding himself, in Wynter's terms, as selected for survival, then he values his life above the lives of others. Take, for example, Charlton Heston's swaggering portrayal of Robert Neville in *The Omega Man*, a 1971 adaptation of the *Legend* story that I discuss in chapter 2. This Neville shoots first and asks questions later. And when he sprays bullets at a shadow flitting across a downtown L.A. window, he reveals how the logic of chosenness is at odds with what Arendt calls the human condition of plurality—and, by extension, with politics. He fails to accept, as Butler writes, "that no one has the prerogative to choose with whom to cohabit the earth" (2015, 111). Indeed, if we look at the scene from the perspective of the shadowy figure in the window, we might see a survivor murdering and terrorizing other survivors. We might see a Last Man insisting that if the reanimation of the dead city won't give rise to a future he recognizes, then it should stay dead. It's this switch in perspective—from (the Last) Man to his Others—that unlocks the hidden pasts and surprising futures encrypted in the apocalyptic city.

In the United States and the United Kingdom, mastering the narratives that emerge from ruined cities became particularly pressing after the 1960s—a moment that Wynter identifies as the first phase of struggle against the story of Man. Spurred by decolonization movements worldwide, she says, the intersecting "isms" that emerged from "the black antiapartheid struggle for civil rights, women's rights/feminism, indigenous and other of-color rights, gay and lesbian rights, and so forth," formed a multipronged attack on "Man's episteme, its truth" (Wynter and McKittrick 2015, 23). James Berger agrees, characterizing the sixties as apocalyptic for American history, in particular. As an example he cites protests against the Vietnam War, which constructed the nation as haunted by legacies of imperial violence, including enslavement, genocide, and Indigenous erasure. The effect, he writes, was "an echo chamber of trauma and apocalypse" that undid the American progress narrative (1999, 140). Making a similar argument, Slotkin points to articulations of racialized spaces: print and TV journalism of the late sixties paired footage of urban uprisings in cities like Detroit with images of urban warfare in Saigon and Ben Tre. These visual connections captured how the crisis of legitimacy spurred by the Vietnam War rippled into U.S. domestic policy, suggesting that "in the War on Poverty as in the war in Vietnam—American political leaders had misunderstood the nature of the forces with which they were dealing" (1992, 535). American streets became sites of protest, outrage, and revolt in the sixties—scenes that conjured other times and places and, in the process, exposed the violent contradictions underpinning the American edition of Man's story.

The unraveling of the American progress narrative reverberated across the Atlantic, finding fertile ground in an England wearied by the war and shaken by global decolonization movements. As Stuart Hall and his colleagues observe in *Policing the Crisis* (1978), the "hippie 'golden summer' had scattered the seeds of disaffiliation far and wide"—and, in 1968, there was "a remarkable cataclysm: a parting of the waters" (237). Black Power arrived in the United Kingdom during this period, finding purchase among the children of the Windrush generation whose claims to belonging were challenged by racially coded immigration reforms. And the student protests of 1968 resulted in a nightly television spectacle: "images of helmeted and shielded riot-control police advancing on lines of students with headbands and combat jackets, looking down the muzzles of machine-guns or scattering before the [tear] gas" (Hall et al. 1978, 238). So British streets, too, were sites of youthful revolt and racialized insurgency. And politicians and journalists responded by projecting nightmare futures modeled on American crises. As in conservative MP Enoch Powell's 1968 "Rivers of Blood" speech, which conjures a British "we" horrified by the unrest in American cities, events in Britain were read "as *incipiently* 'American' in character" (Hall et al. 1978, 29, emphasis original). This projection of an apocalyptic horizon across the Atlantic supported the shift toward authoritarianism that Hall and his colleagues see as beginning in 1969—and paving the way for Thatcherism.

Confronted by a politics of the street, Man's story of humanness was slipping and stuttering on both sides of the Atlantic.[19] So, in the 1970s, a conservative story about ruined cities emerged to shore it up—one that rewrote what Butler calls "sudden assemblies" as scenes of apocalypse (2015, 22). My decision to investigate American and British apocalypse films, specifically, derives from the transatlantic circuit reactivated by this story. The securing of neoliberal hegemony under Ronald Reagan and Margaret Thatcher can be traced, in part, to a feedback loop in which tales of ruined cities and wayward families began to dominate mainstream media in both the United States and the United Kingdom. And these circulating end-times visions tapped into a story that was already hemispheric in scope: Wynter's account of the inventions of Man takes the Atlantic world as, to borrow Paul Gilroy's phrasing, "one single, complex unit of analysis" (1993, 15). I take my cue, then, from the transatlantic shape of black feminist and black radical inquiry, which shows that both Man's world and imaginings of its end require an interpretive approach that exceeds the nation. So while I focus on cinematic depictions of devastated American and British landscapes, I articulate these sites of ruin with the broader Atlantic histories and geographies in which they're embedded. In chapter 3, for instance, I draw on the figure of the zombie to read Danny Boyle's *28 Days Later* and its sequel as reanimating histories of revolt in Europe's Caribbean colonies—as depicting an island uprising, in short, that uneasily recalls others. In this sense, the transatlantic context of Anglo-American apocalypticism lays the groundwork for reimagining the apocalyptic storyline that, in the 1970s, mobilized unruly cities in support of an emerging neoliberal ideology.

The neoliberal project of welfare reform hinges on an articulation, forged in response to the social movements of the sixties, that linked burning streets and willful, often racialized young people to a perceived crisis in the patriarchal family. In the British context, Hall and his coauthors observe that politicians, journalists, and lawmakers began linking inner-city decline to family structures framed as broken. The "ghetto" and the deviant family, they argue, converged as "public images": "a cluster of impressions, themes and quasi-explanations, gathered or fused together" to ostensibly account for social crisis (1978, 118). In the United States, this link was made, contested, and remade in the debates following the 1965 publication of the Moynihan Report, with some conservatives even drawing on Moynihan's assessment of a crisis in black family life to account for the Watts Rebellion in August of that year.[20] The raced and gendered narrative that emerged from the Moynihan Report provided the contours of what would become a familiar charge in the decades that followed: the meddlesome welfare state enables young poor women—especially racialized women—to have babies outside of marriage. Whether "mother" had entered the workforce, was raising her kids alone, or both, she was symptomatic of a crisis in the family wage system that had provided postwar capitalism with a stable social foundation. According to Melinda Cooper, this is the "convergent perception of crisis" that, in the 1970s, animated the alliance between American neoliberals and new social conservatives (2017, 20). Cooper argues that this alliance emerged in response not to the welfare state itself, but to the liberation movements of the 1960s, which were collectively imagining a "politics of redistribution" disarticulated from a heteronormative family structure (21). What American neoliberals began working toward in the 1970s, then, was a (re)establishing of "the private family as the primary source of economic security and a comprehensive alternative to the welfare state" (9).[21] In other words, a shifting, spiraling set of associations between race, crime, ruined cities, and wayward families provided neoliberalism with one of its key narrative arcs: *there's a problem with mother,* the story says, *and the kids are not alright.* And if the solution at the level of the family is the restoration of patriarchal authority, then the state, too, should be remade in a fatherly image: fiscally responsible, security minded, authoritarian.[22]

This neoliberal "family" story is, in a sense, a veil thrown over the ruined city—a narrative meant to suppress what shimmered into view with the street scenes of the sixties: a world after the end of Man. Everyday uses of the word "apocalypse" emphasize large-scale destruction and depopulation. But the term derives from the Greek word *apokalupsis*, usually translated into English as revelation or unveiling. As Berger explains, "the apocalyptic event, in order to be properly apocalyptic, must in its destructive moment clarify and illuminate the true nature of what has been brought to an end" (1999, 5). The 1960s unveiled the apocalyptic counternarrative encrypted in Man's story: from the perspective of the peoples whose lands and bodies were stolen in the wake of 1492—from what Wynter calls a demonic ground perspective—the invention of Man is world-destroying. It was this perspective that had to be suppressed (again) to restabilize economic Man and his world. So the stories about ruined cities that emerged in the 1970s shifted the locus of threat from Man to his Others. In the United States, gatherings in the streets—and the social movements and political mechanisms that supported them—became evidence of dangerous mutations in an otherwise perfect political project. These new narratives exploited what Berger identifies as a centuries-old split in the American apocalyptic imaginary: early Americans framed the country as a new Jerusalem formed out of the "apocalyptic break from Europe" even as they projected an apocalyptic confrontation to come (1999, 133). According to this split, the United States is a postapocalyptic utopia menaced by threats that are "external, or internal but non-intrinsic" (Berger 1999, 134). From communism to a wayward federal government, drug addicts to welfare queens, postwar conservatives cast the bad futures menacing the United States as unfolding from a contaminated American Dream. There's no fatal flaw in the dream itself, this story insists: if anything, the catastrophe of the 1960s calls for a back-to-basics reboot that doubles down on economic Man.

In popular film, apocalyptic storytelling is animated by these tensions between ending and rebooting Western modernity. Envisioning the end of Man's world threatens to expose the alternatives that seethe beneath its surface. In this context, familiar roles—the patriarchal provider-protector and the women and children who need him—work toward a remastering of the ruins. But affective unease abounds in stories of dead or dying worlds. And narrative instability tends to gather, in particular, around the figure of "mother" and the future(s) she represents. For example, the love triangles in American films like *The World, the Flesh, and the Devil* (1959) and *Last Woman on Earth* (1960) mean that different possible futures flash into view as the triangles find their way (or don't) toward resolution. In Britain, stories of apocalypse that emphasize remaking home and family were prevalent enough in the postwar period that science fiction writer Brian Aldiss coined the term "cosy catastrophe" to describe them (1973, 292). Aldiss was particularly referencing novelist John Wyndham, whose *Day of the Triffids* (1951), which was adapted into a film in 1962, softens the reproductive imperative with a romantic storyline. But Wyndham also provided the source material for *Village of the Damned* (U.K. 1960), in which an alien invasion constructs the reproductive women of Midwich as conduits through which to manipulate English—and then global—futures. It may be aliens who impregnate the women without their consent, but their doctors condescend to them while their own husbands and neighbors accuse them of all manner of immorality. With romance out of the picture, the patriarchal power underpinning "cosy" end-times scenarios shows its teeth.

If women in apocalypse films are located along a narrative axis defined by the poles of consent and coercion, then young people are navigating an intersecting axis that stretches between hope and doom. Apocalyptic storytelling often strains against the ideological coupling of (some) children with good futures, playing with the figure of the demonic child—popular in postwar horror films—to amplify the sense of a world undone.[23] The menacing, telepathic kids of Midwich have creepy cousins in the folk horror subgenre that emerged in British cinema in the late 1960s and 1970s. Here, too, young people featured in depictions of a rural England haunted by pagan pasts, repressed nightmares, and sexuality run amuck.[24] And folk horror films like *Blood on Satan's Claw* (1971) had futuristic counterparts, including *A Clockwork Orange* (1971), that reiterated and expanded the links between deviant young people and social devolution. These links were formed in the United States as well. In 1968, George Romero's *Night of the Living Dead* shocked audiences with the sight of a zombified white girl turning on and eating her father. A few years later, *A Boy and His Dog* (U.S. 1975) offered an American echo of *Clockwork* with its depiction of a sexually violent teenager navigating a postapocalyptic wasteland. In the end, the possibility of a romantic coupling between *Boy*'s protagonist and its female lead dissolves when he murders and then cannibalizes her. My point is not that all young people in apocalypse films are evil, nor am I interested in locating revolutionary potential in teen rapists. But genres develop as stories accumulate so that, as Slotkin writes, "the imaginative possibilities of the generic terrain are both expanded and mapped for future reference" (1992, 233). So in this book I hold on to the sense, available within the genre, that young people are suspect; that they're threateningly, promisingly alien. As we see in *28 Weeks Later* (U.K. 2007), a zombified child and an act of patricide—a reconfiguration of the broken family featured in *Night of the Living Dead*—might encompass both horror and hope.

Ruined cities, benevolent patriarchs, suspect mothers, and wayward children: these are the tropes that animate the bad futures from which neoliberalism promises to save us. They've complexified since the 1960s and 1970s, accruing new possible meanings and resurfacing old ones as they circulate across storytelling contexts. This means that encrypted within now hegemonic neoliberal storytelling are tropes that can, and often do, take on a life of their own. And sometimes they can illuminate, from the perspective of still-unfolding legacies of dispossession, that neoliberalism itself is only the latest in a string of bad futures.

In apocalypse films, storytelling mutations are all the more likely because apocalypticism is a notoriously mutable belief system. As Paul Boyer points out, "The same apocalyptic texts offered the disinherited a means of systematizing their grievances, the powerful an avenue of advancing their goals, and believers far from the public arena a language for expressing their deepest spiritual longings" (1992, 55). It's beyond the scope of this book to present an exhaustive account of the history of Anglo-American apocalypticism, but a few examples underscore its protean nature. Going back to the early days of Christianity, the vision of apocalypse recorded by John in the Book of Revelation prophesies the end of Christian persecution at the hands of Roman authorities. But Boyer traces how Christianity earned a more "favored" status under the Roman emperor Constantine in the third century, so, "increasingly linked to imperial power, the post-Constantinian Church downplayed its apocalyptic legacy" (48). Similarly, apocalypticism surged during the English Reformation in the sixteenth century, and Protestant polemicists busily constructed the pope as Antichrist. But the elements of apocalyptic prophecy tend to keep in step with the times, so later, as the American struggle for independence was gathering steam, colonial prophecy interpreters were affixing the Antichrist label to an array of British political leaders. Jumping ahead to the Cold War era, Boyer notes that American prophecy belief surged again after 1970. Feeding conservative reactions to the social movements of the 1960s, prophecy popularizers linked developments in Russia with warnings about a counterculture that was remaking U.S. cities in the image of Babylon or Sodom and Gomorrah. And this brings me back to the layers of dead city with which I began this section—back to readings of urban space that cast Harlem as Babylon and Handsworth as Harlem.[25] These readings charge a politics of the street with destroying the city and, very often, locate salvation in the reauthorization of economic Man.

But conservative interpretations of dead cities can't exorcise the utopian edge of the apocalyptic imaginary—the dimension that registers a critique of the existing order of things and anticipates a better future. This was the dimension mobilized by the subaltern visionaries of Atlantic modernity to breathe life into insurrections and decolonizing dreams. In a short essay on the Paiute prophet Wovoka, who introduced the apocalypse-inducing Ghost Dance to Indigenous America at the end of the nineteenth century, Mike Davis underscores how Indigenous subjects negotiating imposed forms of Christianity repurposed the idea of "revelation." Wovoka, he argues, reinterpreted Western history "from the vantage-point of an already visible future" in which catastrophe piles on catastrophe; and beyond this ruined landscape, he projected a new beginning for the Americas in which white people will have been "only a bad dream" (2002, 31, 23). This articulation of apocalypticism with the end of colonialism and white supremacy also spurred slave revolts in the French colony of Saint-Domingue, where the eighteenth-century Maroon leader Makandal rallied his followers by prophesying a black future for the island that would become Haiti.[26] Frederick Douglass, too, in his 1845 autobiography, linked the end of American slavery to the end of whiteness, predicting that the institutional rape of black women would result in a slave system collapsing under the weight of its own mixed-race issue. What's unveiled in these prophecies is the veil itself: Man's world becomes visible, in all of its fragility and contingency, as a "great mirage"—a "bad dream" (Davis 2002, 30).[27] From the vantage points of the peoples and lifeworlds dispossessed by Man's New World vision, apocalypse has been unfolding in massacre, rape, and plunder since 1492. From a demonic ground perspective, mainstream visions of apocalypse mark the end, not the beginning, of postapocalyptic time.

BEGINNING AGAIN FROM DEMONIC GROUNDS

The "struggle of our new millennium," Wynter writes, is a struggle between securing the continued well-being of Man and securing "the well-being, and therefore the full cognitive and behavioral autonomy of the human species itself/ourselves" (2003, 260). And since Man's story of humanness constructs blackness as subhuman—dysselected—the reproduction of this story hinges on the ongoing "blocking out" of black counternarratives (268). Drawing on the work of W.E.B. Du Bois, Frantz Fanon, and Aimé Césaire, Wynter observes that those who are made to inhabit the narrative slots of Man's dysselected Others experience the "doubled consciousness" of being both normally and abnormally human (Wynter and McKittrick 2015, 56). What unfolds from this psychic dissonance is a self-questioning consciousness. Du Bois understood this as deriving from the "vast veil" that separated him from white America—a veil that, according to African folklore about children born with a caul, painfully gifts the black subject with a revelatory "second-sight" (1903, 6, 7). Black subjectivity takes shape, Du Bois writes, in the process of seeing oneself "through the revelation of the other world" (7). The veil figures the violent separations through which Man emerges in opposition to his Others. And it generates a perspectival doubling in the dysselected subject—a demonic ground perspective, to return to Wynter, from which the world as it is comes into view as contested and changeable. From this perspective, world-ending violence has already happened; Man's world is already postapocalyptic terrain teeming with stories of survival in the wake of disaster. Popular visions of apocalypse conjure these familiar but suppressed histories of violence to imagine The End—and often the rebeginning—of Man. But each telling of this story risks unveiling more than it can manage.

Demonic grounds are, by definition, narrative locations from which the story that seems settled comes into view as unresolved. As McKittrick has shown, they site a terrain of struggle, exposing how the seemingly mapped landscape seethes with fugitive movements, alternative geographies, and incipient futures. McKittrick's *Demonic Grounds* (2006) extends Wynter's work, arguing that attention to black women's geographies "opens up a conceptual arena through which more humanly workable geographies can be and are imagined" (xii). Black women were (and are) violently recruited into Man's world in a particular way—fixed in place, in the context of slavery, as a "seeable body-scale" that stabilized a white masculine sense of place (40). But, McKittrick argues, black women have always contested this recruitment by surviving, remapping, escaping, and hiding within Man's geographies, which means different spatial stories simmer beneath the surface of Man's colonial fictions.[28] They open up sight lines from which seemingly mastered terrain becomes, instead, "an interpretive alterable world" (xiii). Black women's stories of survival are encrypted in Man's story, threatening to (demonically) possess the dominant narrative and scramble the codes of its current iteration.

Undead Ends draws on the counternarratives that arise from demonic grounds both to hack a genre that keeps imagining The End (of Man's world) and to speculate on potentially radical rebeginnings. With each chapter, the Last Man is increasingly disfigured. And if his function is to orient audiences to the ruins, telling us where hope and danger lie, then the destabilization of this trope makes room for multiple perspectives on an undone world. So as (the Last) Man's grip on the filmic imaginary loosens, what Kara Keeling describes as the "black femme function" makes its presence felt (2007, 5). Keeling argues that black queer femininity makes perceptual trouble, jerking viewers out of an immersive experience because our typical repertoires of visual storytelling are ill-prepared to contain her—to manage what she means. And if she can't be recruited into habitual ways of seeing, if her appearance can't be "mutilated" enough to become a cliché, then she opens up a gap in the story (Keeling 2007, 33). What Keeling terms the "black femme function" names the presence that presses on the narrative from elsewhere, the trace of a surviving-otherwise that puts pressure on the world we know (or think we know). For those of us who feel alienated—in different ways, to different degrees—from Man's story, such an appearance might activate the gap between the story into which we're recruited and the one(s) we live every day. It might induce in us queer feelings, which, following Georgis, opens up the possibility of learning. "Learning," she writes, "is the crisis of not being able to hold on to what you think you know and bearing it enough to make way for insight" (2013, 17). Revising the stories we live by requires that we bear their unraveling—that we unravel along with them, and bear, too, the disorientation this entails. But in exchange for vulnerability and courage, we have the freedom to write better stories, map surprising worlds, and dream different futures.

Let me say a few words about my approach to these films, then. The story at the heart of each chapter began as the end-times imagining of a white American or British storyteller. So even when the film's director is differently located in the world, he's navigating source material that arises from one of those national contexts.[29] But my intention here isn't to suggest that a particular worldview can be stably mapped onto the creator's social location or national identity. I don't discuss, in fact, these creators' biographies. Nor do I emphasize production-related issues around funding, studios, or national film industries. (These aren't uninteresting questions; they're just not my questions right now.) I'm interested in the stories white people are telling about disaster, threat, survival, and hope because these stories have tremendous cultural influence. They still dominate the mythmaking landscape in two of the most powerful film industries in the Western world. And since these stories touch the lives and imaginations of millions of people, I'm curious about both the unexamined assumptions they reproduce and the counternarratives they make available, sometimes intentionally and sometimes not. In some ways, I see stories of apocalypse authored by white people as "occupied" by Man's story of humanness: it infiltrates even those films with progressive leanings, sowing the seeds of its reproduction in the figures of the patriarchal survivalist, the heteronormative family, the white savior, or the dangerous Other. So in this book I aim for what Sarah Juliet Lauro describes as a "counteroccupation of mythical space" (2015, 25).

My approach is inspired by Toni Morrison's collection of essays on early American literature, *Playing in the Dark* (1992). Morrison wonders how the racial ideologies that saturated the new nation informed the storytelling of its white writers, asking herself, particularly, how their representations of black characters are entangled in a literary project that she describes as "the architecture of a *new white man*" (15, emphasis original). Reading as a writer, Morrison says, she arrived at an important insight: "The subject of the dream is the dreamer. The fabrication of an Africanist persona is reflexive; an extraordinary meditation on the self" (17). Morrison's insights have led me to see white American and British filmmakers as metabolizing Man's story of humanness, a process that propels them into a fraught negotiation of the roles played by Man's Others in their tales. As Jayna Brown points out, the "dystopian landscape of many black lives offers a template for apocalyptic parables of a global scope" (2013b, 122). And since "those least served and most often violated by social systems make fantastic dissidents," black women are uniquely suited to the role of "the dystopian *l'étrangère*, or outsider" (123, 126, emphasis original). Often this means white storytellers put black women characters to work in films that contemplate the end of Man's story only to renovate and resecure it. They tend to reanimate, in the process, the racist representations that Hall has called "a very ancient grammar" (1981, 41). And yet, as Morrison's dream metaphor suggests, the stories we tell always exceed us. To put it in Wynter's terms, all of us have internalized a story of humanness that induces in us "reflex responses of *desire/aversion*" that both are and are not our own (Wynter and McKittrick 2015, 49, emphases original). And while that means these films tap into Man's storytelling repertoire in ways the creators may not see, it also means they activate ways of seeing and knowing that Man's story has suppressed.

This book begins with *The Road* (U.S. 2009), a film in which the Last Man secures his investment in a familiar story of humanness by foreclosing on, in his own words, the "other tale" suggested by his despairing wife. He clings to a logic of chosenness that the film, in the end, reinforces, which makes *The Road* the most conservative film I explore in this book. But it's also an occasion to map the coordinates of the Last Man's worldview and notice the trouble that mothers and children make. So we start there. But in the next chapter, on *I Am Legend* (U.S. 2007), the Last Man begins to unravel. The 1954 novella on which *Legend* is based offers a last-minute revision of its protagonist as a monster, a boogeyman who haunts the new world taking shape around him. And since this revision hinges on Neville's relationship to a racialized feminine subject, all of *Legend*'s film adaptations anxiously navigate sexual and racial difference as they try to contain the radical possibilities suggested by their source material. In the 2007 film, then, the casting of Will Smith as Robert Neville means *Legend* is telling more than one story. This proliferation of perspectives and storylines continues in chapter 3. *28 Days Later* (U.K. 2002) recalibrates the Last Man by undermining the ideological links between survival and patriarchal power—a disarticulation that makes room to imagine a future in which a young black woman and a white teen girl survive together. And in *28 Weeks Later* (U.K. 2007), this same disarticulation allows a multiplicity of perspectives on the ruined world to coexist. *Children of Men* (U.K. 2006), the film at the center of chapter 4, visibly unlinks the camera from its identification with the Last Man. This strategy brings the cinematic background into focus, drawing viewers' attention to the context in which the film's "other" protagonist—a pregnant black refugee—struggles for survival. And finally, with *Beasts of the Southern Wild* (U.S. 2012), the Last Man gives way to a kid named Hushpuppy, a black girl-king who's busily imagining future humans for whom her life story will be a source of insight. The film is haunted by racist representations of black people as animalistic and primitive—an inheritance it struggles to reckon with—so in that final chapter I think with black feminist criticisms of the film to assemble a different story for Hushpuppy. It's a story, as Wynter might put it, for After Man.[30]

All of these films walk right up to the edge of Man's world. Some of them, like *The Road*, panic and turn back, forcing a familiar ending. Others, like *Children of Men*, linger uncertainly on the brink. Every film in this book offers an occasion to discern the workings of the story outlined by Wynter. Each one opens up, too, the possibility of telling what Georgis (2013) calls a "better story" about humanness and survival—and humans surviving together. So in this book I see myself as both critic and storyteller. I think with adaptations, discarded endings, and Atlantic histories to discern story-potentials that run like fault lines through seemingly coherent narratives. I try, in short, to reinvent them from within. Working in the spaces between white people's stories and black feminist thought, I offer a slantwise perspective that brings unexpected endings—and futures—into view.

1 • TELLING OTHER TALES

Rememory in *The Road*

Early in John Hillcoat's *The Road* (U.S. 2009), the unnamed protagonist flashes back to the moment his wife left him, choosing suicide over survival. The Man (Viggo Mortensen) stands atop a freeway overpass—the concrete ruin of a lost civilization—and, with a fingertip, pushes his wedding ring to the edge of the barrier. Then we're watching perhaps his most painful memory. The Man and the Woman (Charlize Theron) are arguing in soft voices to avoid waking their son.[1] He's pleading and she's numb. Eventually she walks away, the white of her nightshirt fading into postapocalyptic darkness. "She was gone," he says in voiceover, "and the coldness of it was her final gift. But she died somewhere in the dark. There is no other tale to tell." With the exception of a brief erotic dream later in the film, this is the last time the Woman appears on screen. Already relegated to the Man's dreams and memories, she all but disappears at around the thirty-minute mark when her husband deliberately brings her story to an end, refusing us any further access to who she was or what she wanted. But what does *The Road* look like if we look from this suppressed place? How does the Woman haunt this story of a dying father keeping his son alive at all costs? And what can this haunting presence tell us, in fact, about the cost of survival? Encrypted in the narrative background and whispering untold horrors, the Woman is a lodestone for the bad feelings the Man—and the film—can't fully admit. She conjures ghosts that threaten to tell "other" tales about the unraveling of the world.

Based on the 2006 Cormac McCarthy novel of the same name, *The Road* presents a Last Man clinging to an obsolete story of what it means to be human. In my introduction I discussed the work of Sylvia Wynter, who argues that the modern world is shaped by a story of good humanness that evolved, in stages, out of medieval Europe's conception of the human as Christian. The protagonist of this story is a colonial figure Wynter calls Man, currently understood as *homo oeconomicus*, or "optimally economic Man" (2003, 314). Economic Man seeks to master natural scarcity through practices of extraction and accumulation. And his story is animated by a logic of chosenness that obscures the violence this entails: Man is naturally selected for survival, which means the Others he dispossesses and kills are, naturally, "dysselected" (Wynter 2003, 310). In the United States, this story permeates a national mythology that links economic progress with spatial expansion. As Richard Slotkin has shown, the myth of the frontier is structured by "the twin mythologies of bonanza economics and regeneration through savage war"—a pattern of accumulation and violent (re)authorization that's shaped key eras in U.S. history, from westward expansion to the Reagan Revolution (1992, 642–643). *The Road* uneasily taps into this myth. In the aftermath of an unspecified event that's reduced America to ashes, the accumulation of resources is almost impossible because everything is dead. But rather than turn to cannibalism, as many of his fellow survivors have done, the Man scavenges among the ruins. His travels take on aspects of a "savage war" as he journeys into a wasteland full of subhuman Others—a journey he narrates for his son as a tale of "good guys" who are "carrying the fire" across a hostile land. Don't get me wrong: the Man is no John Wayne. He's broken and paranoid; a desperate father with failing lungs. He may not even be at home in this story of humanness anymore. I suspect he isn't. But he clings to it because he has no idea how else to narrate the gloom into which his child was born. And by keeping that story alive, he invests himself with patriarchal power and makes others killable.[2]

The Man's fantasy of survival is that the world he remembers will live on through, in his own words, the "old stories of courage and justice" he passes on to his son. So both his survival and the violence that supports it are authorized by his status as paternal protector. As he explains in voiceover at the beginning of the film, "All I know is the child is my warrant. And if he is not the word of God, then God never spoke." The story the Man is telling himself is one in which the Boy (Kodi Smit-McPhee) is all the good left in a corrupt world, which means his life is more valuable than the lives of all the others they meet along the road. The "we" this story conjures is limited to the father/son duo at the heart of the film—a limitation the Boy can't abide. In this sense, the Boy makes trouble for *The Road*'s conservatism. He pushes back against his recruitment into the Man's story as "the word of God," a figuration that provides, in Wynter's terms, "extrahuman" authorization for his papa's violence (2003, 264). But the film ultimately recaptures the Boy, drawing him in its final moments into a second family unit with another patriarch at its head. Though the Man dies before this new family materializes, its appearance seems to confirm the rightness of his worldview. Slotkin observes that, in myth, the "narrative of the hero's action exemplifies and tests the political and/or moral validity of a particular approach to the use of human powers in the material world" (1992, 13–14). The connection between "savage war" and "bonanza economics" seems broken in *The Road*, which makes it a strange fit, perhaps, for an investigation into the ideological coordinates of neoliberal storytelling (642, 643). But the film turns, instead, to one of the primary sites of accumulation in the long history of capital: the family. As Silvia Federici has shown, the patriarchal family is a site of primitive accumulation in that it harnesses women to the labor of reproducing workers while mystifying this labor "as a natural resource or a personal service" (2004, 8). Writing specifically about American neoliberalism, Melinda Cooper similarly argues that the history of capital "entails the periodic reinvention of the family" and that, in the 1970s, American neoliberals worked to "reestablish the private family as the primary source of economic security and a comprehensive alternative to the welfare state" (2017, 17, 9). The entropic world of *The Road* might mean that economic Man is finished, but the film's investment in the patriarchal family holds open the possibility of beginning his story all over again.

I'm drawn to *The Road* because it stages—and suppresses—a familial conflict. The Man and the Woman see the end of the world differently. And while the film manages this difference by making the Woman ghostly, it lingers nonetheless in *The Road*'s unsettled emotional register. For the Man, paternal love transcends horror. In a 2007 interview with Oprah Winfrey, McCarthy described his Pulitzer Prize–winning novel as "a love story to [his] son." Approaching the film adaptation, Hillcoat and Mortensen took McCarthy's cue, drawing on their respective relationships with their own sons for creative and affective insight.[3] But this love story is haunted. The Woman infuses it with a gothic undercurrent that amplifies the terror her husband tries to contain. So while the Man claims in voiceover that "cannibalism is the great fear," a flashback shows the Woman anticipating a future in which one horror cascades into the next: "They're going to catch up with us and they're going to kill us. They're going to rape me and then they're going to rape your son and they're going to kill us. And eat us." In both its literary and cinematic forms, *The Road* is bleak. But with the exception of this one bit of dialogue, Hillcoat's film suppresses organized rape as a feature of the postapocalyptic world McCarthy imagines—one that activates that "other" postapocalyptic timeline that, I've argued, is encrypted in the story of Man. The New World accumulations of *homo oeconomicus* are premised on legacies of dispossession that include the institutional rape of enslaved black women. From this perspective, postapocalyptic time has been happening for centuries. In this context, the end of Man's world is also, potentially, the end of his world-destroying story. But the colonial violence encoded in "old stories of courage and justice" comes into focus only if we attend to the ghosts (plural) that haunt *The Road*. The Boy is open to this haunting. And it takes the shape of a question mark written by his mother's suicide into his papa's story of survival.

The Boy is born into nuclear winter.[4] His arrival is entangled with other emergences—cannibals, slaveholders—that reanimate realities and fantasies belonging to the birth of a now defunct nation. An early sequence establishes this convergence as the source of the Woman's horror, the reason her suicidal plans included an infanticidal wish. In a flashback, she screams in protest at the Boy's birth. The sounds echo into the present, where her husband awakes to the ominous rumble of a diesel engine coming through a darkened tunnel.[5] The road gang that emerges—a small assemblage of armed (mostly) men, one wearing a gas mask, another a balaclava—is as close as Hillcoat comes to the *Mad Max*–style visualizations of apocalypse that, he says, he deliberately chose to avoid. But Hillcoat's aversion to the "big cannibal armies" of George Miller's *Mad Max* franchise leads him to leave out of his film a moment from McCarthy's novel in which all the Woman's fears are condensed into a single spectacle.[6] Shortly after the Man recalls the conversation in which his wife insists that infanticide is "the right thing to do," he and the Boy hide by the side of the road as an "army in tennis shoes" tramps past (McCarthy 2006, 48, 77). There are phalanxes of pipe- and spear-carrying men. And then "behind them came wagons drawn by slaves in harness and piled with goods of war and after that the women, perhaps a dozen in number, some of them pregnant, and lastly a supplementary consort of catamites illclothed against the cold and fitted in dogcollars and yoked each to each" (78). McCarthy's vision of "slaves in harness" on a forced march recalls the New World scenes of migration and white settlement that produced a profitable place in the midst of a supposed wilderness. The scene haunts Hillcoat's adaptation of *The Road*, suggesting the future of sexual servitude and forced reproduction the Woman anticipates is what Toni Morrison, in *Beloved*, calls "a rememory that belongs to somebody else" (1987, 34). The End of the United States is shaking loose sights, sounds, and feelings that are out there, waiting, as Morrison imagines it, for those who remain to "bump into" them (34).

The Road's journey south through the remnants of the United States stages a repeatedly deferred confrontation with the shadows—the blackness—that organize the gothic imagination. As Morrison writes in *Playing in the Dark* (1992), this blackness is shifting and heterogeneous, "a fabricated brew of darkness, otherness, alarm, and desire" that was, in the context of the early U.S. literature she examines, essential to "the architecture of a *new white man*" (38, 15, emphasis original). Drawing Morrison together with Wynter, the gothic genre manifests—and seeks to manage—the emotional ambivalence that permeates Man's story.[7] The American gothic tradition demonstrates that new-world dreams are haunted by what Morrison diagnoses as a "fear of boundarylessness," which is, she says, "the terror of human freedom" (1992, 37). Putting it differently, gothic terror registers the frightening proliferation of possible worlds that arises from postapocalyptic terrain—the ruins Man makes but disavows. The narrative production of savage bodies and landscapes allows colonial Man to project excess and disorder as emanating from elsewhere—a projection that authorizes his violence. Within this imaginary, Man-made ruins become a history-less darkness inhabited by what Wynter formulates as the "naturally dysselected Native/Nigger figure" (Wynter and McKittrick 2015, 47). And Man becomes, in turn, what Leslie Fiedler ironically describes as a "carrie[r] of utopia" into an unproductive, uninhabitable wilderness (1966, 143). So seeing *The Road* through a gothic lens exposes the colonial logic of the Man's injunction, to the Boy, to keep "carrying the fire." In the face of his terror, the Man tries to stabilize a future he won't see by claiming the Boy as his "warrant" for survival, elevating his son, as a carrier of the fire, above the monstrous Others who menace them from the shadows. But the gothic is a notoriously slippery genre. The feelings it mobilizes tend to slide in unexpected directions. And when the Boy begins to see that some of the others they meet are just as frightened as his papa, that his papa sometimes terrifies just like the "bad guys," the emotional underpinnings of (the) Man's story come loose.[8]

The Boy's capacity to revise his papa's story derives from his mother's ambivalence about survival. This chapter excavates that maternal inheritance, prying open a claustrophobic vision of the end times by listening to a ghost. But here's the thing about ghosts: there's never just one. I read the Woman who haunts *The Road* as, to return to Morrison's language, possessed by rememories that aren't her own. In her reading of *Beloved*, Avery Gordon writes that the concept of rememory speaks to how "social relations as such are not ours for the owning. They are prepared in advance and they linger well beyond our individual time, creating the shadowy basis for the production of material life" (1997, 166). Before the world ended, the Man and the Woman lived a presumably middle-class life in a nation structured by white supremacy and settler colonialism.[9] At world's end, they're forced to confront—or continue to defer—those shadows. In conjunction with the Woman's desire to kill her child, her suicide opens up a question within the narrative that she doesn't explicitly ask: *When is it time to stop?* The question pushes on *The Road* from the outside, from an American gothic tradition that's been repoliticized by Morrison's agitations, in fiction and theory, for critical narratives that attend to what Wynter might call the "hidden costs" of Man's story (Wynter 1994, 60). Morrison's *Beloved* explores these costs by asking, as Gordon puts it, "What is too much?" (1997, 140–141). And how might this too-muchness—too much history, too much horror—find expression in the imagining of a child's death as warding off a wounding future? Clearly there are important differences between the white, formerly middle-class woman in *The Road* and Morrison's ex-slave protagonist, Sethe, who cuts her baby's throat rather than see her claimed by her former master. I'm proposing a method of reading that attends to ghostly presences, narrative traces that belie *The Road*'s mechanisms of closure and containment. By detouring into another tale, I discern questions that intrude their shape on the story in spite of the fact that the Man doesn't hear them and the Woman doesn't exactly ask them.[10] Phantom questions. Hearing them might prompt us to hear, too, the story behind the story: the devastating violence that the white family in *The Road* is living with, in a sense, belatedly. Because reckoning with the end of Man's world means exposing the cost of its beginnings.

MAN, OR, *HOMO OECONOMICUS* AT WORLD'S END

Beneath layers of rags and grunge, the Man, like his son, is far too thin. His hair and beard are matted and his face is sheathed in grime. So when, at about the midpoint of the film, the Man and the Boy discover an underground bunker behind a ransacked farmhouse—when they can eat their fill, rest, bathe, and cut their hair—*The Road* offers its viewers our first and only moment of respite. In a scene that dramatizes the Man's longing for a lost world of sensuous pleasures, he sits dressed in a dinner jacket, takes a drag from a hand-rolled cigarette, and enjoys a shot of Jack Daniels. Looking across the table at his son, recognizing he's reexperiencing a life the Boy may not believe ever existed, he remarks, "You think I come from another world, don't you?" That world, represented until now by a single can of Coca-Cola™ discovered wedged in a vending machine, has suddenly rematerialized in the underground space around them. And it's a world written in brand names: Dole™ and Del Monte™, Spam™ and Vitamin Water™ are all clearly readable on the packages that save *The Road*'s protagonists from starvation. Hillcoat's unyielding visualization of what McCarthy describes in his novel as an "ashen scabland"—a "looted, ransacked, ravaged" country "rifled of every crumb" (13, 109)—means the bunker and its contents arrive on screen as a kind of miracle; that these products with their corporate logos are, truly, salvation. Prompted by the Boy, who offers up an ad hoc prayer of thanks to those who built and stocked the shelter, the Man puts his hands together, looks to the ceiling above him, and whispers, "Thank you, people." I'm not dismissing the Man's joy and relief. (I'd be thrilled about a bag of Cheetos™ in this context, too.) I'm just interested in what this scene reveals about *The Road*'s investment in a particular story of the human and what it says about whose lives matter, who gets to have a future. If the "good guys" are materially bound to the vestiges of capitalism, then how do we understand the cannibals that the Man—and the film—demonizes? How does *The Road*'s good guy/bad guy binary reanimate Man's colonial story at a moment that screams for new narratives of humanness?

By reducing survival to a stark biological imperative—eat or be eaten—*The Road* presents a limit case for *homo oeconomicus*. On the one hand, it reactivates that figure's roots in the eighteenth- and nineteenth-century rise of the biological sciences. Even before Darwin, the Malthusian notion of natural scarcity spurred a new "descriptive statement" of the human as a living organism driven to overcome scarcity at all costs (Wynter 2003, 262).[11] This secular story of humanness revises the Christian tale that dominated medieval Europe: natural scarcity replaces original sin as the source of human suffering, which means that the "new and present plan of salvation is, therefore, that of the unceasing mastery of natural scarcity by means of ever-increasing economic growth" (Wynter and McKittrick 2015, 26). On the other hand, though, natural scarcity is clearly unmasterable in the world of *The Road*, which means that *homo oeconomicus* has become

FIGURE 1. The Man (Viggo Mortensen) finds salvation in a fully stocked underground bunker. Still from *The Road* (Dimension Films, 2009).

an impossible fiction. And at this grim, grimy limit, the violence inherent in his "plan of salvation" comes into view. In a postapocalyptic environment defined by drastically increased and steadily increasing entropy, everyone is negotiating the biological reality that energy circulates through consumption.[12] Survival in this context takes shape as a project of deflecting the cost of existence onto others who are imagined as less worthy of life. The Man's story of humanness belongs to a time when these deflected costs—the simple fact that his accumulation and consumption entails that others starve or are consumed—could disappear (from his sight) into the complex circuitry of a global economy. The fact that his humanity was underwritten by the dehumanization and suffering of others could be disavowed. This disavowal is impossible in the world of *The Road*, which means that *homo oeconomicus* needs a new—or perhaps an old—Other onto which he can project his shadow side.

The Man's story, according to which he and the Boy are "good guys" who are "carrying the fire," recalls imperialist discourses in which civilized "torch-bearers" brave a dark unknown populated by cannibalistic savages (Hulme 1998, 7). After the Man and the Boy escape an old plantation house inhabited by, as Hillcoat puts it, "the bourgeoisie of cannibalism," the civilized/savage opposition underwriting the Man's worldview becomes all but explicit.[13] Troubled by all they've just witnessed, the details of which I'll return to shortly, the Boy rehearses his papa's story:

BOY: We wouldn't ever eat anybody, would we?
MAN: No. Of course not.
BOY: No matter how hungry we were?
MAN: Uh uh.
BOY: Even if we were starving?

MAN: We're starving now.
BOY: Because we're the good guys.
MAN: Yes.
BOY: And we're carrying the fire.
MAN: Yes.

Trying on his papa's logic, the Boy slips from a refusal of cannibalism to being one of the "good guys" to "carrying the fire," a chain of articulations that taps "a vein of latent ideological power" (Slotkin 1992, 2). The dialogue that ends in affirmation begins with the denial on which the good/bad binary pivots—one that underscores the otherness of *The Road*'s cannibals. As Peter Hulme explains in his analysis of the coloniality of the "cannibal scene," "otherness is dependent on a prior sense of kinship denied, rather than on mere difference" (1998, 6). The Man's "good guy" story thus reopens the racial and civilizational fault lines that, beginning in the fifteenth century, remade the human at the threshold of the New World.

The New World cannibal was a monstrous figuration of appetite without limits, an Indigenous screen onto which Europeans projected their anxieties about a story of the human—and a map of the world—that was deeply shaken in the aftermath of 1492.[14] In her psychoanalytic history of the imperial voyages of discovery, Anne McClintock argues that projections of cannibalism worked in tandem with feminizations of the land found in European travelogues, maps, and paintings. Imagining others as monstrous and obsessively mapping the "impossible" spaces of the New World betrays, she posits, "acute paranoia and a profound, if not pathological, sense of male anxiety and boundary loss"—a "fear of engulfment" by the unknown that finds expression in the trope of cannibalism (1995, 24, 27). Analyzing a sixteenth-century drawing by Belgian artist Jan van der Straet, McClintock illuminates the psychic splits and displacements that facilitate the (seeming) coherence of Man's story. The drawing depicts Italian explorer Amerigo Vespucci encountering a naked, female "America" as cannibals roast a human leg in the background. "Suspended between a fantasy of conquest and a dread of engulfment, between rape and emasculation," McClintock writes, "the scene, so neatly gendered, represents a splitting and displacement of a crisis that is, properly speaking, male. The gendering of America as simultaneously naked and passive *and* riotously violent and cannibalistic represents a doubling within the conqueror, disavowed and displaced onto a feminized scene. [And] the fear of being engulfed by the unknown is projected onto colonized people as *their* determination to devour the intruder whole" (27, emphasis original). McClintock emphasizes the paranoid rage of imperial masculinity in crisis, an affective and ideological inheritance that would later find expression in early American storytelling from gothic tales to frontier myths. The story the Man tells his son about goodness, hope, and "carrying the fire" doesn't just authorize his violence. It manages his terror. He holds himself together by holding himself apart from others—a paranoid distancing that, as we'll see, collapses the cannibals and their victims into a single category of threat.

The Road enacts what McClintock describes as a "splitting and displacement" that suppresses the possibility of critique lurking in its vision of American capitalism in ruins. The good guy/bad guy binary allows the Man to long for the lost pleasures afforded by an economic system premised on land theft, resource extraction, and exploited labor by displacing the violence of consumption onto the cannibal. Though *homo oeconomicus* must accumulate, though his appetite must be insatiable, the cost of his mode of being human—its reduction of Others to consumable or exploitable parts—has to remain hidden. The cannibal, a figure shaped by what Crystal Bartolovich describes as a "disgust/desire nexus" (1998, 223), becomes the repository for these hidden costs. But there are signs throughout the film that the Man's horrified distancing of himself from his cannibal Others doesn't quite hold up. Everyone in *The Road* is negotiating the vacuum created by the end of consumer culture. Some are scavenging among the wreckage, taking whatever crumbs remain so that, unavoidably, those who come after them will continue to starve. Others have altogether abandoned consumer culture and its myth of endlessly available goods by directly consuming the bodies of others. And while *The Road* renders the Man-as-scavenger vaguely heroic by casting the cannibals as monstrous, the distinction falters if we look carefully at the two underground spaces that organize it. The bunker full of brand-name goods—the space in which viewers, as much as the protagonists, find a moment of relief—has a subterranean counterpart earlier in the film: another space secured by a padlocked hatch. If we see the well-stocked bunker as a troubling echo of the cellar of an old plantation house, a space "stocked" with partially eaten captives, then the Man's scavenger/cannibal opposition begins to collapse.[15]

The scene at the plantation house exposes the violence of the Man's framing of the Boy as his "warrant" for survival. When father and son find a padlocked hatch in the kitchen floor, the Man rushes out to the yard in search of tools with which to break the lock, missing, in his haste, details the Boy notices. Screenwriter Joe Penhall specifies that these include "a forty gallon cauldron on the blackened remnants of a fire" and "a wooden smoke house with thin wisps of smoke coming off it" (34). Once in the cellar, they're overcome by the stench of captivity and rot, the horrors of which are distilled into the sight of a naked man "with his legs gone to the hip, their stumps blackened and burned, cauterized" (35). The awful scene is shot and edited according to horror conventions: firelight flickers, alternately revealing and concealing emaciated figures; some of these figures grope desperately at the Man and the Boy, their cries for help obscured by a more prominent, zombie-like growling that pervades the scene; and the musical score offers a discordant, high-pitched swell of strings. The starving and half-eaten captives become, themselves, the source of terror, leading the Man to bolt back up the stairs, slam the hatch back down and, what's more, slide a piece of furniture across it to prevent their escape. The Man performs these actions *before* he sees what Penhall describes as a group of "suspiciously well fed" people coming across the yard (36). Before he knows how close the danger is, the Man not only refuses to align himself with these traumatized strangers, but also contributes to their ongoing suffering. Yet, hiding himself and the Boy away in an upstairs bathroom and pressing a gun to his son's forehead in anticipation of their capture, he's saved when those he's just abandoned in the cellar manage to force open the hatch. The distraction allows father and son to flee the house undetected. So the Boy's spared life is firmly entwined with the Man's slamming of the cellar door and the "hideous shriek . . . coming from the house" later that night (41). Curiously, the shot of the fleeing pair originates from an attic window, as if the house itself is watching them run, a witness to their abandonment of the emaciated people inside—and so, too, to their uneasy complicity with the "suspiciously well fed."

This scene begins to trouble constructions of cannibalism-as-savagery-as-darkness, a destabilizing of the Man's "good guy" story that ripples, later, into the space of the bunker. The enormous cauldron and the smoke house evoke the role of the plantation in the rise of industrial capitalism. And this conjuring of a history of slavery means the bodies waiting to be consumed in the cellar align the main part of the house with the terror of white supremacy—with a power that took the form of the ability to control and consume the bodies of others.[16] These aren't histories the Boy knows, but the horrors of the plantation house now live in him anyway. And his picture of unfree, gravely injured bodies is encrypted with rememories. As the ex-slave Sethe explains to her daughter, Denver, in *Beloved*, "if you go there—you who never was there—if you go there and stand in the place where it happened, it will happen again; it will be there for you, waiting for you" (Morrison 1987, 34). What was waiting for the Boy isn't the same as what would have been waiting for Morrison's Denver. He's in real danger of being captured, violated, and consumed, yes. But what lurks in that cellar is also a brutal logic of accumulation that might possess him first as its victim and then possibly, if he survives, as its agent. So when the Man discovers yet another padlocked hatch in the ground, this one opening onto the bunker, the Boy is horrified. The Man works excitedly at the lock, failing to see his son's stricken face, his small backward steps, the "No" that barely forms on his lips. And while the bunker turns out to be their salvation—a place stocked by "good guys" who, the Man assures his son, would want them to have their stuff—it also highlights the sacrificial economy in which the Man is embedded. Like the Survival Condo Project with which I opened this book, the bunker is a privatized solution to the problem of world-ending violence. It reinforces what the Man takes for granted: that survival is at odds with community. As Elaine Tyler May argues in her analysis of the nuclear family in the Cold War–era United States, basement and backyard bunkers replaced government plans for public shelters, an idea "quickly abandoned as impractical" (1988,

90). Modeled on the reliable readiness of "Grandma's Pantry," the bunker is premised on acts of hoarding and articulates survival with the private family (91). It's a materialization, in space, of an us/them logic that pivots on a "sense of kinship denied" (Hulme 1998, 6).

By framing the Boy as his "warrant" and "the word of God," the Man recruits him into a once dominant narrative that's slipping into incoherence. And while the Boy is meant to shore up the faltering story of economic Man, he's also its most unstable point. Even as he anchors his papa's status as a paternal protector, the possibility of infanticide, which ghosts the Boy wherever he goes, points to an aporia in the logic of patriarchal authority. Samuel Kimball explains that a "person is a father only if he has a child. If he kills his child, he ceases to be a father. The category of father thus depends on the category of child. The logic of paternal transcendence, however, requires that the father be categorically independent of all other categories" (2007, 22). *The Road* stages this contradiction. As the life to be protected at all costs, the Boy authorizes the Man's sacrificial attitude toward the lives of others. "I'll kill anyone who touches you," he whispers as he washes another man's blood and brains out of his child's hair. "That's my job," he says, though his face betrays that maybe, this time, they've passed into the realm of too much. But each time the Man fears capture and threatens to preemptively kill his son, he verges on destroying the life that legitimates the violence on which their survival seems to depend. With his papa's gun to his head, the Boy is seconds away from unravelling, in death, the paternal authority that sanctions the Man's violence toward—and violent disregard for—the others they meet along the road. In this light, the Woman's infanticidal impulse is more than a symptom of her despair. I propose we see it, instead, as indirectly interrogating the sacrificial imperatives that drive (the) Man's story of survival.

WOMAN, OR, BEING UNDONE

There's an especially unsettling scene in McCarthy's novel that Hillcoat, after fighting to keep it in the screenplay, decided to leave out of the film's final cut. From a distance, the Man and the Boy see three men and a visibly pregnant woman traveling behind them. After remaining hidden and allowing the group to pass, father and son approach their campsite the next day, prompting the others to flee and leave behind only "whatever black thing was skewered over the coals." The Boy is the first to see it: "a charred human infant headless and gutted and blackening on the spit" (McCarthy 2006, 167). Hillcoat explains in his commentary that, for him, the scene at the plantation house "said about everything there is to say about cannibalism," which made the controversial "baby on the spit" scene feel "redundant." But if we look at *The Road* from the vantage point of the grieving mother who haunts the story—a figure who is, herself, haunted by rememories lingering in the land—then this scene evokes the sexed specificities of slavery economies. Pictured alongside the coffle that's also left out of the film version of *The Road,* the infant roasting on the spit reanimates the impossible pressures placed on black mothers in the context of slavery, women constrained to what Kimberly Juanita Brown formulates as a "sliver of space between production and reproduction" (2015, 94). In this postapocalyptic world, new life is either immediately consumed or channeled into a lifetime of embodied servitude (slaves in harness, pregnant women, a consort of catamites). And in such a context, reproductive labor is entangled with corporeal experiences of being anatomized: hands that work, wombs that grow, flesh that nourishes. This is a vision of white patriarchal survival that swarms with the traumas of American slavery and its afterlife, which means the Woman's suicide is a question that opens onto another postapocalyptic timeline. We'll need to detour from *The Road* to get at the shape of this question because it's one that the Man can't bring himself to hear. So here's another story.

Toni Morrison's Pulitzer Prize–winning novel *Beloved* imagines infanticide as an attempt to keep a horrifying past at bay—a past that arrives in the form of "the four horsemen" of the apocalypse (140). Morrison's protagonist, Sethe, is an ex-slave who, eighteen years before the narrative present, "recognized a hat, and split to the woodshed to kill her children" (150). The hat she saw coming down the road belonged to one of the four horsemen: schoolteacher, who, armed with the 1850 Fugitive Slave Act, had crossed the Ohio River to reclaim "the breeding one" and her "foal" (216).[17] In an event that would become known in the local black community as "The Misery," Sethe collects her children in the woodshed at 124 Bluestone Road with the intention of putting them beyond schoolteacher's reach: "She just flew. Collected every bit of life she had made, all the parts of her that were precious and fine and beautiful, and carried, pushed, dragged them through the veil, out, away, over there where no one could hurt them" (155). Morrison's rewriting of the history of Margaret Garner, an ex-slave who cut her baby's throat to keep the child out of her former master's reach, explores infanticide as an apotropaic gesture—an act, that is, meant to ward off an evil that's both already and not yet occurred. In her reading of *Beloved,* Kathleen Marks explains that an apotropaic gesture "is protective of value, preserving goods from being used up even if at the expense of parts of the self" (2002, 3). But it emerges from a worldview in which time folds back on itself. The apotropaic imagination constructs a seamless continuity between memory and anticipation, projecting past horrors into an imminent future and then deploying acts of self-harm to repel the coming wound. My argument is neither that the Woman in *The Road* faces "the same" nightmare as Sethe in *Beloved,* nor that her suicide should be read as a form of white atonement for the sins of the past. Rather, reading the Woman's worldview as apotropaically structured highlights that the terrors she projects into her family's future are not, strictly speaking, her own. As the source of the gothic undercurrent in *The Road,* she conjures a "darkness" that slips the moorings provided by the Man's "good guy" story. And when it's not affixed to savage, cannibalistic Others, darkness threatens to become legible, instead, as a New World phenomenon forged amid a brutal economic system and proliferating in its aftermath.

The Woman's imagining of a dreadfully near future that will tear her family apart folds back onto a past in which black bodies were reduced to parts—hands, feet, shoulders, wombs—to feed the economic engine of the New World. In *Beloved,* Morrison exploits the gothic trafficking in darkness to redistribute savagery and terror in the young United States, underscoring, in the process, the ways that black subjects bore the disavowed psychic and embodied costs of the American Dream the Woman and her husband once lived. Directly confronting the nature imagery at the heart of American gothic, Morrison reflects, through one of her characters, on the origins of the savagery that white people project onto black bodies:

> Whitepeople believed that whatever the manners, under every dark skin was a jungle. Swift unnavigable waters, swinging screaming baboons, sleeping snakes, red gums ready for their sweet white blood. In a way, he thought, they were right. The more coloredpeople spent their strength trying to convince them how gentle they were, how clever and loving, how human, the more they used themselves up to persuade whites of something Negroes believed could not be questioned, the deeper and more tangled the jungle grew inside. But it wasn't the jungle blacks brought with them to this place from the other (livable) place. It was the jungle whitefolks planted in them. And it grew. It spread. In, through, and after life, it spread, until it invaded the whites who had made it. . . . Made them bloody, silly, worse than even they wanted to be, so scared were they of the jungle they had made. The screaming baboon lived under their own white skin; the red gums were their own. (188–189)

Stamp Paid's rumination on the tangled jungle of savagery redeploys what Morrison describes in *Playing in the Dark* as an "Africanist" trope, or the conventional mapping, in American gothic, of terrifying darkness onto peoples and landscapes imagined as wild. Here, instead, the tangled jungle becomes an internalized landscape seething with rage and paranoid violence, psychic lives contaminated by the systematic degradations that underwrite the nation-building project itself and that, turned outward, transform the land into a matrix of hatred, shame, fear, and aggression. Invaded by the bloodlust they projected onto others, white Americans massacred, raped, lynched, and burned their way to a new world, claiming the mantle of true humanness even as the stench of "fire-cooked blood" pervaded the land (Morrison 1987, 172).

Morrison's apocalyptic rendering of "The Misery" collapses darkness into whiteness, redistributing gothic feelings across an economic system driven by the relentless accumulations of economic Man. Sethe's mother-in-law, Baby Suggs, senses the four horsemen before they arrive, sniffing the air and smelling schoolteacher, his nephew, a slave catcher, and the sheriff, collectively, as a "dark and coming thing" (131). In her own reading of *Beloved,* Christina Sharpe describes the Fugitive Slave Act as increasing the "atmospheric density" of slavery in the United States, a formulation that leads her to posit antiblackness as "the weather"—"the total climate" (2016, 104). Sethe's desperate effort to hold "the parts of her" together in the face of this encroaching storm is a struggle against what Saidiya Hartman formulates as "the extensive capacities of property—that is, the augmentation of the master subject through his embodiment in external objects and persons" (1997, 21). Sethe's actions in the woodshed can thus be understood as confronting whiteness with its own sacrificial economy, draining a vulnerable body of life precisely so that it can't be consumed by an insatiable appetite for power and profit. "By the time she faced [schoolteacher]," Morrison writes, "looked him dead in the eye, she had something in her arms that stopped him in his tracks. He took a backward step with each jump of the baby heart until finally there were none" (155). Sethe's apotropaic gesture arrests, even reverses, schoolteacher's relentless advancement into her new home. But her refusal is caught up in the violence that Sethe seeks to evade, a connection Morrison writes into the parallel rhythms of schoolteacher's backward steps and the increasingly infrequent "jump[s] of the baby heart." So the act of infanticide obeys a twisted logic expressed by Sethe herself: "if I hadn't killed her she would have died" (190). This ambivalence about survival—a not-wanting-to-live that isn't reducible to a wanting-to-die—echoes, later, in the weariness of Baby Suggs. Her heart, too, eventually stops in the wake of The Misery. Finally understanding well after his friend's death, Stamp Paid concludes that Baby Suggs "could not approve or condemn Sethe's rough choice. One or the other might have saved her, but beaten up by the claims of both, she went to bed. The whitefolks had tired her out at last" (171). From this place of ambivalence toward survival, from the heartbreaking exhaustion induced by white supremacy, Baby Suggs recognizes what's "wrong" with whitefolks: "'They don't know when to stop'" (97).

The Road revivifies a New World steeped in the stench of "fire-cooked blood," an atmosphere of terror, rage, and shame in which the Woman's suicide poses the question she can't otherwise articulate and that her husband won't hear: *When it is time to stop?* It's a question that arises from the place where the hidden costs of the stories we live by are deposited, from the foreclosed narrative "slot" that Wynter calls "demonic ground" (1990, 364). To be clear, the Woman is not *The Road*'s demonic ground, a narrative location that Wynter specifically allocates to the women of color whose ways of knowing the world are effaced by Man's story. But if the Woman is the figure through whom the possibility of telling "other" tales is explicitly suppressed ("There is no other tale to tell"), then she is, in a sense, the stitch across a narrative opening—the place where a familial past unspools into a longer historical view from which "old stories of courage and justice" are painfully, violently familiar. I turn to *Beloved* precisely because it grapples with historical memory, which *The Road* tries hard to forget.[18] Gordon reads Beloved, the ghost, as both haunting and haunted, a doubleness that allows Morrison to explore the "Middle Passage [as] the decisive episode that establishes the amnesiac conditions of American freedom: emancipation as enslavement" (1997, 169). And James Berger reads her as "the sign of a society—both white and black—that cannot narrate its past and thus is trapped in an ever escalating circle of trauma and symptom" (1999, 201). *The Road* risks unveiling the unresolved histories of conquest and racial violence that built the now-ruined world, but their resurfacing would trouble the colonial story through which the Man is holding himself together. In his terror, he restages the histories of violence he refuses to remember—a repression he achieves, in large part, by foreclosing on his wife's story. Her destroyed body, which the film doesn't visualize, is the wound in the family unit through which "repressed social antagonisms" leak into the story of *The Road* (Berger 1999, 208).

The Woman's ambivalence about survival, her refusal to see it as an unqualified good, runs like a fault line through *The Road*'s tale of paternal love. In a flashback, she contemplates their gun and two remaining bullets and lists the horrors (rape, murder, cannibalism) that she sees in the family's future. In response to her husband's insistence that "we will survive this. We are not gonna quit," she retorts, "I don't want to just survive. Don't you get it? I don't want to. Why won't you let me take him with me?" Unable to hear her critique of a mode of survival imagined, simply, as refusing to quit—as not stopping—the Man whispers desperately, "Listen to yourself. You sound . . . crazy." But if, following Dina Georgis, we "listen to the emotional content" (2013, 51) of a story the Man can't hear, then we might notice that the Woman doesn't exactly articulate a desire to kill their child. Rather, she wants to "take him with [her]" when she leaves the world. Her longing to hold the family together collapses into a proposal to end their lives together—"Other families are doing it," she says—an ambivalence that suggests her "desire is beyond what she knows" (58). She wants something more than surviving-as-not-quitting and she wants, too, not to leave their son alone in a world gone gray. Unwilling to be recruited into the story that allows the Man to go on living but unable to envision a livable alternative, the Woman simply stops.

As the ghostly narrative presence through which "other" tales of survival are conjured and suppressed—the conduit through which rememories of slavery seep into *The Road*—the Woman is the narrative seam that opens onto what Wynter calls a demonic ground perspective. As I explored in my introduction, this is the perspective from which the New World comes into view as postapocalyptic terrain, an unfolding disaster across which the dispossessed live stories of survival, creativity, and courage. From here, we might reimagine the Woman's unspoken question (When is it time to stop?) as the beginning of an ethical alternative to survival-as-not-quitting. As Baby Suggs explains, "'Everything depends on knowing how much,' . . . and 'Good is knowing when to stop'" (Morrison 1987, 81).

FIGURE 2. The Woman (Charlize Theron) struggles to convey to her husband that survival isn't enough. Still from *The Road* (Dimension Films, 2009).

How much horror can a memory hold? How much depletion can a body endure? How much terror is too much terror? And how might the feeling of "too much" shed light on what stopping entails? Nudged by Baby Suggs, the stopping I have in mind isn't really about suicide at all. The Woman's death expresses her *too much* but doesn't, on its own, interrupt the dense circuitry of violence and bad feelings that animates the world of *The Road*. But because she stopped, because her journey ended somewhere behind them, the Boy is prone to backward glances, pauses that disturb the Man's forward motion. And if this relentless movement is driven by terror—fear of capture, certainly, but also the terror that lingering or changing course might let the *too much* overwhelm him—then the Boy's delays are also occasions for emotional reorientation. This, too, is a kind of stopping. When the Boy prompts enough of a hesitation in their journey to come face to face with strangers, he recognizes in these others a version of the *too much* he feels himself. And this recognition that the terror-horror-shame-anguish coursing through what remains of Man's world is a shared condition leads him, in small ways, to try to stop it. Alleviating another's terror requires that he make himself vulnerable, that he open himself to an encounter that might undo him. His mother's ending of her journey writes a *too much?* that ripples into her husband's *at all costs*. The Boy inherits this question, which attunes him to his ambivalence about a story that elevates his life above all others. Stopping with strangers becomes possible from this place of ambivalence. And with stopping comes the chance to rebegin.

BOY, OR, AN "ETHICS OF COHABITATION"

What prompts the Man to leave his wedding ring behind, to exorcise his wife's ghost by refusing to tell more of her tale, is the Boy's expression of a desire his papa can't bear to hear.[19] The two are hunkered down for the night inside the cab of a tractor trailer abandoned on an overpass. Seemingly out of nowhere, the Boy quietly says, "I wish I was with my mom," which the Man translates as,

MAN: You mean you wish you were dead.
BOY: Yeah.
MAN: You mustn't say that. It's a bad thing to say.
BOY: I can't help it.
MAN: You have to stop thinking about her. We both do.
BOY: How do we do that?

Rather than expressing a straightforward wish to die, the Boy articulates a desire to be *with* that resonates with his mother's desire to "take him with [her]" and which, in this case, would entail that he sacrifice his life. Resisting the Man's fearful reduction of this complicated expression of grief and longing to a "bad thing," I suggest it indexes an insight the Boy inherits—and adapts—from his mother's action: that there's a connection between corporeal and psychic vulnerability and being with others. The Woman's refusal of the sacrificial economy of survival is an act of self-harm in which she assumes the entirety of the cost of her biological existence. She's unwilling not only to be violently consumed, but also to "just survive" for the sake of it, consuming resources that will leave others starving. But her total destruction leaves no self with whom the Man and the Boy can share the psychic costs of her act. This is the paradox of the apotropaic gesture: in mimicking what it seeks to ward off, it generates effects akin to the ones that were feared. The Boy's emerging resistance to his father's paranoia can be understood, then, as a measured adaptation of his mother's choice. Knowing when to stop means that both assuming the cost of one's own existence and deflecting it onto others must be limited processes. The Boy doesn't seek his own death, but he does accept the physical and psychic vulnerability inherent in meeting other people. And his acceptance of what Judith Butler calls "unwilled proximity and unchosen cohabitation"—a closeness and togetherness that terrifies his papa—holds open communal possibilities that exceed the patriarchal family (2015, 114).

As a beginning that arrives into a slowly unfolding end, the Boy inserts himself into his papa's story of survival in unexpected ways, changing the terms of the "good guy" narrative so it can admit vulnerability and, therefore, relationality. His insistence on actions that extend his self beyond his family form connects the Boy, however tenuously, to the remnants of what Hannah Arendt describes as a "web of human relationships" shot through with "innumerable, conflicting wills and intentions" (1958, 184). As I explored in my introduction, this web is the condition of possibility of human freedom, the medium across which our actions reverberate, becoming independent of our intentions and telling stories of who we are that can intervene in the origin story into which we've been recruited. For this reason, Butler explains, Arendt sees freedom as "a plural action," which means the "unchosen character of earthly cohabitation is, for Arendt, the condition of our very existence as ethical and political beings" (2015, 112, 111). Admittedly, the overwhelming deadness of the world of *The Road* makes it almost impossible to imagine the rise of a new political scene, perhaps especially one that takes as its concern a more equitable "distribution of precarity" (Butler 2015, 119). But if the Boy seems to be reaching for a more capacious form of community, is this any more impossible than the Man's—and the film's—investment in a familial future? At bottom, the Boy is seeking a form of togetherness beyond the family, perhaps simply because he knows his papa is dying, which will leave him even more precarious than he already is. Or maybe he shares with his mother a recognition that "just surviv[ing]" isn't enough to alleviate the horrors of his world. Or maybe the logic of chosenness that drives his papa to violence is a burden he just can't bear. There is, after all, comfort—and possibility—to be found in the insight that "we are all . . . the unchosen, but we are nevertheless unchosen together" (Butler 2015, 116).

In *The Road*, what Arendt calls the "web of human relationships" is stretched so thin it's almost nonexistent. But the possibility of its renewal arises each time isolated, fearful survivors come face to face in their travels. Fittingly, then, the Boy's emerging resistance to his papa's paranoid worldview becomes evident when they leave the bunker and, loaded with all the food and supplies they can carry, come across an old man who calls himself Ely (Robert Duvall). Weak with hunger, his eyes cloudy with glaucoma, Ely is not a threat. But the Boy has to plead with the Man before being allowed to give away a tin of fruit cocktail. This minor offering is important not because it will save Ely's life (clearly it won't) but because it creates, however fleetingly, a connection of care between strangers that affirms "the ideals toward which we must struggle," including the creation of the "social conditions of livable life" (Butler 2015, 121). The Boy works tirelessly in this scene to intervene in the hardened paranoia holding the two older men apart. Moving near, murmuring encouragingly, and even briefly holding Ely's hand until his papa orders him to let go, the Boy tries to bring Ely into their circle. The Man is suspicious and uneasy, but he begrudgingly offers an arm when the older man struggles to rise and then invites Ely, to the Boy's delight, to join them for a meal (an invitation that prompts Ely to mutter "What do I have to do?"). But while the Boy wants to sustain this new connection, the Man draws the line at dinner and a night of rest. When they separate from Ely the next morning, the Boy angrily insists that "that old man wasn't a bad guy. You can't even tell anymore." The rebuke suggests the Boy's "good guy" story is beginning to diverge from his papa's. And the tale he tells with his actions—leaving Ely with a can of peaches to tuck into his pack—is one in which courage entails self-harm. And justice has something to do with sharing what little is left to be shared.

The Boy's struggle against his papa's paranoia culminates in an encounter with a thief, a meeting animated by ripples of terror that, like the scene in the plantation house, illuminates a "now" charged with "the debts of the past and the expense of the present" (Gordon 1997, 142). The casting of black actor Michael K. Williams as the stranger who steals the protagonists' cart and supplies makes the Man's terror-becoming-rage come into focus, for a moment, as the terrorizing force of white masculinity.[20] Horrified by how close they've come to losing everything but the clothes on their backs, the Man trains his gun on the thief and rages, demanding that he drop his knife. In this standoff between two armed men, it's once again the Boy whose presence makes a minor difference. Though the stranger initially looks like he'd rather die than relinquish his only weapon, the Boy's quiet plea—"Papa, please don't kill the man"—seems to open up the possibility that this might be a different kind of meeting, which prompts the thief to chance making himself (more) vulnerable by dropping the blade. The stranger's pleading gesture of raising his hands into the air reveals that his thumbs are missing, a sign he's an outcast from one of *The Road*'s cannibalistic "bloodcults." But this indication that the thief might be one of the "good guys" fails to placate the Man, who wants the other to feel as exposed as he felt just a few moments before. The ensuing confrontation is haunted by a master/slave dynamic that links the thief's mutilated hands to a history of branding and brutalizing black bodies on American soil. In a shot/reverse-shot sequence, the Man orders the other at gunpoint: "Take your clothes off. Take them off, every goddamn stitch." As the Boy pleads for the thief's life and the latter, pleading for mercy, reluctantly tosses everything he has onto the cart, Hillcoat switches to a wide shot that frames the encounter against the backdrop of the Atlantic Ocean. Between the naked, shivering black man and the paranoid white man holding a gun, a smudge of gray on the filmic horizon stands in for the edge of what was once the New World.

The Man's attempt to repress his own fear by terrorizing another takes the form of an aggressive appropriation of basic necessities, an extension of himself via the claiming of another's things that the Boy clearly sees as too much—as not knowing when to stop. Reducing both his son and the thief to tears, the Man inadvertently demonstrates the truth behind the thief's justifying claim:

THIEF: You ain't gotta do this to me, man. You ain't gotta do me like this.
MAN: You didn't mind doing it to us.
THIEF: I'm begging you. I'm begging, please.
BOY: Papa.
THIEF: Listen to the kid, man. I'm starving. You'd have done the same thing. I'll die out here. I'm gonna die out here.
MAN: I'm going to leave you just the way you left us.

Becoming the "robber" he had assured Ely he was not, the Man takes his revenge, hauling the reclaimed cart and roughly prodding his son away from the scene. As they leave the naked man shivering in the road, he snaps at the Boy, "You've got

FIGURE 3. The Man leaves the Thief (Michael Kenneth Williams) naked in the road. The Boy (Kodi Smit-McPhee) is dismayed by his papa's actions. Still from *The Road* (Dimension Films, 2009).

to learn!" Aware that his death isn't far off and dismayed by what he sees as his son's lack of hardness, the Man frames his actions as a pedagogy of survival that the Boy refuses when he retorts, "I don't want to learn!" This refusal takes concrete shape as a desire to stop rather than relentlessly pursue their course—physical hesitations that prompt his papa to yell at him and a backward glance through which the audience, too, sees the vulnerable human they're leaving behind. Tellingly, when father and son stop to regroup after this encounter, the Man orders the Boy to "stop sulking" because the thief is "gone." The Boy's incredulous look, coupled with his assertion that "he's not *gone*," insists on the lingering presence of those his papa tries to seal into the background of their story. The thief, like the Woman, has become a ghostly figure that's "invisible but not necessarily not there"—a figure laden "with the something to be done that the wavering present is demanding" (Gordon 1997, 179, 183).

Having refused to consign the thief to an unalterable past, the Boy once again, but this time more forcefully, revises his papa's story to make room for others. When the Man implicitly dismisses his son's empathy as the luxury of irresponsibility—"You're not the one," he says, "who has to worry about everything"—the Boy finally asserts himself. "Yes I am," he yells. "I am the one!" The Man's story has elevated his son to the status of a god, which, Ely had warned him, would result in "nothing but a dangerous situation." But the Boy needs what Dina Georgis (2013) calls a "better story," one that makes it possible for him to connect with, rather than transcend, others. His defiance leads the pair to return to the place where they left the thief, who has now fled, and leave his clothes and shoes piled in the road. When the stranger fails to materialize in response to the Boy's calls, the Boy kneels beside the pile and, recalling his offering to Ely, places a tin of food on top of the rags. The single tin stands as a gesture of atonement, the enacting of a new ritual grounded not in sacrifice, but in a material negotiation of asymmetry. Instead of tirelessly guarding himself against potential harm, the Boy allows himself to be undone by empathy, to apprehend in others the *too much* he feels himself. And where his papa uses the insight that "everybody's scared" to justify his own sometimes terrorizing actions, the Boy seeks, instead, to mitigate rather than intensify both Ely's and the thief's fear. He risks himself just long enough for a glimpse of the possibility of community to appear in the midst of apocalypse. By ceding a small piece of the resources that shore up his existence, he keeps alive the fragile "web of human relationships" that makes it possible to tell new stories and give the world a new shape (Arendt 1958, 184).

ENDINGS

The Road ends with a deus ex machina that, as Sarah Dillon writes of the novel's ending, takes shape as the reconstitution of "the nuclear family (if you'll excuse the pun) of times long gone" (2018, 18). The Boy attends to his dying father, who instructs his son to "just keep going south" and "find the good guys." And then he's left alone, which might prompt us to think carefully about the cost of his papa's survival story and the isolation into which it led them. But soon after, a man identified in the screenplay as the "Veteran" (Guy Pearce) arrives on screen and introduces the Boy to his wife, two children, and a dog. On the one hand, the Veteran's wife (Molly Parker) underscores the limitations of the Man's paranoid worldview by informing the Boy that her family had been following them for a while. Indeed, the Boy caught sight of the Veteran's son at one point, and his papa not only didn't believe him, but also chastised him for running off after what he assumed was a figment of the Boy's imagination. So this family of "good guys" makes it clear that, if not for the Man's paranoia, he and his son might have had allies long before this moment. But, on the other hand, this ending folds the Boy back into a white patriarchal family unit in a way that constrains the unruly potential signaled by his willingness to forge unconventional alliances. By channeling his capacity for relationality back into a familiar—and familial—form, *The Road* suppresses the radical possibilities inherent in the Boy's affirmation of our "obligation to live with those who already exist" (Butler 2015, 111). The Veteran's missing thumb might even remind us of the thief, who stands in for an alternative alliance that haunts this too-neat ending.

In pointing out that the end of *The Road* shuts down many of the radical, unexpected futures that the film, if inadvertently, opens up, my aim is not to write this story off. In some ways the forced reestablishment of the white patriarchal family at the end of the film only highlights the demonic dimension that's been undulating beneath the surface of the narrative all along. This ending, then, is instructive. It reveals some of the mechanisms through which mainstream apocalyptic storytelling negotiates discarded pasts to craft the illusion of a blank slate and a fresh start. The key element of *The Road*'s ending, for me, isn't the appearance of a new father figure as much as it is the wife who accompanies him, the figure named in the screenplay as "Motherly Woman." On one level, the "motherly" qualifier simply serves to differentiate this character from the Woman (Charlize Theron), who, through the arrival of a new female character, has suddenly become the "other" woman. But this displacement of the Woman by an implicitly "more" motherly substitute begins to clarify the storytelling work both figures perform. All too often, mainstream apocalypse films anxiously envision the end of *homo oeconomicus* and his world only to project into the future new, somehow purer versions of familiar ways of being. And maternal labor is essential to patriarchal, proto-capitalist visions of rebeginning. New Edens need reproductive bodies and caregiving subjects. They require, in short, Motherly Woman. But Motherly Woman is only on screen for a moment, which suggests that her narrative function is to remain as "blank" as the "blank slates" that economic Man impresses on the worlds he destroys, forgets, and builds over. Reproductive bodies and (the illusion of) a world wiped clean: both serve in colonial fantasies as natural resources from which to extract familiar rebeginnings. From a storytelling point of view, then, Motherly Woman underscores what was troubling about the Woman, who was so narratively unpredictable that our access to her had to be mediated by the Man's dreams and memories. She was ambivalent about his story of survival and refused, as a result, to be recruited into the future that unfolds from that story. The film works hard to manage this loose end, consigning her to dreams and flashbacks and ultimately replacing her with a more recruitable maternal figure. *Undead Ends* begins with *The Road* for this reason: it's a vision of survival that follows the contours of Man's story—a logic of chosenness, the authorization of patriarchal power, the affirmation of white familial futures—and demonstrates the narrative force required, in the end, to (re)secure this fantasy.

The Road achieves its eleventh-hour rescue of Man's colonial story through a conjuring: the arrival of Motherly Woman maintains the illusion that the Woman whose questions, feelings, and desires unsettle the story is securely contained in the narrative background. She's overwritten by the film's ending. This mastering of feminine bodies—and feminized landscapes—is a key dimension of the dominant apocalyptic imaginary. So by way of an ending, let me turn to yet another story. When John of Patmos recorded his vision of The End in the Book of Revelation, he wrote Motherly Woman's demonic opposite into the apocalyptic imaginary: the Whore of Babylon, "mother of harlots" and "habitation of devils" (King James Bible, Rev. 17:5, 18:2).[21] John's writings included what biblical scholars agree is an allegorical substitution in which the violent destruction of the Whore of Babylon stands in for the ruin of the city of Rome. "Babylon" refers to both the woman holding "a golden cup in her hand full of abominations and filthiness of her fornication" and "that great city, which reigneth over the kings of the earth" (Rev. 17:4, 17:18). The monstrous harbingers of apocalypse "shall hate the whore," John wrote, "and shall make her desolate and naked, and shall eat her flesh, and burn her with fire" (Rev. 17:16). Babylon's spectacular, sexualized undoing exposes the narrative violence that generates the intertwined fictions of Motherly Woman and a cleansed world, both ostensibly awaiting the imprint of a newly empowered patriarch. The stripping, burning actions that destroy Babylon seek to exorcise what's vilified as the demonic element—the (dis)organizing principle that "cannot predict the future"—from ruined landscapes (McKittrick 2006, xxiv). But something of the demonic always remains. Dreams. Flashbacks. Inheritances. As compulsively as the Last Man works to manage the pasts that haunt him, as forcefully as too-neat endings seem to foreclose on unfamiliar futures, undead ends persist, whispering other tales of survival.

2 • ADAPTATIONS AND MUTATIONS

I Am Legend's Double Helix

Robert Neville (Will Smith) is hunting deer through the streets of Manhattan in a red Ford Mustang. Francis Lawrence's *I Am Legend* (U.S. 2007) opens with wide shots of desolate New York City attractions—the Flatiron Building, the United Nations Headquarters—before settling into an extended aerial view of Manhattan's rooftops. The faint roar of an engine is, at first, barely discernible amid birdcalls and insect sounds. With his German Shepherd, Sam, on the front seat beside him, Neville is on the lookout for fresh meat, maneuvering the Mustang through grassy streets with one hand and steadying his rifle with the other. In a later flashback sequence, he tells his wife, "This is ground zero. This is my site." Lawrence's adaptation of Richard Matheson's 1954 novella relocates the American apocalypse to the eastern seaboard, shifting the ground of Matheson's story, which is set in Los Angeles, to a site of twenty-first-century American trauma. *Legend*'s island city is quarantined—too late—when a rapidly mutating virus goes airborne, transforming millions of New Yorkers into vampiric creatures with superhuman strength and speed. And unlike previous versions of the story, in which Neville's adversaries mark their connection to him by calling his name, Lawrence's CGI monsters are speechless. On one level, then, this remade *Legend* mobilizes pieces of the post-9/11 American imaginary: unhuman Others assault "ground zero"; and from the perspective of our traumatized protagonist, their actions communicate only mindless, murderous rage. From this point of view, Neville's role as a military scientist in search of a cure is to reassert an American Dream that's been infiltrated by hateful Others. But there is, of course, more to this story.

Legend's evocation of the War on Terror seems to present terrorizing hate as alien to the United States, but this is a projection the narrative can't sustain. The film enacts a "splitting and displacement" (McClintock 1995, 27) that seeks to manage the revelatory function of apocalypse: to suppress, that is, the point where stories of disaster expose a fundamental truth about the now-ruined world. At stake, as in the last chapter, is the American edition of what Sylvia Wynter calls the story of Man, a story about what "we" are that defines humanness according to Western bourgeois norms of self-governance and economic productivity. Those who fail to approximate these norms are, in Wynter's terms, the "dysselected" that shore up a narrative in which Man is chosen to bring reason, light, and (economic) freedom to dark places (2003, 310).[1] So the American Dream is underwritten by the narrative construction of nightmarish Others, boogeymen who shapeshift across time: the savage Indian, the rebellious slave, the Islamic extremist. Man can see himself as a builder, rather than destroyer, of worlds because he scripts Others as destructive terrorizers. What Patrick Wolfe terms a "logic of elimination" is thus encoded within Man's story, condemning the dysselected to disappear either through murderous violence or assimilation (2006, 387). In this context, Jodi Byrd argues that American Indians are foundational to the U.S. imperial imaginary; that the latter repeatedly "make[s] 'Indian'" those who thwart Man's world-building (2011, xx). So Byrd's insights suggest that every conjuring of the post-9/11 terrorist can't help but summon, too, the American Indian: "the original enemy combatant who cannot be grieved" (2011, xviii).[2] This is where *Legend* gets interesting. Neville's vampiric Others are the disastrous result of a viral cure for cancer run amuck, which means the monsters that undo the world arise from within Western medical science. Cinematic echoes of 9/11 then seem to deflect this terror that springs from within onto "uncivilized" outsiders, resulting, as Ian Olney observes, in many critics reading *Legend* as a "neo-con fantasy" that channels the "bunker mentality of the Bush-Cheney years" (2017, 72).[3] But if, following Byrd, the American Indian forms a blueprint for the post-9/11 terrorist, then the film's projection carries within it a rebound effect. The terror of an invading horde slides from Islamic extremists to Indian savages. And only our (assumed) identification with Neville, the military scientist, prevents terror from sliding all the way to the "original" invading horde in the New World—coming to rest, that is, with the settler state erected by Man. But what if the Neville with whom we align ourselves doesn't fit so neatly into Man's story?

The 2007 version of *Legend* gives us, for the first time, a black Robert Neville—a Last Man who oscillates between resecuring Man's New World vision and resurfacing the histories of racial terror it disavows. A metaphor offered in the film's prologue exemplifies this ideological slipperiness. Dr. Alice Krippin (Emma Thompson) explains her ill-fated cure for cancer, a genetically engineered version of the measles virus, as follows: "If you can imagine your body as a highway and you picture the virus as a very fast car being driven by a very bad man, imagine the damage that car could cause. But then if you replace that man with a cop, the picture changes, and that's essentially what we've done." Seconds later, Krippin's explanation issues into the wide shots of a ruined Manhattan that establish the film's narrative present. It's a "changed" picture that visually uncouples the ideo-

FIGURE 4. Robert Neville (Will Smith) with his companion, Sam, on the hunt for deer in postapocalyptic Manhattan. Still from *I Am Legend* (Warner Brothers, 2007).

logical links between cop and "good guy" that Krippin had presumed. And it might prompt us to wonder, when Neville comes speeding into the visual field in his "very fast car," exactly what kind of driver our protagonist is. As a former representative of the security state, Neville's insistence on remastering the unruly city suggests, perhaps, an authoritarian Last Man: "I'm not gonna let this happen," he says as the city riots.[4] But in my introduction I examined how authoritarian responses to the riotous city are raced and gendered. In the Cold War era, conservatives located bad futures in black familial dysfunction and other pathologies associated with the inner city, all the while disavowing the historical traumas that resurface in urban uprisings. This is where the casting of a black Robert Neville sends *Legend*'s story spinning off in a few directions at once. Because a counter-reading that sides with the monsters and sees Lieutenant Colonel Robert Neville as a conduit of state violence doesn't really hold up, either. It wavers under the pressure of *Legend*'s depiction of a lone black man whose movements through the city are constrained by the presence of a terrifying, pale-skinned majority. In other words, both Neville and his monstrous Others signify in (at least) two ways at once, which means that neither can stabilize what the other means within the story. So what do we do with a Janus-faced Last Man?

Simmering beneath the surface of its gestures to the War on Terror, *Legend* makes available two more readings that run in opposing directions. On the one hand, we have Neville the military man enacting an assimilationist agenda, which includes experimenting on a "savage" population that's undone Man's story of humanness. But on the other hand, we have Neville the black man terrorized by a vampiric horde that evolved directly out of Western fantasies of scientific progress. One narrative strand invites us to reinvest in colonial Man; the other offers glimpses of the deadliness of Man's story. It's Will Smith's recruitment into the telling of this tale that makes both strands discernible. The resultant instability is exemplified by *Legend*'s negotiation of the meaning of Matheson's title. "I Am Legend" derives from the twist that ends the novella: it expresses Neville's belated insight that, from the perspective of the new society he's been systematically destroying, he's a boogeyman; that he occupies a place in their story akin to that of the vampire in his. *Legend*'s cinematic adaptations all sidestep the implications of this insight, variously absorbing Neville-as-legend back into the story of Man. But in the 2007 film, Will Smith's Robert Neville has a soundtrack: Bob Marley's *Legend* album. Late in the film, Neville explains that Marley "had this idea. It was kind of a virologist's idea. He believed that you could cure racism and hate, literally, cure it, by injecting music and love into people's lives. . . . 'Light up the darkness.'" This coupling of "racism and hate" splits the film's organizing metaphor. Hate-as-virus maps fairly well onto *Legend*'s gestures to an unhuman assault on "ground zero," recalling, as it does, the oft-repeated post-9/11 American question, "Why do they hate us?" But racism-as-virus dovetails with Krippin's ill-chosen "cop" metaphor—(police) racism-as-virus—which threatens to twist *Legend*'s story and unveil the repressed traumas at the heart of the American experiment.

And that's just the thing: *Legend* is, from the beginning, a twisty tale. The insight that arrives at the end of Matheson's novella ripples back through the narrative, activating a counternarrative that was there all along. From the point of view of the end, Neville is always in the process of being revised as a monster, of becoming-legend for an unfamiliar future. And if the function of the Last Man is to orient viewers to the ruined world, then this revision activates a perspectival shift in which terror and hope begin to slide around, looking for new narrative slots. The first cinematic adaptation of *Legend*, *The Last Man on Earth* (U.S./Italy 1964), forecloses on this storytelling mutation. The film does convey that the new society is afraid of its protagonist, Robert Morgan (Vincent Price), but this does nothing to shake his worldview; he dies calling his killers "freaks" and "mutants." *The Omega Man* (U.S. 1971) similarly tries to neutralize the emotional insight at the heart of Matheson's story, rewriting Neville (Charlton Heston) as what Wynter might call a "donor figure" that can be projected into the past to anchor Man's rebeginning (Wynter and McKittrick 2015, 36). In this chapter I discuss *The Omega Man* rather than *The Last Man on Earth*. Where the latter anxiously avoids referencing its own historical moment, *Omega* talks back to the countercultural upheavals of the 1960s.[5] And its (re-)revision of Neville hinges on the narrative recruitment of black femininity to confirm the universality of Man's story. But this recruitment activates the counternarrative encoded in *Legend*'s storytelling DNA. The 2007 film inherits this tension, offering a black Robert Neville who is, as a *Time* magazine cover in his house wonders, a "Savior?" If the film aims to present the United States as terrorized to justify its imperial reach, then Will Smith's blackness seems, on one level, to reassuringly uncouple this project from its origins in white supremacy and colonialism. But what threatens to appear in the place of Neville-as-military scientist is a cinematic image of blackness that, as Kara Keeling writes in her discussion of the visual life of the Black Panther Party, "intensifie[s] the adversarial valence of the Black" (2007, 75). In a stateless postapocalyptic context, an armed black man contending with whitened monsters will mutate any story that reduces survival to a reboot of the American Dream. Especially when that story is specifically designed to mutate.

SEEING DOUBLE: RICHARD MATHESON'S *I AM LEGEND* (1954)

Robert Neville is knocking back glasses of whiskey and developing a theory about the vampires lurking outside his house. Drunkenly playing the professor while the undead prowl his lawn, Neville muses that the vampire is hated because it's profoundly feared—"a minority element if there ever was one, and there was one" (Matheson 1954, 31). He temporarily forgets his loathing, identifying instead with the thirstiness of those outside his walls, and offers an ironic "thesis": "Vampires," he opines, "are prejudiced against" (31). Matheson's *I Am Legend* (1954) constructs Robert Neville as an angry, lonely Last Man. Neville was a Los Angeles factory worker and military veteran in his former life, and his world fell apart when the plague of 1975 left him surrounded by corpses, both the still and the reanimated. Published in the early days of the civil rights movement, Matheson's novella gives readers narrative access to the psychic life of a white man who experiences himself as inundated by otherness and realizes, belatedly, that he's been displaced from the category of "normal." It dramatizes the end of Man as the dominant "genre" of the human.[6] And *Legend* is animated by an insight that arrives at the end of the story and reverberates back across the narrative, shedding critical light on all of Neville's actions. Captured by a "new society" (158), the evolution of which he's completely failed to discern, Neville finds himself reoriented by the emergence of another perspective on the undone world—one that prompts him to see himself as a monstrous anachronism. Finally grasping that he's failed to distinguish between the undead and the still-living in whom the bacterial plague has mutated—that he's been murdering them all in what he understood to be a cleansing of the city—Neville suddenly sees himself as a "terrible scourge," an "invisible specter who had left for evidence of his existence the bloodless bodies of their loved ones" (169). He recognizes on the faces of those who await his execution the terror that he, too, has felt, leading Neville not only to accept that Man's story of humanness—his story—has reached its end, but also to see its violence for the first time. How Neville arrives at this double vision, seeing himself as both Man and monster, creates the blueprint for the visual afterlife of Matheson's story.

Legend's portrayal of a racialized uprising is also the story of a breakdown in social reproduction, which means female bodies are points of intensity in this postapocalyptic landscape. Even in his drunken ramblings, when Neville reframes his monstrous Others as a "minority element" forced into violent revolt—the vampire "has no means of support, no measures for proper education, he has not the voting franchise"—he ends his ironic ventriloquism of postwar liberalism with a revealing question: "Sure, sure, he thought, but would you let your sister marry one?" (32). Neville's interior monologue evokes the supposed purity of white womanhood to highlight the contaminating influence of a racialized minority group, a construction that articulates with a postapocalyptic scenario in which, in his words, "black bastards" (35) are literally infected with plague. So Neville's attempts to ward off the unfamiliar future taking shape around him crystallize in his treatment of his wife's corpse. Unable to dispose of Virginia's body in the same burning pit into which he routinely throws the others—an inability that, in the narrative past, resulted in her undead return to their house—Neville instead keeps her corpse contained behind the iron doors of a crypt. At one point, prompted by fear that her dead body has been desecrated, an enraged Neville imagines razing all of Los Angeles to ensure that Virginia remains untouched. From the new vantage point that opens up at the end of the novel, this fantasy comes into view as a claiming of what Judith Butler formulates as "the prerogative to choose with whom to cohabit the earth"—a choice that is "always a genocidal practice" (2015, 111). It raises questions, too, about Neville's entombment of his wife. His compulsion to keep her "pure" and immobilized is synonymous with a need to end her story. To borrow the words of the Man in *The Road*, Neville ensures "there is no other tale to tell" about Virginia—certainly not one that involves his wife roaming the postapocalyptic streets of L.A., mixing with the "black bastards" who've inherited the world.

Neville's efforts to control his wife's story betray anxieties about his own future, a drama that animates a sexually violent imaginary in which he sees himself as besieged by undead seductresses. When he retreats into his fortified home at night, he's surrounded by bacterially reanimated bodies, including that of his former neighbor, Ben Cortman, who calls on Neville to come out and join them. Living a life of "forced celibacy" and fighting off the "mindless craving of his flesh," Neville experiences this ritual hailing as sexualized: "In the beginning he'd made a peephole in the front window and watched them. But then the women had seen him and had started striking vile postures in order to entice him out of the house" (19). The "lewd puppets" (19) that seduce him at night are objects of violence and, later, experimentation during the day. In what begins as a project of extermination but turns, over time, into a layman's investigation into causes, symptoms, and possible cures, Neville moves systematically through the city's residential neighborhoods in search of inert vampire bodies. In one fit of "experimental fervor," he violently pulls a woman out of bed by the wrists and, when she unconsciously digs her nails into him in protest, "drag[s] her the rest of the way by her hair" (39). Gazing at her on the sidewalk, observing the effects of sunlight on the vampire body, he "notice[s] her figure" before bitterly channeling his desire into the ostensibly detached, calculating gaze of the scientific observer (40). Neville's need to control the feminized, sexualized cityscape—to master female corpses and hold the city still—can be understood as a compulsive effort to manage his own desire for contact. This desire manifests repeatedly as a self-destructive impulse to leave his house at night. His sexually violent fantasies are symptomatic, then, of a colonial project of (self-)mastery, an unstable shuttling between drunken rages and scientific coldness that holds him apart from others and permits only death-dealing, probing forms of touch.

Neville's postapocalyptic lifeworld is riven by tensions between his stagnant, housebound existence and the terrifying "boundarylessness" induced by social collapse (Morrison 1992, 37). And these tensions rush to the surface when Neville meets Ruth. Late in the novel, after three years of living in isolation, Matheson presents a protagonist unmoored from the "multidimensional scope" (120) of time in which memories and imaginings jostle for purchase on the present. He inhabits a long, suspended "now" devoid of what Hannah Arendt calls "the web of human relationships" in which our actions, witnessed by others, tell stories of who we are (1958, 184). At this point, Neville barely has a story left with which to piece himself together. All he has, really, is Ben Cortman—the only person in the world who still calls him by name. And it's in this context, in which "hunting for Cortman" (119) has become the flimsiest of threads connecting him to the world outside his head, that Neville finally meets Ruth, an infected survivor sent by the new society to investigate their boogeyman. Neville's struggle to integrate Ruth into his wavering worldview—to fit her into a story that's suddenly lurched back to life—is exemplified by his use of a strangely clinical imperative. Caught between paranoia and hope, he muses about a potential future: "if she stayed, if they had to establish a relationship, perhaps become husband and wife, have children . . ." (139, ellipsis original). The unfinished thought conjures a procreative couple that overwrites the more radical relational possibilities that Neville himself once evoked. Sometime before Ruth's arrival, the sight of an uninfected dog had filled him with longing, reminding him that "always, in spite of reason, he had clung to the hope that someday he would find someone like himself—a man, a woman, a child, it didn't matter. Sex was fast losing its meaning without the endless prodding of mass hypnosis" (101). Though Neville's desire for closeness has shifted through the narrative, becoming more open and capacious in the absence of social conventions, Ruth's appearance seems at first to recruit him (back) into a "husband and wife" story that now feels alien (139).

But Ruth isn't a pure female vessel that will reboot Man's world. She's the harbinger of an unknown future. While Neville examines the results of a blood test that tells him she's infected, Ruth knocks him out and flees, leaving behind a letter that explains who she is and warning that her people will come to destroy him. And though the letter describes a drug that's kept her alive by arresting the germ's multiplication, Neville stares into his microscope and surmises that a more fundamental change has taken place: "Bacteria can mutate" (156). Ruth and her people represent a third group that destabilizes the Man/monster opposition organizing Neville's story of survival. As he puts it after reading Ruth's letter, the "framework of his life was collapsing and it frightened him" (156). The existence of this third group—and the sudden understanding that he's a hunted criminal—shuffles the emotional economy of Matheson's story. Neville sees "dark-suited men" piking the vampires outside his house and tries to hold on to a distinction between his own actions over the last three years and the "methodical butchery" taking place on his lawn (158). But latent affinities between Neville and his undead Others are surfacing: their (blood)thirstiness echoing in his alcoholism, his boxed-in nighttime existence mirroring their daytime hiddenness. All of this coheres around the figure of Ben Cortman struggling to escape the slaughter. Neville, for whom hunting for Cortman was "a relaxing hobby," suddenly finds himself emotionally aligned with his prey: "With a sense of inward shock he could not analyze in the rush of the moment, he realized that he felt more deeply toward the vampires than he did toward their executioners" (119, 158). And when Cortman finally goes down, Neville "almost felt the bullets in his own flesh" (159). Watching his own death-dealing actions reflected back to him prompts Neville to see his story from another angle—a vantage point from which he's a terrifying villain. This is the double vision that structures Matheson's *Legend.* Like Neville, who's haunted by a future he can't see, the narrative wavers under the pressure of a conclusion that will double back on it, unlocking perspectives that unfold a second story alongside the first. This doubleness—and the insights it affords—is encrypted in the cinematic versions of *Legend,* threatening to revise adaptations that work against it.

One more word, then, about Ruth, the mutant who embodies a future beyond Neville and the world (he thinks) he knows. In my chapter on *The Road,* a critical perspective on the Last Man's worldview found its way into the story via the ghost of a woman encrypted in the narrative past. In *Legend,* Neville's unraveling begins with an emissary from a future he won't live to see. Even before he knows of her mutation, Ruth's perspective—and questions—make Neville think "strange, alien thoughts" (147). So the counter-reading built into *Legend*'s narrative structure hinges on Ruth's arrival. Her hybrid existence and her letter are the pivots that reorient the protagonist—and the reader—so that the disavowed costs of Neville's survival finally surface. Among them is the revelation that his body count includes Ruth's husband. And even if the new society seems to reflect more than trouble Neville's orientation to an undone world—they, too, are cleansing the earth of "monsters"—Ruth takes critical distance from both the Last Man and the new men. In the end, she flatly refuses Neville's hypocritical judgements about the violence of the "dark-suited men," but she also provides him with the pills to take his own life, which thwarts the spectacular execution planned by her people. It's possible, then, that Ruth is oriented toward a future that isn't as "heartless" as Neville fears (168). Either way, she sends ripple effects back through the story that ask us to look, again, at everything Neville's said and done. And because Ruth is the narrative mechanism through which *Legend* undoes Man's story, it's Ruth—this time called Lisa—whom *The Omega Man* has to contain to achieve its refiguration of Neville as a white savior.

STAYING LOW: BORIS SAGAL'S *THE OMEGA MAN* (1971)

Robert Neville (Charlton Heston) is wandering through the women's section of a downtown L.A. department store. His roving eyes eventually come to rest on a brunette mannequin in a dusty bikini. As he settles his hand on the small of her waist, looking wistful, the sound of glass breaking underfoot causes him to whip around and survey the room. A medium shot features a dozen mannequins in various postures, two of which have afros and dark skin. As Neville scrutinizes one of these figures, her eyes slide toward him. They size each other up and then she bolts. This is Neville's first glimpse of Lisa (Rosalind Cash), the adult leader of a group of children who are resistant, though not immune, to the plague that's stricken the world. Her first on-screen appearance in *The Omega Man* alerts us to a fugitive mode of survival that's taken shape, in part, in response to Neville's monopoly on daytime movement in the downtown core. In this version of Matheson's story, Neville is a military scientist saved from the ravages of germ warfare by an experimental vaccine of his own creation. As far as he knows, he shares L.A. only with the Family, a group of black-robed, albino mutants led by former TV news anchor Jonathan Matthias (Anthony Zerbe). They believe they're chosen to complete the global purification begun by the plague, which leads them to cast Neville as "the last of scientists, of bankers, of businessmen"—a remnant of the establishment that must be eradicated. But Neville, too, operates according to a logic of chosenness that frames the Family as "vermin" to be exterminated. He explores the city sector by sector, searching out their "nest" and responding to any movement at all—even a shadow flitting across a window—with a spray of bullets. So when Neville expresses shock that he's been unaware of Lisa's existence for the three years since the plague, her explanation is also a rebuke: "Between the Family at night and you in the daytime shooting at anything that moved, man we had to stay low." Lisa is *Omega*'s critical perspective, a presence navigating the spaces outside and under Neville's urban grid and activating an alternative story of survival that the film works hard to absorb.[7]

Released during the rise of the Black Power movement, Boris Sagal's *The Omega Man* (1971) anxiously inherits Matheson's tale of racialized revolution, evading its most radical implications by demonizing the counterculture of the 1960s. Critics have pointed out that Lisa is styled like Angela Davis; that her multiracial band of infected young people seems to allegorize an insurgent Third World; and that the Family's "book burning, Luddism, and cultish collectivism" evoke "the familiar, propagandistic caricature of Sovietization" (Sully 2016, 105). I propose that *Omega*'s navigation of these Cold War–era coordinates hinges on its conjuring of a contemporaneous and distinctly L.A. demon: the Manson Family. The trial of Charles Manson and his followers for the 1969 killings that became known as the Tate-LaBianca murders began in June 1970 and stretched into the following spring. Filming on *The Omega Man* began in late 1970. And the Family certainly seems to channel the Manson Family's twisted take on the hippie counterculture: the long-haired, darkly Messianic leader; the followers who demonstrate their togetherness by speaking and singing in unison; their "nest" is even in the Civic Center, the downtown complex that includes the Hall of Justice where the Manson trial took place.[8] Perhaps more importantly, though, Manson's apocalyptic beliefs offer a template for the imagining and invalidating of black revolution. The Beatles-inspired apocalypse that Manson called "Helter Skelter" was a war of black against white: as one of his followers explained, "'what it meant was the Negroes were going to come down and rip the cities all apart'" (qtd. in Bugliosi 1974, 327). The Tate-LaBianca murders were meant to look as if "'some of the spades from Watts'" had committed them, which Manson hoped would incite white reprisal and ultimately spark a black-white civil war (qtd. in Bugliosi 1974, 328). The Family would wait out the violence in the desert and return as the chosen people. In the mind of Charles Manson, black people would massacre the white establishment and then, "unable to handle the reins of power because of inexperience," turn the world over to Manson and his followers (415). By drawing on the still-fresh memory of the Manson Family, *Omega* reimagines Matheson's uprising as the deluded vision of a depraved, murderous pocket of the counterculture. This lays the groundwork for the film's reinvestment in, as Lisa puts it, "the man—and I do mean The Man."

The Omega Man's displacement of the sixties liberation movements with a Mansonesque caricature happens in the first ten minutes of the film. When Neville goes to the movies looking for company, the marquee announces that he's viewing the 1970 documentary *Woodstock*. Colonel Robert Neville sits alone in the dark, watching half-clothed crowds groove along with Country Joe and the Fish. His face is a mix of emotions as he speaks along with one of the interviewees, an indication that he's seen this film many, many times since the world fell apart. But there's an edge to Neville's melancholy, too, a sense that somehow these vaguely anarchic young people are part of the reason everything went to hell. The film reinforces this sense by carrying over into Neville's postapocalyptic present the "figure of the pressing, threatening crowd" (Sully 2016, 103). At this point we've only seen Neville alone in the city. So the shift from the depopulated urban streets to the crowds at Woodstock activates "a dialectic of the presence/absence of bodies" that animates *Omega*'s portrayal of a besieged Last Man (100). When Neville leaves the theater, he's bombarded by the sound of ringing payphones—an auditory hallucination. It's as if the on-screen crowd has leaked out into the empty streets, making the city around him, even in its stillness, hostile and disorienting. A single overhead shot that seems to originate in the upper-story window of an off-screen building suggests the urban landscape is watching, even enticing Neville to stay out after dusk. And when he finally quiets the ringing in his ears, his anxious exclamation that "they'll be waking up soon!" relays Neville's sense of inundation over to a fearsome "they": the Family that waits for Neville outside his townhouse. From Woodstock to the (Manson) Family, *Omega* draws a line from one of the most famous spectacles of the sixties counterculture to one of the most infamous.

The demonization of Matthias's Family, a foil to the multiracial family that Neville connects with through Lisa, functions in two interrelated ways in *The Omega Man*. By neutralizing the most radical elements of the sixties movements, the Family (seemingly) splits Lisa's Black Power aesthetic away from the revolutionary political imaginings it signifies. This allows the film to absorb blackness into a fantasized future anchored by a benevolent white patriarch. Benevolent whiteness, too, emerges in contrast with the evil extreme signified by the Family's shared paleness. As if to counter Matheson's racialized description of the vampire as "something black and of the night [that] had come crawling out of the Middle Ages" (28), *Omega* visually expresses the Family's condition as a loss of skin pigment—sickening as whitening. So when Matthias's right-hand man, Brother Zachary (Lincoln Kilpatrick), describes Neville's house as a "honky paradise," his leader rebukes him for remembering his blackness: "Forget the old ways, brother, all your hatreds, all your pains. Forget. And remember: the Family is one." The Family is both whitened and postracial. Recalling Manson's vision, Matthias emerges as the white—or whiter—leader of a new society in which there's no place for (further) black revolt. In short, *Omega* sidesteps the most radical implications of Matheson's story by rearticulating revolution to a pathologized whiteness associated with un-American collectives both foreign and domestic. This makes room to present Neville as untroubled by racial diversity even as he maintains all the power and authority of white masculinity. The young group to which Lisa introduces him is a family without a father, a lack that presents Neville with the opportunity to shape the future that will emerge from postapocalyptic terrain. So *Omega*'s answer to the apocalyptic sixties is a racially diverse rebeginning embodied in the pairing of Neville with Lisa. But, like Will Smith after her, Cash's Lisa can't be smoothly recruited into the production of a new New World dream. Though she's potentially pregnant with Neville's baby at the end of the film, Lisa's allegiances, desires, and corporeal future are murky at best, making her the loose end that might yet unravel this tale.

The film works to manage this loose end, to contain the story moves and futures that Lisa breathes to life, by yoking her to Neville as, in Wynter's terms, a "donor figure" (Wynter and McKittrick 2015, 36). According to Wynter, we emerge as a "we" by inventing and projecting behind us a myth of origins, conjuring donor figures that give the present social order a mandate that allows it to hold its shape into the future. A donor figure is thus both exemplary of and apart from the "we" it calls into being. So when Lisa, the children, and a former medical student named Dutch (Paul Koslo) enter Neville's life, contact and connection take shape as corporeal investments—donations—through which Neville "fathers" the postapocalyptic generation. Authorized as both patriarch and donor, Neville ostensibly guarantees that the young people in his charge won't follow in the anarchic footsteps of the hippies in the *Woodstock* footage. In fact, his blood will directly intervene in what the film presents as an otherwise inevitable transformation. When Dutch explains to Neville that their group is resistant to the plague but could "go over" any time, becoming the "tertiary cases" that he's seen in the Family, Neville begins making a serum out of his own vaccinated blood. Lisa's younger brother, Richie, is at an advanced stage of infection, so he becomes the first vessel meant to carry what Neville jokingly(?) describes as his "genuine, 160-proof old Anglo-Saxon" blood into the future. Lisa, too, will eventually need Neville's Anglo-Saxon vitality because she spontaneously "goes over" at the end of the film. But even before this, *Omega* gestures to another exchange of bodily fluids when Neville and Lisa banter about being the "last boy" and "last girl" in the world and then have sex. The next scene underscores the reproductive implications of this encounter when, while raiding a drugstore, Lisa laughingly tosses aside a package of birth control pills. So Neville's blood now runs through Richie's veins and Lisa is potentially pregnant with his child. Evoking a history of American anxieties about miscegenation, *Omega* projects a postwhite future anchored, nonetheless, in the restored patriarchal and scientific authority of white masculinity. In this version of the story, Neville becomes the "founding father" of a new mixed-race family while his "genuine, 160-proof old Anglo-Saxon" blood becomes the material basis of that family's origin story—an inheritance destined to become, literally, the stuff of legend.[9]

The Omega Man offers a new New World origin story by constructing a racially diverse "we" that unfolds from a benevolent scientist who dreams of a new Eden. But this emergent collective is contested. When Neville informs a recently healed Richie that the bloodlines of their family will not extend to the Family, whose members he describes as "half-dead already," Richie retorts, "You know what, Mister? You're hostile. You just don't belong. . . . There are times you scare me more than Matthias does." Of course, the film's conjuring of the Manson Family undermines Richie's critique. Any doubts we might have about the Family's evil intentions are put to rest when, in response to Richie's attempt to organize a parlay between Matthias and Neville, Matthias orders the boy killed. But Richie's actions, like those of the boy in *The Road*, tell a story of vulnerability, care, and compassion that brings into relief the violent exclusions shaping Neville's fantasy of a fresh start. Richie's had the embodied experience of "going over" and coming back, a lived experience of duality that induces in him the dream of a "we" capacious enough for everyone left alive, including the sick. In contrast, Neville insists on withholding health from the city's "vermin," a move that establishes his new Eden as a biopolitical project that divides the fit from the unfit. And this division animates Neville's fantasy of reviving civilization in an untouched, ahistorical space: "Someplace nobody ever bothered with. A river nobody ever dammed, a mountain nobody ever built any bloody freeways to." So while Richie is unable to forget those who would be left behind, Neville's dream is entirely premised on forgetting: a space beyond L.A. that was always unpopulated, an empty land "nobody ever bothered with," is, at root, a colonial fantasy. It projects a blank slate that suppresses, again, the originary peoples and lifeworlds of what we now call the Americas.

Neville dies at the end of the film, striking a Christ-like pose and bequeathing his Edenic dream—along with the serum and a now "turned" and possibly pregnant Lisa—to Dutch. But *Omega* ends with a deferred transaction: the injection that would cure Lisa is implied but not delivered by the narrative, raising questions about her figuration as the receptacle that will extend Neville's bloodline in predictable directions. Lisa "belongs" with the Family at the end of the film but lingers, inexplicably, by Neville's body as he bleeds out. This lingering is what makes her available to be collected by Dutch the next morning, but it also suggests allegiances that are multiple and contradictory. It suggests, even, that Matthias's grip on her, signaled a few scenes before by her zombie-like response to his voice, isn't as total as it seems. Lisa's divided loyalties at the end of the film echo the radically inclusive stance that Richie died for, opening up the possibility that Lisa, too, desires a mode of survival that isn't premised on abandonment, forgetting, and apartness. After all, Lisa has a history of criticizing Neville's survivalism that reverberates uneasily across her recruitment as the "last girl" to his "last boy." When they meet face to face at the midpoint of the film and Neville recognizes her as the department store "mannequin," she snidely describes herself as his "living Playtex doll," a savvy articulation of the way Others are objects to be used or destroyed in Neville's imaginary. Given the sexual violence that seethes beneath the surface of Matheson's source material, and in light of a history of the institutionalized rape of black women in the New World, the last girl's ironic self-description as a living doll haunts the awkward romance that unfolds across the second half of the film. *Omega*'s unconvincing love story can't com-

FIGURE 5. Lisa (Rosalind Cash) confronts "the man—and I do mean The Man." Still from *The Omega Man* (Walter Seltzer Productions, 1971).

pletely suppress the critical, gun-toting Lisa who's survived for three years in spite of Robert Neville.[10]

The Lisa who calls herself a living doll and rebukes Neville for his trigger-happiness points to alternative modes of sociality and survival, allowing us to feel the presence of a story that *this* story can't imagine. While *Omega* works hard to separate Lisa's corporeal style from the radical political imaginaries of Black Power, her on-screen appearance in a red leather alligator-skin pantsuit and Angela Davis–like afro is too much for the film. Especially given Davis's appearance on the FBI's Most Wanted list in 1970 and the widely circulated mugshot that resulted, Lisa offers a glimpse of revolutionary blackness that resonates with the broader visual disruptions effected by Black Power.[11] As Kara Keeling puts it, images of "blacks with guns" in the 1960s jarred loose the common sense frames, or stereotypes, through which blackness had previously appeared in American culture: "the cinematic appearance of blacks with guns made visible one of the black's alternative pasts, rendering the past called forth to support the habituated perception of the black 'not necessarily true'" (2007, 74–75). The glimpse of an alternative past gestures to the possibility of a new origin story and, in turn, a radically different "we." The image of Lisa with her gun trained on Neville, whom she derisively describes as "the man—and I do mean The Man," isn't easily folded into the last boy–last girl story and its logical extension: a first boy–first girl rebeginning in a new incarnation of Eden. *Omega*'s deferral of Lisa's cure to an off-screen time and place inadvertently jives with the unsettled historical timeline generated by "black with guns," articulating alternative pasts to an indeterminate future and, perhaps, an as yet unimagined world. Lisa's story is unfinished, her future uncertain. If I extend my imagination to an unseen space-time beyond the cinematic frame, she's there, her actions telling better stories than the story of Man—and I do mean The Man.

LISTENING TO MARLEY: FRANCIS LAWRENCE'S *I AM LEGEND* (2007)

Tired of eating canned vegetables for dinner, Robert Neville's loyal canine companion, Sam, recklessly chases a deer into the blackened interior of a crumbling Manhattan apartment building. Neville is gripped by a fear so intense that he nearly abandons his only friend to the creatures that are, in all likelihood, waiting out the daylight in this yawning darkness. Barely suppressing his panic, he creeps through the building, calling for Sam in hoarse whispers and allowing only intermittent flashes of light to orient himself in the space. When the two finally reunite and make a run for it to escape those who've become alert to their presence, Neville aims for the only faint glimmer of daylight he can see, hurling himself through a second-floor window to escape the screeching, clawing creature that's leaped onto his back. In contrast with the raging loneliness of Matheson's Neville and the sardonic swagger of Heston's, Will Smith's Neville is terrorized. He shrinks in fear from the roaring white bodies that control the Manhattan night—as well as its daytime shadows. And this fear of the dark shakes darkness loose from its traditional moorings in the dominant U.S. imaginary.

Legend's geographical shift to "ground zero" evokes an American trauma that also conjures the nation's "formative catastrophes and their symptoms"—a conjuring that asks us "to identify the ideological sutures that hide the damage and repetitions" (Berger 1999, 219). In combination with Smith's casting, *Legend*'s relocation opens up a long history of black life and death encrypted in the New York cityscape. From the African Burial Ground under Lower Manhattan to the rumors of a slave rebellion that, in the mid-eighteenth century, resulted in thirteen black men being burned at the stake and buried there, New York City seethes with a history of brutalized and rebellious black bodies.[12] Given the play of dark and light that organizes Neville's relationship to his Others, Simone Browne's discussion of colonial New York's "lantern laws" is particularly relevant here. In response to an armed slave insurrection in 1712, Browne writes, in "March 1713, the Common Council of New York City passed a 'Law for Regulating Negro & Indian Slaves in the Nighttime,'" declaring that they were not to appear in the streets of New York "'above one hour after sun sett without a lanthorn and a lighted candle'" (qtd. in Browne 2015, 78). Browne notes the way these ordinances governed black and Indigenous life in the colonial city, constructing racialized peoples "as security risks in need of supervision after dark" (78). The logics informing this early surveillance technology articulate whiteness with the right to move freely in the dark and, in turn, demand that racialized subjects make themselves perpetually trackable. In a context in which Neville lives in fear of a violent white majority and in which, without a light source, he risks injury or death, a black Robert Neville conjures the city's colonial ghosts. And this is where the "ideological sutures" keeping those ghosts at bay begin to fray (Berger 1999, 219). *Legend*'s narrative stability depends on the suturing of its black Last Man to the security state he once represented. But the history of the lantern laws, summoned by Neville's need to stay in the light, is a reminder of the racial origins of practices of security and surveillance.[13] In this landscape, with this Neville, racism-as-virus begins to peel away from the post-9/11 intimations of hate-as-virus, opening up *Legend* to storytelling mutations.

Neville's relationship to the state he once represented is unstable. While his gray cargo pants and Belstaff leather jacket don't signify in the same way as Lisa's afro, he is, nonetheless, an armed black man negotiating a hostile city, his appearance potentially evoking an "adversarial valence" of blackness that exposes a projected rebeginning of the American Dream to scrutiny (Keeling 2007, 75). Even in the flashback sequence in which Neville is wearing his military dress uniform, a tense scene underscores his fraught relationship to state power. As he's ushering his wife, Zoe, and young daughter, Marley, past a military checkpoint with minutes to spare before the quarantine takes effect, Zoe's retinal scan shows a false positive for infection. Browne argues that biometric technologies function in ways that reinforce "prototypical whiteness"; that they're embedded in a "visual economy of recognition and verification" that assumes the normativity of white bodies (2015, 110). So we might see in this moment a surfacing of the racial logics that animate biometric technologies, which exposes Zoe to the antiblackness structuring the state's practices of security.[14] The result is a chaotic scene in which Neville's uniform is barely enough to hold the black family together. What threatens to become visible here, even as Neville shouts his "Lieutenant Colonel" rank, is "the precariousness of the State's claim to represent black people" (Keeling 2007, 75). In a postapocalyptic context in which the state has fallen, then, Lieutenant Colonel Robert Neville, virologist, is a trace identity overwritten by the simpler way that Neville describes himself in his radio broadcast: "My name is Robert Neville, I am a survivor living in New York City." Neville's only attachment to his old identity is his ongoing effort to find a cure for the Krippin Virus (KV), a project he carries out in his basement laboratory according to somewhat standard protocols of environmental control, data collection, and testing. But while this might signal a preserved connection to a vanished state, it might also indicate a more unruly, species-wide sense of affiliation. After all, when one of his rats shows decreased symptoms of KV, Neville declares that the associated compound is his "next candidate for human trials," which means that his "we" is potentially more elastic than his former job allowed. As the two endings of this *Legend* attest, Smith-as-Neville might tell an unexpected story—one that's critical of the neocolonial worldview into which the film's theatrically released ending attempts to recruit him.

This Neville inherits the two models of survival embodied by his predecessors in *The Omega Man*: an uneasy twisting together of militarized hardness and black militancy that might, at any moment, come unraveled. On the one hand, Neville's

FIGURE 6. Neville, holding Marley (Willow Smith), demands that soldiers scan his wife's eyes again before the quarantine takes effect. Still from *I Am Legend* (Warner Brothers, 2007).

efforts to subdue and reassimilate his monstrous Others register his implication in Man's colonial story. Though he sees the KV-infected as human rather than "vermin," his search for a cure nonetheless proceeds according to a logic that Sherene Razack identifies as the improvement of the unfit—"or, in an old phrase, the civilizing mission" (2015, 7). "I can still fix this," he insists to his wife as the city falls apart. But, on the other hand, this neocolonial narrative knots up when we shift perspective and see Neville as a black man terrorized by a vampiric, pale-skinned horde. Heston's Neville leaves his balcony doors open so he can listen to the Family's taunts and hurl tumblers of whiskey at them. But Smith's Neville lives a fugitive existence more akin to that of Lisa, withdrawing far into his Washington Square townhouse at night and sliding thick steel shutters across its elegant windows. From this perspective, Neville's attempt to "fix" a world in which he's exposed, daily, to violence and death might transmute a neocolonial tale into one that evokes anti- and decolonial legacies. In the last chapter I argued, following Toni Morrison, that darkness is a multivalent element of the American imaginary; that the savagery and terror it connotes are projected onto Man's Others to suppress the fact that Man himself terrorizes, rapes, and massacres his world into being.[15] From this point of view, we might see Neville as negotiating—and working against—Man's world-destroying darkness. Together, these readings of *Legend* unveil Man's story as structured by both settler-colonial and antiblack violence. There are tensions here that a black Robert Neville doesn't really resolve. Even *Legend*'s progressive ending meets an imaginative limit when it comes to questions of Indigenous futurity. Still, Neville's blackness means that one narrative strand—the one that's attuned to the costs of Man's story—keeps peeling apart from the one that encourages us to reinvest in colonial Man.

The strands of story I've been identifying unfold toward *Legend*'s two very different endings. The difference between them derives from the film's negotiation of an insight that I explored in the previous chapter: risking ourselves can breathe life (back) into the "web of human relationships" in which we contest, stretch, and revise the story of our "we" (Arendt 1958, 184). From the moment a hoodie-wearing mannequin that Neville playfully calls "Fred" appears out of his usual place at a local video store, Neville's feelings for others unravel his orderly world. And the film's endings resolve this unraveling in nearly opposite ways. Recalling the gendered logic of Matheson's source material, I refer to them as the "Virginia ending" and the "Ruth ending." Virginia, remember, was the wife who Neville entombed in an effort to end her story. His treatment of her corpse was emblematic of his impulse to master the city and ward off an unfamiliar future. Ruth, on the other hand, was the narrative mechanism through which Matheson reoriented Neville's perspective on his own actions, inducing a double vision in which he saw himself as both man and monster and prompting him to cede his claim to the city. In the context of the 2007 *Legend,* the theatrically released "Virginia ending" sees Neville become a new founding father, sacrificing his life to support a reboot of Man's world in a walled community in Vermont. The "Ruth ending" is the discarded original ending, allegedly altered due to unfavorable responses from test audiences, in which Neville realizes that the infected are communicating their losses; that they're holding him accountable for the hundreds of test subjects he's killed in his search for a cure. Throughout the second half of *Legend,* and beginning with the loss of his dog, Sam(antha), Neville's relationship to a cluster of feminine and feminized others creates an unstable interplay between his impulse toward mastery and his susceptibility to being undone.[16] The "Virginia" ending resolves this oscillation by ushering in a future of more walls, more security—the rebeginning of Man—and the "Ruth" ending critically revises everything Neville thought he knew.

In this *Legend,* the "Ruth" function—the unexpected feminine arrival whose perspective reorients Neville to the ruined world—is split between an uninfected survivor named Anna (Alice Braga) and an infected test subject sedated in Neville's lab. She's listed in the film's credits as the "Alpha Female." This splitting runs along the fault line of Ruth's characterization in the original story: there's the fantasy Ruth who, Neville imagines, is like him and with whom he may ("have to") start a new human world; and she's displaced by the mutant Ruth who represents the new society. Given that Ruth is the narrative mechanism that unlocks the counternarrative at the core of Matheson's novella, her splitting in this *Legend* can either facilitate a taming of the story or amplify its radical message—an either/or that depends on whether Anna or the Alpha Female is the pivot on which the film's climax turns. Anna is a Brazilian survivor from a Red Cross ship off the coast of São Paulo who's traveling with a young boy named Ethan. After arriving in Manhattan and preventing a disconsolate Neville from following through on what is, essentially, a suicide mission prompted by Sam's death, Anna inadvertently leads the infected to his townhouse. So the climax of the film sees Neville, Anna, and Ethan taking refuge in the basement laboratory. There, they retreat behind the plexiglass partition where Neville's been keeping the sedated Alpha Female, only to discover that his latest serum has worked. But the infected, led by the Alpha Male, are already throwing themselves at the glass wall, uninterested in Neville's cries of "I can save you!" This is where the film splits in two. Both endings play on the butterfly symbolism threaded through the film, which originates with Neville's daughter, Marley. In a flashback sequence earlier in the film, Marley twice tries to get Neville's attention by making a butterfly with her hands. So the direction the story takes depends on whether Marley's butterfly leads him to Anna or the mutant.

The "Virginia ending" released in theaters links the butterfly to Anna, which frames, in turn, the sacrifice that follows as a form of Christian martyrdom that recalls Charlton Heston's Christ-on-the-cross pose at the end of *The Omega Man*. When Anna first arrives on the scene, her message to a bitter, cynical Neville is that "the world is quieter now," which should allow him to hear "God's plan." And though Neville at first rages against this advice, we know from a flashback sequence that he and his family prayed together before Neville sent Zoe and Marley off in a helicopter to escape the quarantine zone. Anna reminds Neville of his familial and Christian roots, then, both of which he lost track of when that helicopter exploded in the air before his eyes. So when the splintering of the glass partition in the lab produces a butterfly shape, Neville notices, for the first time, a small butterfly tattoo on Anna's neck. He installs Ethan and Anna, along with a vial of the test subject's cured blood, behind the thick steel door of a coal chute before pulling the pin on a grenade and throwing himself at the glass wall. In the film's coda, Anna becomes his emissary, delivering the cure for KV to a survivor's colony in Vermont: "We," she says in voiceover, "are his legacy. This is his legend." So in the "Virginia ending" Neville becomes a new Founding Father whose sacrifice restores Man's world, invigorating a future safeguarded by enormous gates, surveillance cameras, armed guards, and the sound of church bells. It's a rebeginning in a walled community on the east coast that anticipates another westward expansion across the continent—one that installs a black "donor figure" to anchor a more inclusive but fundamentally unchanged American Dream (Wynter and McKittrick 2015, 36). On the heels of Neville's attempt to reason with the infected, shouting through the glass that he "can save everybody," "God's plan" takes shape as a restaging of the vision outlined in the 1493 papal bull, which required that "'the barbarous nations [of the Americas] be overthrown and brought to the faith itself'" (qtd. in Weaver 2014, 2). The future projected from New England ground resettles the settler state, recruiting Neville's incinerated body into a postracial fantasy in which a "new and improved" United States rises from the ashes of the old.

But the "Ruth ending," which hinges on the Alpha Female, moves toward imagining a more flexible "we." And this begins with a different butterfly. *Legend*'s discarded ending shows the Alpha Male, injured by the splintering glass, deliberately use his bloodied hand to smear a butterfly shape onto the weakening partition. An incredulous Neville hears his child's voice—"Daddy, look it's a butterfly"—but this time it directs his attention to the "cured" Alpha Female's butterfly tattoo, a vestige of the young person she was before the outbreak. Neville listens, finally, to his Others, which prompts him to arrest the cycle of violence by risking—though not ensuring—his own destruction. He reverses the cure, opens the partition, and moves without protection among the infected, his bowed head suggesting both fear and shame. Neville's stunned, whispered apology elicits an anguished roar from the Alpha Male. The next shot is composed so that Neville's blurred head remains in the foreground while, in the background, a wall covered with photographs of his other test subjects—all dead—comes into view. A visibly humbled Neville looks at the wall and then shuts his eyes tightly against an attack he's sure is coming. But the Alpha Male leads his pack out of the lab and leaves him unharmed. The "Ruth ending" sees Neville recognize the violence of the Western scientific-military apparatus that produces, experiments on, and destroys dehumanized Others. And, acknowledging his part in that dehumanizing violence, he awaits the Other's judgement of his crimes. But in this moment, both characters let go of a story in which their wounds authorize them to destroy the other. Both seem to recognize that they injure as well as suffer injury; that they terrorize as well as feel terror. The result is an act of atonement and an unexpected mercy.

The "Virginia ending" suggests a violent rebooting of the colonial "logic of elimination" through which the dysselected are disappeared (Wolfe 2006, 387). But the "Ruth ending" offers a vision of survival that pivots on the claim of nonviolence. In *Frames of War* (2009), Judith Butler casts nonviolence not as an abstract principle but, rather, as a mode of address. Our capacity to hear this claim depends on our willingness to revise a story in which we've suffered and survived injury—a hero's tale—so that it can encompass, too, the ways we've caused others to suffer. It depends on a sense of self shaped by the insight that we do harm to others even in our hurt. We are, Butler writes, "mired" in violence (171). But this is the condition of possibility of hearing the claim of nonviolence and enacting, in turn, a "crucial breakage . . . between the violence by which we are formed and the violence with which, once formed, we conduct ourselves" (167). If we can hear the disavowed costs—to ourselves and to others—of our story of survival, then we can find our way to a revised story and a new "we." In the coda to *Legend*'s discarded ending, we see Neville, Anna, and Ethan driving out of New York City and hear Anna's voice in a new radio message: "Keep your radio on. Listen to our broadcasts. You are not alone. There is hope. Keep listening. You are not alone." In place of a voiceover that tries to secure our interpretation of Neville's sacrifice, we have the renewal of an open address to unknown others. Anna's "keep listening" recalls, this time, Neville's explicit framing of his return of the Alpha Female as an act of "listening," which suggests that the "you" to whom the broadcast is addressed might be unexpectedly capacious. This ending leaves unresolved the colonial implications of rebeginning in the Americas. But it does make room for the survival—and coexistence—of genres of humanness beyond Man.

If this is the ending toward which *Legend* was headed all along—one in which Neville is neither Man nor monster—then what meaning does it make of Matheson's title? Early in this chapter, I noted that Neville's soundtrack is Bob Marley's *Legend* album. Neville the scientist grooves to "Three Little Birds" as he bathes his dog, creating a pocket of love and calm in the midst of a shattered world. And when he tells Anna that he and Zoe named their kid after Marley, he's stunned by her (maybe a little improbable) failure to recognize the name. This prompts him to share the singer-activist's belief that "you could cure racism and hate . . . by injecting music and love into people's lives"—a belief that he frames as "a virologist's idea." Much of Neville's identity, then, is wrapped up in his relationship to the music and worldview of Bob Marley. There are two points I want to make, in closing, about how *Legend* works in *I Am Legend*. The first is that when Neville quotes Marley's "Light up the darkness," he recalibrates imagery that's often deployed in colonial storytelling. As I've shown, a storyline in which Neville means to bring the light of scientific reason to the "savage" darkness that's taken hold of the world barely holds up in this film.[17] And here Neville rearticulates the project of lighting up the darkness—"a virologist's idea"—to anticolonial, antiracist activism. This suggests that "darkness" is Man's doing. And it opens up space to wonder what might become of Neville's scientific practices when they're freed from the framework of the security state. (I return to the question of scientific futures in chapters 4 and 5.) The second point I want to make is that the inclusion of Marley's music in *Legend* creates a soundscape that reaches beyond the film's progressive ending. Katherine McKittrick argues that the "rebellious enthusiasms" of black music—the beats, rhythms, frequencies, lyrics, and waveforms that refuse black dehumanization—undo Man's ways of knowing and the forms of dispossession they support (2016, 81). "One grooves *out* of the logics of antiblackness," McKittrick writes, "and *into* black life" (89, emphases original). This is part of a much bigger story about black cultural invention and rehumanization in the diaspora, strands of which are threaded through the next three chapters. For now, I only want to draw a line from Neville's listening to Marley—both his kid and the artist after whom she's named—to the insight at the heart of the film's discarded ending: that we can reimagine, altogether, what it means to be human.

CODA: BODIES THAT LABOR

My description of Ruth as a "narrative mechanism" and my naming of the 2007 film's two endings as "Ruth" and "Virginia" draws attention to how femininity works in the *Legend* stories. But I'm also drawing attention to the fact that femininity *works*—that feminine and feminized bodies are put to work by a narrative concerned, for the most part, with a man's vision(s) of the future. So while the 2007 *Legend* offers us a protagonist who troubles the story of Man (and I do mean The Man) in ways *The Road* doesn't, I'm wary of the gendered transactions on which both of the film's endings pivot. In the "Virginia ending," Neville draws a sample of the cured Alpha Female's blood and entrusts it to Anna, who passes it over to an unseen man as soon as she arrives at the colony in Vermont. The camera offers only a closeup of large, white hands. So the dehumanized female mutant is plundered for biological material and then consumed by Neville's self-destructive explosion, and Anna delivers both this valuable blood and Neville's story into (ahem) male hands. But even the more progressive "Ruth ending" is organized by Neville's return of the Alpha Female to her mate. The transaction is suggestive of what Eve Sedgwick calls "the exchange-of-women framework," in which relations between men constitute "the backbone of social form" (1985, 86).[18] I don't mean to suggest that *Legend*'s "Ruth ending" can or should be reduced to this masculine exchange—only that the range of futures that comes into view seems constrained by it. In the end, the white woman is the "mad scientist" whose creation ruins the world; a black woman and child are encrypted in the narrative past; the female mutant is objectified; and Anna never really gets to tell her own story. (What's happened to her over the last three years? How has she kept Ethan alive? What, exactly, are the contours of her Christian faith?) Since this is where *Legend* meets its imaginative limits, in the next chapter I'll consider two films in which a young black woman, a "mad" white woman, and two teen girls play significant roles.

Danny Boyle's *28 Days Later* (2002) and its sequel inherit some of *Legend*'s mutant DNA. Both franchises imagine the apocalypse in terms of what Priscilla Wald (2008) calls the "outbreak narrative." And though neither Matheson nor Boyle refers to his monsters as "zombies," both *Legend* and the *28* films are persistently taken up by fans and critics as part of the "zompocalypse" horror subgenre. I turn to the *28* films next, then, not only because female characters with complex psychic lives feature in their storytelling, but also because they shed light on yet another body that's laboring in *Legend*'s cinematic background: the zombie, a figure that, as Sarah Juliet Lauro argues, was appropriated and put to work by American filmmakers in a "bitterly ironic . . . cultural theft of an artifact that was itself about cultural theft" (2015, 98). In the next chapter, I think with and build on Lauro's analysis of the zombie as embodying, in irresolvable tension, both enslavement and rebellion. For now, I want to notice that (re)reading *Legend* as a contribution to the Americanized zombie myth amplifies the unruliness of a black Robert Neville. In her reflections on George Romero's "incidental" casting of black actor Duane Jones in *Night of the Living Dead* (1968)—a film that, Romero says, was influenced by Matheson's *Legend*—Lauro notes that "this happy accident is precisely what makes the film socially conscious" (99). Outside of any question of directorial intention, Jones's on-screen presence activates the historical content of the zombie figure—particularly its association, crystallized during the Haitian Revolution, with the rebellious slave. I've been following a different line of argumentation about the casting of Will Smith in *Legend*, but reached a similar conclusion: Smith's blackness can't be stably recruited into a domesticated version of a story about race and revolution. Locating *Legend* in the Hollywood zombie tradition only reinforces that argument. As we'll see in the next chapter, no matter how fast it runs, the zombie is never far from its (anti)colonial origins.

3 • REVOLTING REANIMATIONS

The *28* Films

Danny Boyle's *28 Days Later* (U.K. 2002) has an ending that was never released in theatres. The abandoned sequence depicts the death of the film's young white protagonist, Jim (Cillian Murphy), in an empty Manchester hospital. Jim's fellow survivors—a young black woman named Selena (Naomie Harris) and a white teenager named Hannah (Megan Burns)—go to great lengths trying to save him. But in the end, they can't. So in the final shot, Selena and Hannah walk down one of the hospital's long corridors, one carrying a rifle and the other holding a pistol at her side. The long shot captures them from behind, their silhouettes made strange by the red dresses imposed on them when, earlier in the film, an encounter with military men went badly wrong. The camera holds position as the two survivors walk away and then disappear through the double doors at the end of the corridor.

And that, Boyle and screenwriter Alex Garland say, is where the credits would have rolled. But, like *I Am Legend*'s alternate ending, this one was rejected by test audiences and consigned to the Special Features menu of the film's DVD release. In their commentary, Boyle and Garland call this both "an" ending and "the" ending. "The proper ending," Boyle says at one point. And Garland sounds perturbed by test audiences that read this scene as two women "walking off to their doom" in spite of, he notes, "all the evidence" offered throughout the film of their capacity to survive. This chapter is an attempt to think with this seemingly impossible ending—to linger in the gap between "all the evidence" that Selena and Hannah can survive together and the unimaginability of this prospect.[1] What can we learn from how the *28* films deviate from the patriarchal, colonial fantasies of survival that swirl around the figure of the Last Man? And what role does the zombie play in these storytelling interventions?

28 Days Later and its sequel, Juan Carlos Fresnadillo's *28 Weeks Later* (U.K./Spain 2007), are known for introducing into cinemas a new kind of zombie embodiment widely seen as symptomatic of late capitalist crisis. "Variously known as the fast zombie, the rage zombie, or the plague zombie," Ian Olney writes, this

FIGURE 7. Hannah (Megan Burns) and Selena (Naomie Harris) head back out into quarantined England in the alternate ending to *28 Days Later*. Still from *28 Days Later* (DNA Films, 2002).

monster "invites us to contemplate our place in an economy that has spiraled out of control and appears to be on the verge of consuming itself" (2017, 66). The *28* films draw on the visual grammar of rioting in ways that evoke the postwar street scenes I discuss in my introduction. From the student protests of 1968 to the streets of Brixton, Toxteth, and Handsworth in the 1980s, British conservatives read scenes of disaffected youth and racial unrest as portending The End of (white) Englishness. And Boyle's monsters are choreographed in a way that visually conjures these histories.[2] They're speedy, not lumbering. And unlike their emotionally flat predecessors, the *28* zombies are driven by a viral infection called Rage—so they jerk and wrench and twist and snap. Because Jim was comatose in a hospital when the world erupted, Selena has to tell him what happened. And she narrates the outbreak as "rioting" that moved from television screens to "the street outside" until, finally, "it was coming through your window." The trajectory from watching the riots on TV to watching them break into your house reifies the nightmares projected by conservatives in response to urban unrest. As Nadine Attewell observes, Selena's account of the outbreak of Rage echoes the racialized "invasion narrative" constructed by Conservative MP Enoch Powell in the 1968 speech now known as "Rivers of Blood" (2014, 179). In Powell's account, an elderly white woman watches the ruination of her once "respectable" street as "one house after another [is] taken over" by people of color (qtd. in Attewell 2014, 179). The damage spreads from house to house and street to street, ultimately threatening the nation as a whole, which means that what's at first a disquieting spectacle on the TV news will eventually, well, come through your window. In this sense, Rage actualizes what Stuart Hall and his colleagues call the "signification spirals" deployed in conservative storytelling: the framing of an event in terms of its "'threat-potential' for society" and the correlated escalation of that threat-potential from deviance to illegality to, at the outer limit, extreme violence and social breakdown (1978, 220).

But the *28* films open up the possibility of rereading riots as uprisings. This rereading emerges from how the films' emphasis on surveillance articulates with what Sarah Juliet Lauro calls the "the 'un-life' of the zombie myth," or the way it infuses an anticolonial impulse into the Western narratives that appropriate it (2015, 99). I'm not making a claim about Danny Boyle's intentions or political sympathies. When it comes to reckoning with Britain's imperial legacies, the director's body of work is uneven.[3] Rather, the *28* films trade on the same "communal recognition" that Lauro describes in relation to George Romero's zombie classic, *Night of the Living Dead* (U.S. 1968). Like Romero's "ghouls," the infected Britons in *28 Days* and *Weeks* are never referred to as zombies in the films themselves. They're just "infected." But audiences and critics saw them as following a recognizable storyline in which a form of living death "represent[s] both disempowerment and rebellion" (97). So, responding to a subtext about power and revolt, filmgoers placed *28 Days Later* in the zombie horror subgenre. Our task now is to listen for how, as Lauro puts it, "the zombie's origins speak" in this cinematic context (99). And I locate them in the *28* films' interrogation of surveillance apparatuses.

Simone Browne argues that the development of modern surveillance practices is enmeshed in histories of slavery and its afterlife. And she draws on the insights of Sylvia Wynter, whose ideas about the invention of a figure called Man—a Western, patriarchal, bourgeois model of the human—inform my thinking about the function of the Last Man in apocalyptic storytelling.[4] Browne observes that the same colonial narrative that represents Man as the epitome of humanness "fixes and frames blackness as an object of surveillance"—a subhuman threat to be monitored and contained (2015, 7). But the counterpoint to a long history of racializing surveillance is a set of tactics that Browne calls "dark sousveillance," or an equally long history of black subjects co-opting "the tools of social control" to survive, evade, and escape (21). Dark sousveillance has given rise, she argues, to ways of knowing that critique and imagine beyond Man's world. By mobilizing a zombie storyline that repeatedly draws attention to looking relations, the *28* films open up a critique of the race-making surveillance practices authorized by Man's story. In this way, they exemplify what Olney sees as characteristic of the zombie horror subgenre: "that it invites contemplation of white deathliness"—that it both features (un)dead white people and, at least potentially, unveils the terrorizing, death-dealing underpinnings of whiteness (2017, 20). So even as American and British filmmakers appropriate the zombie, putting it to work in films that typically emphasize white subjects and their anxieties, the figure carries with it legacies of survival—and rebellion—in the black diaspora. The zombie "is never merely a cultural appropriation," Lauro writes; "it also infects its occupying host" (2015, 5).

The conduit for this infection is the *28* films' attention to eyes and affect. The Rage virus causes a hemorrhaging of the ocular blood vessels, which means that Boyle's zombies have red eyes. And in *28 Weeks*, when a healthy carrier unexpectedly appears in quarantined London, she has one blood-shot eye and one that's clear. The significance of this motif lies in the origin story of the Rage virus. *28 Days Later* opens with scenes of violence: a necklacing, a hanging, and shots of surging crowds are punctuated by global scenes of confrontation between civilians and militarized police forces. The opening plays on audience expectations, nudging viewers toward the assumption that we're being thrown into the apocalypse in medias res. But the camera draws back to reveal that these scenes of decontextualized violence are playing, looped, on a bank of television monitors. And watching them is a chimpanzee strapped to a gurney.[5] The goal of the experiment in the Cambridge Primate Research Centre is to induce violent rage so it can be studied. As one scientist pleads to the animal rights activists who break into the lab, "In order to cure you must first understand." So the masked activists are the most immediate cause of the outbreak, which might align the film with conservative narratives that link fear of the foreign Other—represented on the screens the chimp is watching—with fear of the estranged insider. But that's not the story these films are telling.

Beginning with the origins of the Rage virus, the *28* films repeatedly shift the locus of horror away from the infected—and the unruly public assemblies they evoke—to indict, instead, the security and surveillance apparatuses that terrorize in the name of keeping (some of) us safe. Invasion narratives conjure a seemingly stable white Englishness by positing what Sara Ahmed describes as an "ordinary subject" in crisis, threatened by some combination of devious outsiders and deviant insiders (2004, 43). They draw their power, then, from the biopolitical logic of Man's story of humanness, which differentiates between good capitalist subjects and Others who wreck and riot. From this perspective, the violence of "security" is seemingly authorized by the need to protect the nation and its forums of competition from the unfit—or from, in Wynter's terms, the "dysselected" (2003, 310). But the opening sequence of *28 Days Later* displaces horror from the scenes of violence on the monitors to the experimental apparatus itself; the one that collects and curates and loops the footage and forces it on a captive audience. I don't disagree with Jayna Brown that the origins of Rage seem more "alchemical" than medical (2013b, 133). But I see the Cambridge experiment as indexing a key mechanism through which Man's Others are constructed as dangerous: the narrative circulation of affect. The apparatus in the lab is a storytelling machine. It pieces together scenes of unrest that are ripped out of context by technologies of visual capture and presents them, through sheer accumulation, as the origin of bad feeling.[6] It frames a global array of Others as senselessly enraged and therefore terrifying—a growing population of disaffected subjects that must be cured, contained, or killed. In short, the chimp is infected by Man's story.

I read Rage, then, as a form of revolt. Dina Georgis posits revolt as an alternative to thinking freedom in terms of resistance. Because resistance tends to take shape as reaching for empowerment, it's structured, she argues, by "an identification with the emotional logic of power" (2013, 107). But revolt operates differently. "It demands change but has no preconceived notion about what that would mean" (109). So revolt makes conceptual room for a subject whose desire exceeds what it knows—a subject whose inclinations have taproots beyond the realm of conscious understanding. There's a whole mesh of psychic experience that derives from the fact that we're born into a social world we didn't choose and recruited into its stories before we can speak. Making a self in these conditions requires that we renunciate feelings and wants that, in the world into which we've arrived, are coded as forbidden—even monstrous. So fashioning a self means loss. And navigating those losses propels us into an endless process of narration. As Georgis puts it, "we never stop projecting our internal world externally in symbolization and we never stop introjecting the outside world in" (106). Drawing Georgis together with Wynter, the self emerges as an always-in-process narrative that works on the stories we inherit, including the threads of Man's story that weave in and out of our everyday lives. But sometimes the costs and contradictions of those storylines shake things loose within the self, inciting questions and, perhaps, acts of revolt. Refusing what psychoanalysis calls the Law of the Father—"the fixed meanings and ideals imposed upon us"—opens up the possibility of reinvention (109). Revolt itself is not reinvention. Revolt breaks things. But in tearing down or tearing us away from existing structures and narratives, it weakens the grip of the stories we live by and makes space for renewal. Following Julia Kristeva, then, Georgis imagines the freedom to rebegin as animated by revolt.[7] Which brings me back to zombies filled with Rage.

The *28* zombies are simultaneously infected by and revolting against Man's story; animated as the objects of terror that story constructs and raging against the world it orders. Key to this interpretation is the fact that Boyle's zombies aren't noted for their consumption of human flesh and entrails. They mostly expel. They puke blood, their mouths drip, and they rip at themselves until they bleed. I read their revolt against the story that infects them in these acts of expulsion—in the spraying bodily fluids that also transmit the virus, transforming Rage from an object of scientific study into a self-amplifying, world-ending force. This dynamic, in which disempowerment coexists with rebellion, is what Lauro describes as "the zombie's dialectic" (2015, 5). And we might understand the affective expression of this dialectic in terms of what Sianne Ngai calls "animatedness" (2005, 89). The speedy, wrenching movements of the infected exemplify an affect that "manages to fuse signs of the body's subjection to power with signs of its ostensive freedom" (100). Ngai reads this fusion in scenes from American stories in which racialized subjects seem externally manipulated and, at the same time, display an embodied elasticity that exceeds outside control. And animatedness, she argues, is transmissible. Contagious. So even as it encodes a racializing subjection to power, it activates, too, a link "between 'animation' and the 'agitation' that subtends our concept of the political agitator" (96). The *28* zombies aren't political agitators. But they're supremely agitated. And in their world-destroying revolt, they reanimate other times and places in which those made by Man's story into objects of terror rise up to demand something else.

THINGS THAT COME BACK: ZOMBIES AND CARRIERS

This chapter articulates the zombie with the insurgent civilian to illuminate how revolt can make room for the estranged insider to reach for another self—and another world. In *28 Days* we see this linkage in three survivors who find themselves aligned with the infected against the violence of a Last Man who aims to reboot the world he knew. And *28 Weeks* gives us a character who embodies this articulation: Alice Harris (Catherine McCormack), a white mother, is a healthy carrier of Rage. Her hybridity confounds the security protocols that organize the American-led reconstruction of England. The problem with Alice, you see, is that everyone lost sight of her. When she emerges from more than six months of isolation in the quarantine zone, all we know is that she disappeared into an unobserved, unregulated space for quite a long time. So when she comes back, no one knows what she's brought with her. And the space-time Alice survives is the same interval that Selena and Hannah are poised to navigate in the "impossible" ending to *28 Days*. So what if Selena and Hannah had met Alice—or someone like her? And in the absence of this intriguing storyline, what can Alice illuminate about a discarded ending in which two young women disappear into a riotous city and survive, perhaps, to tell their tale?

Both the zombie and the carrier illuminate the *28* films' critiques of the terror unleashed in the name of security. Browne's work demonstrates that "how things get ordered racially by way of surveillance depends on space and time and is subject to change, but most often upholds negating strategies that first accompanied European colonial expansion and transatlantic slavery that sought to structure social relations and institutions in ways that privilege whiteness" (2015, 17). The zombie conjures the Haitian Revolution and its afterlife, bringing the colonial coordinates of the surveillance practices that secure Man's world into focus. And the carrier evokes early twentieth-century anxieties about women navigating cities unobserved. In this context, concerns about white women, especially, acting without patriarchal oversight tap directly into the history of "racializing surveillance" identified by Browne (2015, 16). As Priscilla Wald observes, "a communicable disease and a fatherless baby can both introduce the threat of race suicide" (2008, 91). As figures, then, the zombie and the carrier are shaped by security logics and practices that reify the social, spatial, and bodily boundaries that uphold the supposed superiority—and coherence—of whiteness. Framed as threats to be contained, both are also linked to histories of escape and rebellion. They reveal how, from Man's perspective, the unknown narrative territory to which Selena, Hannah, and Alice all point is a breeding ground for wayward futures. So excavating the sedimented histories of which the zombie and the carrier are composed is an exercise in imagining what happens in the interval between revolt and rebeginning. It's an interval marked out by the *28* films' contiguous timelines: the six months during which England is quarantined from the politically organized world. When reconstruction begins on the Isle of Dogs, whatever returns from this abandonment is troublesome. Because what returns *from* that place might be carrying some of what returns *in* that place. A little island revolting against Man's world is not, after all, unprecedented. So let's start with the zombie.[8]

The zombie is unique among movie monsters because, as Lauro argues, its history as a myth "uncannily parallels its own substance" (2015, 17). The zombie is a folkloric figuration of the experiences of enslaved Africans, a figure that inhabits—and embodies—a borderline where biological life meets social death.[9] In the early twentieth century, this figure was appropriated by U.S. filmmakers to explore the experiences of the (usually) white American subject under capitalism. The zombie, Lauro concludes, "is therefore not just a myth about slavery, but a 'slave metaphor': usurped, colonized, and altered to represent the struggles of a distinctly different culture" (17). During the Great Depression, Hollywood began capitalizing on the often sensational stories of Haiti contained in the memoirs and travel narratives written by Americans during the U.S. occupation. William Seabrook's *Magic Island* (1929) includes a now famous description of "dead men working in the cane fields" as well as a story about zombies—"ragged creatures" who are "vacant-eyed like cattle"—working at the Haitian American Sugar Company, HASCO, outside Port-au-Prince (92, 95). Early cinematic representations of the zombie drew on this "twin vision of the colonial slave and the corporate employee," leveraging zombie tales to speak to American subjects in the grip of capitalist crisis (Lauro 2015, 79). Victor Halperin's *White Zombie* (U.S. 1932), for example, is set in Haiti and features a white zombie master running a sugar plantation worked by black zombies.[10] As the film's title suggests, though, it's primarily concerned with the zombification of its white American characters. Patricia Chu reads *White Zombie* as mapping white masculine anxieties about agency in the context of mass democracy onto "the fear of becoming nothing but a body endlessly consenting to its own lack of autonomy" (2006, 29). But the stolen metaphor threatens to turn on the storytellers who appropriate it. As Ian Olney observes in his discussion of American zombie films of the 1930s and 1940s, typically in these films "white colonials emerge not as agents of civilization or enlightenment but as dead and bringers of death" (2017, 28). And while much has changed in the genre since then, the zombie is marked by the traces of its past articulations. They linger like nodes awaiting activation, itching to counter-occupy a host story busily imagining The End of Man.[11]

What returns with the zombie is the Haitian Revolution and, with it, what Chu calls the "back story of modern Western subjectivity" (2006, 9).[12] The figure that Wynter calls economic Man has a disavowed double, a modern subject that emerged from the uprising in the French colony of Saint-Domingue at the end of the eighteenth century. In other words, the New World birth of the Euro-American entrepreneur was shadowed by a second birth, and this "new New World man was a black, anti-colonial nationalist" (Chu 2006, 10). Largely suppressed by dominant historical narratives of the Age of Revolution, this "unthinkable" rebirth haunts the Western world. It represents an alternative beginning from which the meanings of key political terms like "freedom" are contested, if not entirely unmoored.[13] If enslavement constitutes a form of living death and, in such a context, death represents the liberation of the enslaved, then, as Lauro explains, the liberty-or-death opposition deployed in Euro-American revolutionary rhetoric becomes, in Saint-Domingue, "liberty-in-life/liberty-in-death" (2015, 52). No wonder, then, that contemporaneous European accounts of the Haitian Revolution cast the revolutionaries as monstrous in their determination: "as either superhuman and uncannily courageous or subhuman, blindly following orders" (61). Either way, they were seen by the armies that faced them as a relentlessly advancing horde. The living dead in revolt. From the European perspective, then, economic Man was challenged by a monstrous Other, the subject of an unthinkable anticolonial narrative of humanness and freedom.

What was unveiled by the end of the French colony was a different sense of the place that was becoming Haiti—a countermapping of the island organized by, to borrow a term from Carolyn Cooper, "resistance science" (1995, 4). Cooper is referring specifically to "marronage, that tradition of resistance science that establishes an alternative psychic space both within and beyond the boundaries of the enslaving plantation" (4). As Greg Thomas points out, Cooper's formulation expands understandings of maroonage that restrict it to the physical spaces where ex-slaves made community. "It is, 'resistance science,' generically," he writes, "animating 'psychic space' in whatever 'physical spaces' in need of this antiracist and antislavery resistance tradition" (2016, 73). We might see Haitian Vaudou, then, as one of the branches of this science.[14] In Saint-Domingue, survivors of the Middle Passage recombined fragments of West African cosmologies and ways of knowing the world. So Vaudou epistemologies encompass, among other things, the soul-capture myths that are the likely antecedents of the zombie figure; the botanical expertise from which the *bokor* or *houngan*, the Vaudou practitioner, derives his or her power; and a way of seeing—second sight—that belongs to the realm of the dead.[15] Even before the Revolution, the story of the 1757 insurrection led by the maroon leader Makandal exemplifies the potency of "resistance science." Famously emboldening his followers by linking them to the protective dead via Vaudou ceremony, Makandal orchestrated the mass poisoning of white planters and their livestock. His extensive knowledge of plants and their properties meant that the toxins used were derived from the very soil that was making the colonists rich. Lauro observes that prior to this attempted insurrection, the writings of planters and colonial administrators emphasized the "bogus nature" of Vaudou and its plant-based medicines and poisons. But after 1757, "accounts of Vaudou practices, in particular, those later implicated in the creation of zombies—death-defying demonstrations, suspicious body-snatching, the inducement of paralytic trances—were henceforth interpreted as a weapon decidedly not supernatural but terrifying nonetheless" (2015, 58). Decades later, a 1791 Vaudou ceremony at Bois Caïman spurred a revolution that was read, by Europeans, as an outbreak in need of containment.

Resistance science countered the terrors of whiteness, exposed the colonial order as alterable, and whispered of antiracist, antislavery futures. But since Man's story can admit none of this, resistance science also propelled the colonizers into what Thomas formulates as a "crazed dialectic—absolute addiction to slavery's profits; absolute shock, hysteria, and denial in the face of endemic African revolt and maroonage" (2016, 74). Drawing on Wynter, Thomas notes that the history of European writing on black revolt amounts to a compulsive "mystification" of both the motivations and the science behind it (74). Many eighteenth-century Europeans interpreted the Makandal affair not as organized rebellion but, rather, as a wave of homicides perpetrated for the sake of "individual interest: vengeance, jealousy, reduction of the work load, infliction of economic loss on a master," and so on (Fick 1990, 68). This is consistent with the larger pattern of response identified by Michel-Rolph Trouillot, who writes that from the European perspective, "enslaved Africans and their descendants could not envision freedom—let alone formulate strategies for gaining and securing such freedom." And from this perspective, Trouillot observes, the quest for collective black liberation is "unthinkable" (1995, 73). To maintain this unseeing in the face of all the evidence against it, colonizers enacted what Anne McClintock calls a psychic "splitting and displacement" (1995, 27). The violence and terror of the colonial order splits away from Man, who becomes the embodiment of reason, enlightenment, and benevolence. And terror sticks, instead, to those who revolt—from the enslaved whose desire to escape was so nonsensical that it was diagnosed as a disease to those, like Makandal, who surreptitiously returned carrying the tools of organized rebellion.[16] Island uprisings threatened to end Man's world. Subjects seen as subhuman threatened to redefine humanness altogether. In this context, salvaging the illusory coherence of Man's worldview meant conjuring monstrous Others: harbingers of bad futures.

Man's reading of black revolution as terrifying, world-ending violence is encoded in contemporary representations of the zombie apocalypse. So a rebellious counternarrative—a counternarrative of rebellion—lies just beneath the surface of this imaginary. A more radical vision becomes discernible if we wonder about the economy of terror that shapes zombie tales. Christina Sharpe writes that "in much of what passes for public discourse *about* terror we, Black people, become the *carriers* of terror, terror's embodiment, and not the primary objects of terror's multiple enactments" (2016, 15, emphasis original). Sharpe is writing about the United States in our own historical moment, but her observation holds for the European take on an eighteenth-century French colony in upheaval. And it's relevant, too, to postwar British invasion narratives like the one concocted by Enoch Powell, in which "the contagiousness of blackness" overwhelms and undoes the (white) nation (Attewell 2014, 180). In all of these contexts, a public discourse that constructs black people as "carriers" of terror displaces the origins of violence from Man to his Others. The splitting and displacement that facilitates the European unseeing of black revolt is precisely what animates the enactments of "racializing surveillance" that, Browne argues, continue to organize Man's world well after legal emancipation (2015, 16). And in the early twentieth century, the figure of the carrier itself took shape in ways that reactivated many of these logics and practices of social control. Like the zombie, this figure has an unruly, expansive narrative life. The carrier circulates in what Wald (2008) describes as the "outbreak narrative," a blending of popular and scientific discourses focused on the spread of contagious disease. In the context of the *28* films, Alice is the first known carrier of Rage. But much of what happens to Alice happens off screen—during the six months in which she's presumed dead and survives cut off from Man's world. So what happens in the relatively brief time we can see her offers some indication of just how much terror swirls around the fact of her survival and return.

In the prologue to *28 Weeks*, which takes place within the time frame of the first film, Alice is abandoned by her husband when the infected overrun the cottage where they're hiding. She bangs on an upstairs window, screaming for him to come back, but he flees. We don't see her again until, twenty-eight weeks later, she's discovered living in the attic of her former home in London. By then Alice is emotionally unhinged by all that time alone in the quarantine zone—and by whatever happened to leave those bite marks on her body. And she returns carrying suppressed pasts: a husband's shame; the human cost of quarantine; a still-active virus. So the woman who's already survived abandonment, terror, injury, and prolonged isolation is met with yet more violence. Screaming in outrage, she undergoes a brutal decontamination shower at the hands of the military before she's strapped to a gurney and locked in an observation room. And when her repentant husband, Don (Robert Carlyle), arrives seeking absolution, their kiss initiates a second outbreak of Rage. It begins with a now infected Don beating his immobilized wife to death. The violence inflicted on Alice stops only when her corpse is incinerated by firebombs dropped by the military in an effort to contain the new outbreak. So what does her return signify that it's met with such unrelenting violence? Why, exactly, is Alice a problem for District One, the seed of a reconstructing nation taking root on the Isle of Dogs?

The carrier narrative has an archetype in which anxieties about women's bodies—where they're going, the futures they're carrying—intersect with visions of urban space as rife with transgressive possibilities. As Wald explores in *Contagious* (2008), the archetype of the carrier is Mary Mallon, the Irish immigrant to the United States who became publicly known as "Typhoid Mary." The first documented healthy carrier, Mallon was "discovered" in 1906 by Dr. George Soper of the U.S. Army Sanitary Corps, who traced her through a series of typhoid epidemics in the houses where she worked as a cook in and around New York City. And the portrait of Mallon that Soper fleshed out over many years established the narrative coordinates through which the carrier emerged as suspect—a public menace. Typhoid is spread through the ingestion of food or water contaminated by an infected person's feces, so Mallon was coded as "dirty" in ways that articulated with the early twentieth-century racialization of Irish immigrants to the United States. And alongside an emphasis on the "dirt and disorder" of her New York City rooming house, Soper lingered over the "disreputable-looking man" who was the unmarried woman's lover (qtd. in Wald 2008, 84). What's more, Mallon was uncooperative, assuming an alias and disappearing sometime around 1912. So when she was rediscovered a few years later, her willful evasion of public health authorities only reinforced the picture that was emerging of a contaminated, unrepentant woman. Her disappearance underscored what was already troubling about the healthy carrier: the threat she represents is invisible. Mallon dropped out of sight and came back, tying the danger presented by her infectiousness to her capacity to move, undetected, through the city.[17]

"Typhoid Mary" has an antecedent in what Wald describes as the "unattached woman," a figure that emerges at the intersection of early twentieth-century sociological work on single women in the city and contemporaneous public health discourses concerned with venereal disease. Her narrative arc, Wald observes, is that of the fallen woman—a story that maps sexual promiscuity onto "spatial promiscuity" (94). (A dirty rooming house, a "disreputable-looking man.") The young woman arriving in the big city provided early American sociologists with a potentially scandalous storyline: the girl who's left family and community behind might be prompted—perhaps by unchecked desire, perhaps by desperate loneliness—to seek out what sociologist W. I. Thomas called "unapproved stimulations" (qtd. in Wald 2008, 90). Writing in 1906, Thomas argued that because women were dependent on community for regulation, "an unattached woman has a tendency to become an adventuress" and, what's more, she can "pass from a regular to an irregular life and back again before the fact has been noted" (qtd. in Wald 2008, 89, 90). So the unattached woman is defined not only by a trajectory away from the regulating effects of family and community surveillance, but also by her capacity for return. And in between, unwatched, she navigates an urban landscape defined by the intermingling of strangers across boundaries of class, race, religion, nationality, gender, and sexuality. In this context, Wald concludes, "implicit in her ability to disappear is the threat of her circulation and of what she might bring back. When she returns from wherever she has been, the community that had lost sight of her will not know what she might be *carrying*" (90–91, emphasis original). She goes and comes back—an "adventuress" carrying a range of possible futures that, from the perspective of the existing social order, must be detected and contained, cured, or killed.

There doesn't seem to be anything dirty or disreputable about Alice before the outbreak. She was a white Englishwoman who lived in a nice London house, which should make her an ideal subject to mother the reemerging nation. But by disappearing into unregulated space and coming back, she earns the scrutiny of a security-and-surveillance apparatus with long colonial roots. It marks her as suspect because she's returned transformed, opening up questions about what humanness and community could look like in the aftermath of Rage. Remember: Alice is undone by revolt and (the first time, at least) survives it. So she opens up narrative space in which to imagine a more flexible, creative rebeginning than that suggested by the repatriation taking place on the Isle of Dogs. And though Alice doesn't survive a second outbreak—in fact, she was slated to be executed by the military, but Don got to her first—the trouble she makes persists in the form of her two children. This is part of what makes the carrier figure so unnerving from the perspective of Man's story: as early researchers noticed, women who have borne children—"in other words, *mothers*"—are statistically overrepresented in the healthy carrier category (Wald 2008, 94, emphasis original). I argued in my introduction that conservative storytelling deploys problems with "mother" to authorize greater social control. From the perspective of the security apparatus charged with eradicating revolting bodies, the carrier-mother is a contaminated, contaminating figure. Alice smuggles into the rebeginning nation the possibility of coexisting with Rage; of sharing one's skin with, rather than disavowing, a monstrous version of the self. It's a possibility that undoes the psychic "splitting and displacement" that animates Man's story of humanness (McClintock 1995, 27)—and one that Alice transmits to her kids as a simultaneously corporeal and affective inheritance. But before we get there, Alice's return from quarantine sheds retrospective light on *28 Days*' seemingly impossible ending, too. What if Selena and Hannah survived? And what if, like Alice, they came back carrying experiences and feelings that estranged them from the reconstructing nation? After all, the terrors they face in the quarantine zone have more to do with Man than his zombified Others.

"THE ANSWER TO INFECTION": *28 DAYS LATER*

Major Henry West (Christopher Eccleston) has a plan. His unit was assigned to a blockade outside of Manchester, but when communications were cut and the city started to burn, he moved the remnants of his company to a nearby estate and secured the property with tripwire, landmines, and floodlights. From there, he began broadcasting a recorded message promising "the answer to infection" and "salvation" for survivors who could find him. So when Jim, Selena, and Hannah follow the direction provided by the broadcast, they find nine military men camped out in an English mansion—soldiers who are weirdly enthusiastic about the arrival of "three survivors: one male, two female. I Repeat. One male, two female." By this point, Jim's initial incredulity about the absence of organized power has been replaced by the conviction, which the film invites us to share, that Rage has sparked a global apocalypse. So when West informs him that, "secondary to protection, our real job is to rebuild, start again," Jim seems a little unsettled but mostly relieved. As it turns out, West's assumption that Rage has wiped out the world is incorrect. But in the grip of that delusion, he's aiming to twist his circumstances into what Brian Aldiss has called a "cosy catastrophe" scenario (1973, 292). Once the infected die of starvation, he intends to "bake bread, plant crops, raise livestock." And in this vision of a back-to-basics reboot—in which he retains and, in fact, boosts his patriarchal authority—he needs women. Because, as West explains to a speechless Jim, "women mean a future."

In this fantasy, West is the patriarchal head of household, his men are his sons, and "mother" is missing. The answer to infection, then, is to violently recruit Selena and/or Hannah into that role. Because what else is there? "What do nine men do," West muses, "except wait to die themselves?" In the climactic scenes of *28 Days Later*, horror slides from the infected outside the estate to the threat of rape that suffuses the inside of the house. From West's perspective, rape is authorized by the need to turn this ragtag group of survivors into a family unit. Behind the horror of organized sexual violence, then, is a terrifying imposition of the patriarchal family form. The family emerges here, in Eve Sedgwick's terms, as "an object of struggle, not a given" (1985, 111). And this is where *28 Days* leverages the radical possibilities of the horror genre. Drawing on Robin Wood's identification of classic horror film conventions, Diana Adesola Mafe observes that horror films usually present "a state of so-called normality" threatened by "the 'return of the repressed' in monstrous form" (2018, 20). The resumption of normality depends, of course, on the vanquishing of the monster.[18] But rather than presenting the patriarchal family as an emblem of "normality" to be safeguarded against threat, *28 Days* makes the family itself into a site of horror. Mafe sees West's mansion as a manifestation of what Carol Clover calls the "Terrible Place" where, especially in slasher films, women protagonists survive and sometimes avenge masculine violence (qtd. in Mafe 2018, 22). Mafe elaborates that if "the classic haunted house is built on patriarchal foundations, it can also be an 'intrauterine' space in which female and female-allied characters find an 'uncanny' agency despite their entrapment" (22). By locating horror in the patriarchal household and activating "elements of a rape-revenge film" (21), *28 Days* prepares the way for an alliance between its monstrous and feminine characters. And this begins to illuminate the stakes of the film's "impossible" ending.

What would two women do in a burning city teeming with monsters? And how might what happens there reshape the stories they tell about themselves and the world around them? Selena and Hannah escape their horrifying recruitment (back) into the familial roles defined by Man's story of humanness. And then, the discarded ending offers, they disappear into a city in revolt. If they survive the quarantine period—if they, like Alice, come back—will the stories they've lived, the feelings they carry, estrange them from a national rebeginning structured, once again, by Man's hierarchies? How will they feel reentering a world that purchased its security by leaving them to die? Does what screenwriter Alex Garland describes as "all the evidence" of their capacity for survival make room, too, for the possibility of their revolt and reinvention? Exploring these questions is more than a matter of noticing that Selena has proper machete skills and Hannah drives like a boss. It's about attending to the ways the film opens up imaginative space by aligning viewers with what Barbara Creed (1993) calls the "monstrous-feminine" that disturbs and transgresses the patriarchal order of things. Thinking with Creed, Mafe connects the blood-spraying infected with "a primal and abject femininity" and then draws a line from the zombies to Selena (2018, 21). Mafe sees Jim, too, as implicated in the monstrous-feminine, arguing that "the film shows an exponential association between Selena and Jim as agents of female empowerment who collaborate to undermine 'hysterical masculinity'" (24). United against West's patriarchal fantasy, Selena and Jim are each propelled into a becoming-monster that expands our sense of what's possible in this postapocalyptic world.[19] These becomings—and the potentialities they entail—are tied to the film's deviations from (the Last) Man's story of humanness.

28 Days Later plays with the conventions of apocalyptic horror by offering Jim as a Last Man who metamorphoses into something "closer to a Final Girl" (Mafe 2018, 30). A figure identified by Carol Clover, the Final Girl is the character who survives the Terrible Place and takes revenge against her terrorizer.[20] And to reach a finale in which, with the help of the infected, Selena and Jim undo the patriarch and his house of would-be rapists, *28 Days* first establishes a pattern of meaning that disarticulates security and survival from father figures. It all begins when Jim, a twentysomething bike courier who was in a coma and missed the apocalypse, wakes up alone in a hospital.[21] When he leaves the building—amid the now iconic shots of a still and silent London—he repeatedly yells "hello" as he tries to grasp what's happened to the city he knew. It's the only word he says in his first ten minutes of screen time. Then, inside a Catholic church, Jim finds himself confronted by a priest who approaches him far too quickly. So the second word he utters is "Father?" Where "hello" signifies a sweeping desire for connection, "Father" channels this desire toward familiar forms of authority. But Jim's utterance is as much a question as a form of address, and it's followed by a lurching, snarling attack that forces him to fight back and then flee. The film then reinforces this sense that "Father's house" is unsafe when Jim, having been rescued from the infected by Selena and Mark (Noah Huntley), returns to his family home. When the trio

FIGURE 8. Selena catches her breath after killing a fellow survivor before he becomes enRaged. Still from *28 Days Later* (DNA Films, 2002).

camps out in the house overnight, Jim becomes lost in a memory of being in the kitchen with his parents. Boyle gives us visual access to the banal scene, shooting it in flickering, sepia-toned eight millimeter—and then shatters it when a former neighbor crashes through the kitchen window and tackles Jim. Mark is wounded in the ensuing struggle, so Selena hacks him to death with her machete before he can turn. After twenty-eight days of social breakdown, Selena's survival instincts are close to the surface, which keeps Jim alive while he recalibrates. And Jim's first two encounters with the infected signal the depth of the recalibration required. When even the good father figure turns later in the film—Hannah's lovely dad, Frank (Brendan Gleeson), is infected at the blockade just as West's soldiers make their appearance—"Father?" is indisputably uncoupled from survival. So by the time we meet Major Henry West, we should be wary of "the answer to infection."

When West takes Jim on a guided tour of the estate, the cost of reestablishing the patriarchal family amid the ruins comes into view in layers of uneven power relations. First, after describing the weaponized grounds around the mansion, West pats Jim on the head. The strange gesture puts Jim in his place as a son, aligning him with the raucous soldiers who are driving donuts in the loose gravel around the house. It also implicitly invites him into the intergenerational bargain that structures patriarchal power: the son's submission in the present clears the way for his future ascension to the role of patriarch.[22] But not all sons are created equal. The next one we meet, in the kitchen, is Private Jones (Leo Bill), an off-kilter young white man wearing a pink apron. The feminized cook hints at what's missing from West's domestic scene, a lack that comes into focus when, at dinner that evening, Jones serves eggs that are "off." The symbolism of rotten eggs—"I thought the salt might hide the taste, sir"—points to the cook's incapacity to properly perform the caregiving services demanded of feminized subjects.[23] It's not long before we learn that West and his men intend to transfer this set of demands to Selena and Hannah as its "proper" objects. But first, there's one more stop on the tour. At the outer limit of this power structure is Private Mailer (Marvin Campbell), a recently infected black soldier chained by the neck in a yard outside the house. In the context of the familial fantasy that organizes the estate, and in light of histories of representing black subjects as animalistic, Mailer is positioned as an uncanny twist on the family dog. And like the chimpanzees in the Cambridge lab, he's a test subject. This "futureless" former soldier, West tells a startled Jim, will indicate how long the infected take to starve to death. Expelled from but still captured by the family, Mailer is the monstrous Other who exposes the coloniality of West's patriarchal power. And it's Mailer who becomes an uneasy ally when "Selena and Jim enact the culminating and castrating revenge of the Final Girl" (Mafe 2018, 31).

Mailer's bloodshot eyes exemplify the zombie's dialectic, simultaneously registering his infection (disempowerment) and, in a key scene that shows him staring through a window into the house, his claiming of the right to look (revolt). Mailer is the racialized test subject meant to be observed by West in the mode of makeshift military scientist. And the collar around his neck evokes the histories of coffles and racial terror with which zombies are historically entangled. As bell hooks writes in *Black Looks* (1992), white power in the context of slavery meant controlling the black gaze so that "black people learned to appear before whites as though they were zombies, cultivating the habit of casting the gaze downward so as not to appear uppity" (168). West reestablishes these asymmetrical looking relations. He can direct his scrutinizing, knowing gaze at Mailer whenever he decides and Mailer, held in place by brick walls and a chain, has only a limited view. As hooks observes, this arrangement is zombifying. But the zombie's eyes, even when they seem unseeing, suggest more than abject disempowerment. In *Tell My Horse* (1938), Zora Neale Hurston describes reputed Haitian zombie Felicia Felix-Mentor, whom she photographed in the late 1930s. Hurston lingers over "the dead eyes" that appear "as if they had been burned with acid" before finding herself overwhelmed as an observer: "the sight of this wreckage was too much to endure for long" (206).[24] Note that Felix-Mentor is resistant to Hurston's ethnographic gaze. The sight is too much. The eyes, in particular, are haunting. The *28* films intensify this by depicting zombified eyes that are infected and enraged, not dead. So when Mailer ultimately claims the right to look—the "wreckage" looking back—he revolts against the security and surveillance apparatuses that underwrite West's rebuilding plans. And when he returns to the house from which he's been expelled, he unmaps the spatial arrangement of white patriarchal power.

Jim becomes-monster by freeing Mailer and insinuating himself into the infected soldier's revolt against West's vision, activating the zombie's suppressed origins in the service of undoing a patriarchal survivalist fantasy. When it becomes clear that Jim isn't on board with his plans for Selena and Hannah, West orders two men to take him into the woods and shoot him. But Jim escapes his inept executioners and breaks the chain holding Mailer in the yard, which leads to both of them darting around the house, peering in windows, and attacking the men inside. This new alliance is visually confirmed by the grainy, low-resolution imaging through which a bloodied, half-naked Jim begins to look like one of the infected.[25] So much so that when he finally locates Selena and murders her guard, she isn't sure, at first, if Jim's turned. But in a sense, he has. West's execution order made Jim as disposable as Mailer, which leads him to revolt *like* the infected, *with* the infected, against his scripting as "dysselected" (Wynter 2003, 310). This realigns audience sympathies with the monsters. And at the heart of this realignment is the fact that Jim is animated by an emotional insight that completely escapes Major Henry West. The logic of chosenness according to which West operates—his delusion that the world has ended and he's selected to begin it all again—protects him from a reality he can't bear: he's been abandoned by the very apparatuses of power from which he derives his authority. Like the infected and other survivors, West has been dysselected by a biopolitical logic that abandons some in the name of securing the rest. And because he can't see or experience himself this way, the future he envisions replicates the very power structures that left him to die. So, in alliance with Mailer, Jim revolts against this postapocalyptic reinscription of Man's story—and revolt brings down both Father and his house.

Jim's becoming-monster works in tandem with the survival strategies Selena employs inside the mansion. Like Jim, Selena performs the role in which she's been cast in the hopes of opening up room to maneuver. As West's men force her into a tight-fitting red dress, she kisses one of them, very roughly, before requesting time alone with Hannah so they can change in private. In the context of a large estate controlled by a white patriarch who intends to breed her, Selena's manipulative seduction evokes the figure of the jezebel, or, as Patricia Hill Collins elaborates, the "sexually wanton Black woman" (2004, 56). A figure deployed to justify institutionalized rape in the context of slavery, the jezebel is what Collins calls a "controlling image"—one of a number of stereotypes of black femininity that, in the postslavery present, "become texts of what not to be" (139). My claim is not that Selena finds agency in approximating a white fantasy of black feminine sexuality. Rather, playing this role opens up a sliver of space that allows her to step into another one: zombie master. Selena is a pharmacist, an occupation that, as Jayna Brown points out, "signifies the black woman as nurturer, witch, or oracle" (2013b, 133). When the men leave the room, Selena drugs Hannah with Valium. Feeling that sexual assault is inevitable, she puts Hannah into a drug-induced stupor in the hopes that the girl will feel what's about to happen less deeply. So to support Hannah's psychic survival, Selena reanimates a history of zombie-making and its pharmacological underpinnings.[26] And what they're surviving isn't the infected, but men still drawing power from the roles defined by Man's story. They have something in common, then, with Mailer and the others who are raging against Man's world.

It's a fragile link, perhaps. But it threatens to outlast the infected themselves—to preserve something of their world-ending revolt well beyond the time of quarantine. Rage might die of starvation. But what if its affective residue clings to survivors like Selena and Hannah? Jeffery Jerome Cohen writes that "the monster polices the borders of the possible" (1996, 12). *28 Days*' impossible ending is one that sees Selena and Hannah, left to their own devices in the quarantine zone, potentially amplify their connection to the monstrous-feminine. After all, this is exactly what happens to Alice.

ASK ALICE: *28 WEEKS LATER*

The first thing you notice about Alice Harris is her eyes. *28 Weeks* opens with a match flaring to life in the darkness, the flame illuminating a close-up shot: one is blue; the other a deep brown. So we begin with the eyes of a survivor, which suggests that Alice's perspective on this world is important. And the different colors anticipate that the perspective she offers might be somewhat strange, even split. The Chief Medical Officer in District One will speculate that the "genetic abnormality" that manifests as heterochromia iridum—differently colored eyes in the same individual—is somehow linked to Alice's becoming an asymptomatic carrier of Rage. Just as *28 Days*, after its prologue in the Cambridge lab, starts with an extreme close-up of Jim's eye fluttering to wakefulness in the hospital, its sequel, too, seems to offer viewers an anchoring perspective on the postapocalyptic world. But at the end of the prologue that perspective disappears. And when it returns, when Alice enters the tightly regulated District One from the still unsanitized area across the Thames, she's taken becoming-monster to a whole new level. We have no idea what Alice has seen since that time in the cottage when, her eyes wide open in shock and terror, she watched her husband choose flight over fight. But when she comes back one of those eyes is bloodshot, signaling that Rage courses through her system. So even as Alice manages, somehow, not to turn, her body harbors monsters.

One bloodshot eye, one clear. A survivor who stares at the reconstructing nation. What does Alice see on the Isle of Dogs? How is it informed by what she saw on the quarantined British mainland? If the Last Man establishes a vantage point that orients viewers to the ruined world, then *28 Weeks* plays sleight of hand with this function, sliding it from Alice to Don to their kids so that multiple perspectives on ruins and rebeginnings coexist in the film. One of these perspectives is shot through with shame. Others are stretched between loss and hope. All of them register the nearness of Rage. The Harris family is struggling over how to articulate what happened before with what's happening now. And the struggle generates an unstable, ramifying perspective that confronts a security apparatus with a troubling array of futures.

It begins with the shift from Alice's eyes to Don's. A failed paternal protector, Don's way of seeing is soaked in shame about the past, which propels him into a quest to annihilate the witnesses to his disgrace—to kill the futures in which his actions will be remembered. In my introduction I argued that neoliberal storytelling aims to control narratives of disaster, inviting us to see ruins as sites of renewed competition: freedom-in-the-making. The protagonist of this story is the one Wynter describes as economic Man, the enterprising subject who stakes his claim to true humanness on his mastery of natural scarcity; the one who secures both his property and his dependents through the accumulation of resources. *28 Days* presents a critique of this narrative by refiguring economic Man as a deluded patriarchal survivalist. Its sequel takes a different tack by envisioning a father who can't transcend disaster—who can't compete—and then rages against his scripting as a failure. When we lose sight of Alice at the cottage, we catch a last glimpse of her from Don's perspective as he looks over his shoulder, fleeing the infected who've overrun the property. She's screaming for him behind an upstairs window, her eyes wild with fear. This sight—this look—will haunt Don for the rest of the film. When he tells his children that he watched their mother die, a jump cut to Alice at the window underscores the dissonance between what he says and what he saw—and what she saw, too. So when Don becomes infected, he directs his violence at the eyes of the woman whose return unraveled his story of survival, pushing his thumbs into them in a horrifying, protracted act of murder. The second outbreak begins something like the first, then. Don is infected by Man's story—a narrative that tells him how to be a father and then casts him, for his failures, as dysselected. And he violently revolts against this casting.

Since Don is guilt-stricken, I read him as animated by debt.[27] I understand his guilt as shaped by an internalization of the imperatives of the "enterprise society" that, according to Michel Foucault, is proper to neoliberalism (2008, 147). Neoliberal storytelling posits freedom as derived from competition, a notion that generates a social fabric pervaded by what Foucault calls "surfaces of friction" (149). Scenarios of apocalypse can be read as taking the enterprise society to its nightmarish extreme: amid exponentially multiplying "surfaces of friction," Man must make his familial enterprise viable by capitalizing on opportunities to accumulate and secure. But Don can't do the job. So his guilt expresses his failure to successfully compete and, what's more, his indebtedness to the state for his security and that of his family. Don is animated by guilt, tethered to a story of humanness that marks him out as a failed Man. Once infected, though, he revolts against the very story that's pulling his strings. This is in part

FIGURE 9. Alice (Catherine McCormack) sees her husband fleeing in terror and screams for him to come back. Still from *28 Weeks Later* (Fox Atomic, 2007).

because Don's guilt—or indebtedness—runs in two directions at once. He feels beholden to the security state, which makes him easily recruitable into the militarized rebeginning happening on the Isle of Dogs, where, his daughter teasingly reminds him, "you're the caretaker." But he feels guilty about Alice, too. And this drives him to use the access card that comes with his job for an unauthorized visit with his wife. This is when guilt twists into Rage, a murderous aggression that unravels his paternal identity along with the security apparatus that was shoring it back up. After killing Alice, Don spends the rest of the film stalking his children.

The shift from Alice's terrified-outraged look to Don's guilty-infected look is followed by the introduction of two additional perspectives—ways of seeing that exceed the security zone's limited sense of what could happen next. Young Andy (Mackintosh Muggleton) and the teenage Tammy (Imogen Poots) were away on a school trip in Spain when the outbreak began. Having spent months in a refugee camp, they're reunited with Don on the Isle of Dogs shortly after the film's prologue. Andy has eyes, like his mum's, that are two different colors, which makes him the harbinger of a monstrous future. But it's his orientation to the past—his desire to see his mum's face just one more time—that sets off the chain of events that unravels District One. Aiming to collect some items from their family home, the siblings sneak past the military checkpoints that sever the Isle of Dogs from the rest of London, slipping into what one official describes as the "forbidden" zone across the Thames. So the excursion that results in Alice's return begins with Andy and Tam's willful evasion of a militarized regime of surveillance. Like the "unattached woman," they disappear and come back, stirring up, in the interim, the suppressed pasts that linger in unwatched spaces. When

Andy discovers Alice in the attic of their old house, joy mingles with uncertainty and the recognition of paternal betrayal—ambivalence that crystallizes in an ambiguous hug between mother and son. It's possible to read Alice's hug, which mutates into a desperate, clutching squeeze, as foreshadowing the threat she ostensibly poses to District One. But I suggest an alternative reading. What if Alice's embrace revolts against the experiences of abandonment that constitute her largely untold story? Left for dead first by her husband and then by everyone else, Alice tries to reestablish connection. And that connection becomes unstable only as the distant sound of a helicopter becomes louder and then settles over the house. Spied from the rooftops as they were leaving, Andy and Tam bring an arm of the security apparatus home with them. So Alice's hug "zombifies" when the security apparatus reasserts its mechanisms of surveillance and control. As *28 Days* suggests with the origin story of the Rage virus, security regimes animate the very monsters they purport to keep at bay.

The zombifying effect of security apparatuses derives from the distance between eyes that look from a place of embodied vulnerability and the cold, hard gaze of technologies of surveillance. In *28 Weeks Later*, this distance is a function of height. The film establishes a topography in which the military controls the airspace and rooftops and deploys technologies of long-distance visual capture. The streets are for the civilians and, later, the infected. In contrast with those first shots of a ruined London in *28 Days Later*, which we see, with Jim, from the ground, our first glimpses of the city in *28 Weeks* are aerial views. Similarly, we first see the Isle of Dogs through the scopes of rooftop snipers. So Andy and Tam's foray into the London streets is our first indication that audiences might identify, in the end, with those on the ground. Because when the outbreak begins, the military gaze that frames all civilians as suspect—the one that's been tracking the repatriation process via CCTV cameras—zombifies the crowd. "Code Red" begins with the movement of civilians to containment areas and a military attempt to distinguish between the infected and "friendlies." But as the situation deteriorates, General Stone (Idris Elba) gives the command to "target everyone at ground level. No exceptions." The problem is that Andy and Tam, as the first children to be repatriated, were exceptional the minute they stepped foot on the Isle of Dogs. Their arrival was noticed first by the Chief Medical Officer, Scarlet (Rose Byrne), and then by a rooftop sniper, Doyle (Jeremy Renner). During Code Red, both Scarlet and Doyle refuse the "no exceptions" command and leave their posts to protect the kids. This shifts the topographical arrangement of the film, reorienting the audience's view of what's happening by offering a ground-level perspective. Down here, in the pathologized urban streets, an unstable mixture of civilians and infected tries to survive the sniper shots and firebombs that rain down from the film's upper regions. Caught in the grip of a military machine bent on annihilation, Andy and Tam might as well be monsters.

Andy and Tam are extensions of the trouble Alice makes. They embody familial pasts that unspool into national and colonial imaginaries that link deviant children to uncertain futures. Hannah Arendt's principle of natality, which I discuss in my introduction, grounds the possibility of political freedom in the fact that we're "born into the world as strangers" (1958, 9). Children are strange arrivals brimming with potentially world-altering newness. And kids who activate unpredictable beginnings threaten the progressive timeline that animates Man's story of humanness. If the destruction of the British mainland ripped a hole in this story, then the reboot on the Isle of Dogs means to suture the gap and ward off the monstrous futures bubbling up in the ruins. From this perspective, the outbreak is readable in terms of what Wald calls "thirdworldification" (2008, 45). Conservative storytelling often deploys a pathologized "Third World" landscape—broken infrastructure, ransacked buildings, hordes of figures seen as human-like but not human—to imagine a nightmare "First World" future. So thirdworldification frames the end of the so-called developed world as a backward slide through time occasioned, especially in the context of epidemiological horror stories, by globalization and its unnerving proximities. This is part of the imaginary to which the *28* films respond. As Jayna Brown observes in her discussion of *28 Days*, the film engages with "a paranoid nationalism in America as well as Britain"—a longing, spurred by globalizing capitalism, "for a time when boundaries between racial and national bodies were stable, when the difference between 'us' and 'them' was clear" (2013b, 122). But rather than bolstering this nostalgia, the *28* films implicate it in the making of monsters. It's the compulsive telling of Man's paranoid story, represented by the Cambridge lab experiment, that proliferates threat, violence, and dis-ease.

By aligning the audience with the kids, *28 Weeks* interrogates the familial-colonial coordinates of the bad futures projected by conservative storytelling. On the surface, Andy and Tam are good white English kids, embodiments of the symbolic Child that underwrites what Lee Edelman calls "reproductive futurism"—the presupposition that the existing social order must survive, which marks out an ideological limit of the politically organized world (2004, 4). But since particular, historically situated children are rarely able to carry this symbolic load, Claudia Castañeda's work on "figurations" of the child comes at these questions differently. Castañeda investigates the layers of context-specific meanings and practices that generate child-figures about which we tell stories and through which we build worlds. These figures, then, should "also be considered in terms of their uses—what they 'body forth' in turn" (2002, 3). Because children are typically figured as adults-in-the-making, becomings rather than beings, they're uniquely positioned to "body forth" both desirable and dystopian futures. And like perspectives that see The End in terms of "thirdworldification," visions of children as inexorably oriented toward adulthood are underwritten by developmental time. Castañeda explores how the rise of the biological sciences led to imaginings of the child as "a bodily theater where human history could be observed to unfold in the compressed time-span of individual development" (13). According to this logic, children illuminate not just an individual past—that of the adult who was once a child—but also a collective past racialized as "primitive" or "savage."[28] So conservative storytelling leverages the racial logic of developmentalism to cast deviant children as agents of social devolution. And Wald demonstrates that outbreak narratives tend to reify this link. Reading American journalist Geddes Smith's 1941 tract *Plague on Us*, Wald notes that in the context of thinking about healthy carriers, Smith "defines children as 'immigrants into the human herd—immigrants whose susceptibility dilutes herd resistance and so helps to keep certain diseases in circulation'" (2008, 22). Between mothers who evade patriarchal oversight and children who arrive into the world as strangers, the "agents of the community's reproduction carry the threat of its annihilation" (23).

Andy and Tam's capacity to "body forth" an array of rebeginnings derives from their insistence on connection in the face of terror—a togetherness that counters the logic of quarantine. I see this as a maternal inheritance, an echo of Alice's actions at the cottage, where she stopped to help a child trapped in a closet while her terrified husband begged her to leave the boy behind. And then he left them both. So the last time Alice appears in *28 Weeks*, haunting the cinematic present, she's spliced into the midst of the climactic scene in which her husband attacks their son in a darkened Tube station. As an armed Tam approaches Don, who's pinned Andy to the floor and is sinking his teeth into the child's neck, the film cuts to Alice's horrified face in her moment of abandonment at the cottage. On screen for less than a second, she screams his name in protest, her voice resonating with Tam's yell in the present. Synchronizing Alice's "Don!" with Tam's "Dad!," the scene cuts directly from mother back to daughter, zooming in on Tam's eyes as she hesitates with the gun. That shot of Alice's face indexes a past to which Tam has no access, which means that Don's memory triangulates the mother/daughter parallel for the viewer. It's a perspective from which Tam's eyes compound the shame that Don already associates with Alice's. The scene is crosscut with sight lines, affording the viewer access to the perspectives of three of the four members of the Harris family, including one who's dead and one who's monstrous. And to preserve the fourth perspective—clinging to the possibility that Andy will open his eyes in the aftermath of Don's attack—Tam reluctantly kills her father. A daughter becoming-monster.

So Andy becomes a carrier at the end of the film—his mother's weird genes holding Don's Rage at bay—and Tam reveals that becoming-monster can entail both revolt and reinvention. In keeping with the *28* films' uncoupling of father figures and survival, Don's spiraling shame, spraying outward in unrelenting acts of aggression, stands between the siblings and their futures. So Tam commits patricide to hold open the possibility of any kind of kinship at all. And in spite of

Andy's now dangerously hybrid embodiment, she keeps her brother close, even shielding him from view when they finally reach help. Closeness, not quarantine. Tam's decision echoes Alice's ambiguous hug in the attic of their former home. Given Andy's capacity to infect others, including Tam herself, her shielding of his telltale eyes is readable as dangerous. But in preserving Rage to preserve her brother, Tam reanimates Alice's revolt against Man's practices of abandonment and surveillance.

A final word about Alice, then.

CODA: KISS

The second outbreak of Rage begins with a kiss between husband and wife. But what do we do with that kiss? Alice is strapped down in a locked room when her husband lets himself in, tearfully telling her how scared he was and how sorry he is. And when she replies that she loves him, they kiss. I'm not saying that Don's sorrow is disingenuous. He's not very brave, but that doesn't make him unsympathetic. Nor am I convinced that Alice's barely audible "I love you" is false. But Don is seeking absolution from a traumatized woman who's completely immobilized. And he has a key to the room in which she's being kept. The scene is structured by a glaring power imbalance, which means that Don becomes infected while claiming access to Alice's body when she's unable to consent. And it leads me to wonder if the resulting transmission of infection is readable as revolt—as Alice's (perhaps) unconscious refusal of gender norms that make wives responsive to, even responsible for, their husbands' bad feelings. Because Don's fear has cost Alice dearly. And his implicit demand, in the present, that she assuage his guilt is asking a lot. So Alice might still love her husband. She might even understand that his terror brought out his worst self. But maybe the Rage in her body—the monster she harbors—taps into layers of feeling beyond what Alice knows. Don pulls away, reeling and jerking. And Man's world, which has been costly to him but more costly to her, begins ending again.

Alice isn't the only woman in the *28* films for whom kisses are complicated. Selena uses one to manipulate the men who plan to rape her. And later, when Jim and Selena reunite and kiss each other, Hannah is so unsure of what she's seeing—is he biting her?—that she attacks Jim. In a sense, though, Selena *is* menaced by this kiss. Its conjuring of a heterosexual couple threatens to overwrite all the evidence that Selena is a survivor; to activate a storytelling apparatus in which men rescue damsels in distress and, for their trouble, win love. But the "damsel" role is typically reserved for white women, so this refiguring of Selena as Jim's love interest only highlights, perhaps, the "controlling image" that's haunted her all along: the "Strong Black Woman" whose capacity to endure terror and abuse is somehow naturalized, resulting, potentially, in an unseeing of her labor and her courage (Collins 2004, 139, 208). The kiss propels Selena into an impossible storytelling tension, stretching her between the character-flattening stereotypes of the damsel in distress and the black woman with "outsized corporeal or emotional strength" (Brooks 2018, 11).[29] It seems to me that part of what's impossible about the film's impossible ending—"the proper ending," Boyle says—is its opening up of "story potentials" that exceed these stereotypes (Scott 2004, 32). This highlights how forced the theatrical ending is: the one that sees Jim, Selena, and Hannah awaiting rescue in a small cottage in the Lake District. A film that's located horror in the English countryside ends in what Nadine Attewell describes as "an iconically English landscape." And in a film that's shifted terror onto the patriarchal family unit and the forms of gender violence it feeds, this ending might be seen as performing "a return to England-as-home as well as to the home-as-institution" (2014, 192). But I'm inclined to see homes as haunted, uncanny spaces, so I also agree with Mafe that "vestiges of the monstrous-feminine are not entirely absent, even in the tranquil final scene" (2018, 42). Selena sits at a sewing machine, stitching curtains into letters to spell out the word with which we began: Hello. But this work is "grounded in her survivalist ethos. She is not darning Jim's socks here—she is manufacturing a distress signal" (42).

In some ways, the persistence of the monstrous-feminine at the end of *28 Days Later* anticipates that its sequel will unravel every source of security offered by this ending. The cottage is overrun. The heterosexual couple splits and a (white) woman survives alone. The military becomes a murderous machine. And in the end, quarantine fails. *28 Weeks* leaves us with a wrecked chopper—the one that carried Andy and Tam across the Channel—and a shot of the infected racing through the Chunnel that connects a "diseased little island" to the rest of Europe (*28 Days*). It dramatizes, in short, the breakdown of what Attewell calls "island solutions" (2014, 35). It's not so much that England, like Manhattan in *I Am Legend*, is amenable to quarantine (until it isn't). The "island solution" is more about how "the (quasi) insular geography and architecture of District One reflects its orientation towards the future and away from the past" (209). That is, island solutions rest on a seemingly clear differentiation between inside and outside, "us" and "them"—a spatial demarcation bolstered by a forgetting of the pasts that haunt the nation's claims to coherence. As the next chapter, on *Children of Men* (U.K. 2006), explores, forgetting Britain's imperial history to carve out a seemingly purified national inside is an unsustainable project. And this is true in *28 Weeks Later* as well, a film in which the white family, a microcosm of the nation, can't hold itself together because it's already infiltrated by feelings that unravel and estrange. Attewell concludes her discussion of *28 Weeks* by meditating on "the possibility that the family is strange, the stranger, as in the classic horror scenario, already inside the house, there among us, there inside us" (210).

Don is undone when too much terror transmutes into too much guilt and too much Rage. Alice's Rage is barely controlled, exercising, perhaps, a will of its own. Tam is patricidal. Andy is a mutant. (And what happened to that chopper, exactly?) The white family comes apart at the seams, undoing the neat divisions through which Man's story differentiates human from monster, chosen from cursed. So the next chapter thinks with a film that explores what kinds of human connection—what new understandings of humanness—might emerge from this undoing.

4 • MATERNAL BACKGROUNDS

Children of Men

Alfonso Cuarón's *Children of Men* (U.K./U.S./Japan 2006) ends with a deferred encounter. In the final shot, an African refugee named Kee (Clare-Hope Ashitey) is adrift in a rowboat off the coast of Bexhill-on-Sea. In 2027, *Children*'s present, Bexhill is a refugee camp where an authoritarian, xenophobic England deposits those who have fled the global chaos induced by an unexplained crisis in female fertility. Generational time has come to an end, so the youngest person in the world is now eighteen years old—until, that is, Kee gives birth in the middle of an uprising at Bexhill. So in the final frame, she's cradling to her chest the first child to arrive in the world in nearly two decades. And coming into focus in the middle of the shot is a hospital ship disguised as a fishing boat called *Tomorrow*. It's crewed by emissaries of the Human Project, a collective that, until now, was just a rumor. On the right side of the screen, a light on the buoy that marks their designated meeting place flares once before the scene cuts to black.

For some critics, this is a hopeful ending. Slavoj Žižek sees the *Tomorrow* as the perfect political "solution" to Kee's plight because it's "rootless"—a complement to Kee's statelessness.[1] In a more skeptical vein, Zahid Chaudhary objects to what he sees as Cuarón's representation of an "oceanic plenitude" that offers a "theological solution to material conflicts" (2009, 93, 87). But an ending that sees a black woman meeting a ship full of scientists seems fraught with peril. While appreciative of the film's critique of xenophobia, Jayna Brown writes that it also "reinforces the ways black women have been defined by their physiological function, evaluated according to the usefulness of their sexual reproductive bodies" (2013b, 127). From this perspective, *Children*'s final image is structured as a deferred encounter between two vessels that evokes histories of slavery, including the legal doctrine of "*partus sequitur ventrem* (that which is brought forth follows the womb), in which the Black child inherits the non/status, the non/being of the mother" (Sharpe 2016, 15). Indeed, scholars of transatlantic history might wonder about Žižek's characterization of the *Tomorrow* as "rootless" given the submerged oceanic landscape it traverses. For thinkers from Édouard Glissant to

FIGURE 10. Kee (Clare-Hope Ashitey) and baby Dylan wait for the *Tomorrow* off the coast of Bexhill-on-Sea. Still from *Children of Men* (Universal, 2006).

Katherine McKittrick to Paul Gilroy to Christina Sharpe, the time of modernity begins to take shape in the crossings of ships navigating the Atlantic basin—in the terrors of the ship's hold and the bodily traces strewn across the ocean floor.[2] In this context, the film's final image might ask us, following Walter Benjamin, "to seize hold of a memory as it flashes up in a moment of danger," alerting viewers to a rebeginning animated by familiar forms of violence (1968, 255).

My aim here isn't to replace hopeful interpretations of *Children*'s ending with a reading of Kee and her baby as doomed.[3] I'm inspired, instead, by the watery gap that Cuarón sustains at the end of the film. The space between Kee and *Tomorrow* makes imaginative room in which to contemplate a range of threatening-promising possibilities that confront this new mother and her miraculous infant.[4] Some of these possible futures are, no doubt, exploitative and horrifying. For Brown, "we do not see Kee being lifted on the ship, but our limitless horizon has been blocked, occupied by the looming representation of science and militarism" (2013b, 131). I don't disagree. There are grounds to read the arrival of the *Tomorrow* as stabilizing a storyline in which, guided by Western science, bodies coded as primitive redeem a fallen world. *Children of Men* opens itself up to such a reading. But since this interpretation, as Brown writes, "occupies" the horizon of possible rebeginnings that opens at the end of the film, I have questions that I hope move toward a "counteroccupation of mythical space" (Lauro 2015, 25). What kinds of scientists are on board the *Tomorrow*? What kind of project is the Human Project? Is there distance, perhaps, between the humanness it imagines and the more restricted understanding embedded in the film's title?

In this chapter, I return to Sylvia Wynter's insights about Man's grip on our definition of the human, this time emphasizing what I described in my introduction as the theological underpinnings of Man's story. For Wynter, the figure that currently dominates our understanding of humanness is economic Man, the successful entrepreneurial subject. And this secular figure, she argues, is a redescription of the human that carries with it the narrative components of medieval Europe's conception of the human as Christian. These include the postulation of a "significant ill"—natural scarcity rather than original sin—and a correlated "plan of salvation" that hinges on the unrelenting accumulation of resources (2003, 265).[5] The novel on which *Children of Men* is based, P. D. James's *The Children of Men* (1992), resurfaces the Christian version of this narrative arc. So the question of how—and how much—Cuarón's film deviates from Man's story requires a consideration of how it mutates the symbolic register established by James. The novel begins with reflections on Western science as a failed "god"—a false idol whose worshippers are "outraged and demoralized" by its inability to pinpoint the cause of human infertility (James 1992, 6, 5). And it ends by locating salvation in the reconstitution of the white patriarchal family through the baptism of a baby boy. This storytelling inheritance propels the film into what Chaudhary describes as a "journey from the earlier triad of white man–white woman–white child to white man–black woman–black child" (2009, 74). Along the way, the references to both Western science and the Nativity that give James's story its ideological shape become key coordinates in Cuarón's counternarrative. For some critics, the film still ends with a too-neat "narrative of redemption" that forecloses the questions it raises about race, alterity, and political conflict (92). But I wonder if the cinematic *Children*'s redemption arc is as stable as it seems. I'm not sure that it survives, intact, the invention of Kee—the one main character who has no counterpart in James's novel and whose "hyperbolic excess," Diana Adesola Mafe suggests, "arguably transcends the director's intentions" (2018, 72). Kee ushers into the film what Wynter calls a "demonic ground" perspective, a story-place from which it becomes possible to imagine human futures that strain against the titular reference to Man.[6]

How we see Kee in this film is related to how we see a character I've delayed introducing: Theo Faron (Clive Owen), *Children*'s lethargic Last Man, anchors the redemption storyline. Once an activist, Theo lost his child to a flu pandemic and lost his faith in the world as a result. But then his estranged ex-partner, Julian (Julianne Moore), approaches him to help Kee find safe passage to the coast. So his story is a conversion narrative that follows a trajectory from nihilism to hope. But interpretations of the film that center Theo's emotional journey tend to write his resurrection across Kee's pregnant, precarious body. The first move in such a reading is usually to posit the infertility on which the story pivots as a metaphor for the spiritual barrenness of Western modernity. Even though Žižek takes issue with this "obvious spiritualist trick," his materialist corrective—"the true infertility is the very lack of meaningful historical experience" under late capitalism—similarly relegates Kee to the background of Theo's journey. If the "true infertility" in the film derives from the "ideological despair of late capitalism," then listless, apathetic Theo exemplifies this sterility.[7] Žižek sees Theo as a Last Man in the Nietzschean sense: a passionless being who values survival over the riskiness—and heartbreak—of worldly engagement. Within this framework, the story of his conversion is one that sees him reinvest in the world in response to the miracle of new life. And when the film concludes, Theo's investment seems to pay dividends when Kee decides to name her baby girl Dylan after his dead son. So even as the Last Man dies from a gunshot wound in the rowboat—in that final shot, he's a corpse slumped across from Kee and the baby—Dylan confirms that Theo will live on. From such a vantage point, the martyred protector shares in Kee's fecundity. By sacrificing himself, Theo potentially becomes what Wynter calls a "donor figure"—the ghostly paternal ground of a new human origin story (Wynter and McKittrick 2015, 36). From this angle, *Children* seems to offer a postwhite future that somehow reaffirms the power and benevolence of white masculinity.[8]

But Cuarón's use of the long take, his lingering with backgrounds, opens up the possibility of decentering Theo and bringing Kee more firmly into focus.[9] After all, Theo isn't just a Nietzschean Last Man. In this book I've been considering the various strategies through which apocalypse films play with and often destabilize the Last Man as a convention of the genre, a figure whose perspective typically orients viewers to the ruined world. In the previous chapter, I argued that the *28* films reimagine and distribute the Last Man function across multiple characters, creating a ramifying perspective that brings multiple views of the ruined world into coexistence. *Children* comes at this differently by noticeably disarticulating the camera from Theo's point of view. The film opens with a fixed shot of the patrons of a London coffee shop, their mournful eyes glued to a TV announcing the stabbing death of "baby Diego," the world's youngest person, in Buenos Aires. Theo enters the visual frame, orders and pays for his coffee, and then exits the shop with the camera following. But outside on the street, when Theo turns left, the camera conspicuously turns right. It takes in a state-sponsored message about reporting "suspicious activity" before finding our protagonist again as he's about to splash booze into his morning coffee. Immediately, then, Cuarón establishes the camera's relative autonomy from the Last Man. These overt deviations from Theo's point of view, which continue throughout the film, have prompted a number of critics to attend to *Children*'s background. As Chaudhary observes, the film's "structure of visibility [is one] in which the background of the frame, rather than the putative object of cinematic focus, carries the weight of signification" (2009, 80). Down the street, an explosion decimates the coffee shop Theo's just been in and the camera backtracks without him, reconnecting with what was happening behind the protagonist's back.

This chapter extends and intervenes in discussions of *Children*'s background by focusing on the raced and gendered "histories of labor" that shape Kee's navigation of the narrative present (Ahmed 2006, 49). My approach is inspired by Sara Ahmed, who, like me, is leery of readings of the film that convert the *Tomor-*

row into a symbol of hope to stabilize the story of Theo's redemption. Meditating on the unconfirmed existence of the Human Project, Ahmed interprets Kee's journey as proceeding "on the whim of a rumor," but clarifies that "something beyond the technology of belief is expressed here" (2010, 180). Contact with the Human Project happens through "mirrors"—a relay system of clandestine meetings and whispered exchanges between activists. So the rumor indexes a history of work: "the future is what happens through the work required to get close enough to hear the whisper, which is always a whisper that somebody else must have heard" (180). Theo gets close enough to hear the whisper through Julian. But this chapter is about the histories that bring Kee and Julian herself into range of the whisper. What Ahmed refers to, in another context, as "histories of labor" asks us to attend to the conditions of arrival that shape our worldly encounters: "we need to face the background of an object, redefined as the conditions for the emergence not only of the object (we might ask: How did it arrive?), as well as the act of perceiving the object, which depends on the arrival of the body that perceives" (2006, 49, 38). For Ahmed—and for me—it's a matter of undoing the "acts of relegation" that make backgrounds in the first place (2006, 31). It's about questioning the storytelling habits that collude in subordinating what's behind (in space) and before (in time) to the object or event that comes into focus through that very subordination: a ship that arrives seemingly out of nowhere; the technology of (Theo's) redemption. But Cuarón's visual lingering with the cinematic background invites us to see Theo's heartbreak as just one feature in a landscape of ruined and precarious lives that includes piles of smoldering animal carcasses, activist white women undone by their documenting and protesting of state violence, racialized revolutionaries rising up against the biopolitical state, and refugees held in camps and cages.[10] And Kee activates this background in ways Theo can't.

In place of a stable, knowable origin, Kee indexes what Michel Foucault describes as "a profusion of lost events" that exposes national identity as an unsustainable—and so endlessly reiterated—fiction (1984, 81). The problem isn't (only) that Kee is black. Alert to how stories can be spun, one activist in the film warns that "the government will take her baby and parade a posh black English lady as the mother." In the context of global depopulation, Britishness can likely accommodate black maternity—especially posh black maternity—provided it belongs to a national "inside" mapped out by "racially coded immigration laws of the 1960s and 1970s" that attempted a "re-closure of the nation" in the aftermath of empire (Smith 1994, 23, 24). As I'll explore in the next section, Nadine Attewell argues that postwar immigration reforms that grounded citizenship in the British Isles were meant to conserve the whiteness of Britishness in the face of "demographic panic" (2014, 169). What Attewell calls "island solutions" locate control over national identities and futures in spatial formations premised on apartness (35). While the fiction of a posh black English mum could undermine the illusion of a racially pure—white—Englishness, it keeps intact a national identity underwritten by the spatial closure that, in 2027, Britain still relentlessly polices. But Kee is a refugee from an unspecified African country, an heir to the "black 'invader'" figure imagined by Enoch Powell in the 1960s (Smith 1994, 8).[11] Her presence attests to the permeability of the boundaries of the nation and, in turn, to the instability of the national identity the island purports to anchor. What's more, she claims not to know who fathered her child: "I don't know half the wankers' names," she tells Theo. This statement obscures both paternal identity and the circumstances in which Dylan was conceived, gesturing to a nebulous what-happened-before that can't be shaped into a stable origin story. So the film's redemption story arc centers on Theo, presenting him as a "donor figure" that secures a postracial rebeginning (Wynter and McKittrick 2015, 36). But something else is happening behind his back. A future animated by unknown pasts—one that attests to the porousness of geopolitical boundaries—is reshaping the island as a threshold onto the world.

(I) ISLANDS

"You know what they do to these cows? They cut off their tits." Kee's disembodied voice addresses Theo as the camera tracks his progress into a cattle barn, revealing hay, milking apparatuses, and dairy cows before settling on Kee herself. Standing inside a pen with the animals, she's visible from the waist up, captured from a distance and framed by milking machines as she reflects on the violence of industrial agriculture: "Four tits fits the machine. It's wacko. Why not make machines that suck eight titties, eh?" Then Kee disrobes to reveal her swollen breasts and belly to a startled Theo, the camera tilting up from a bovine snout and a tagged ear as she comes into focus from the background of the shot.

The image of a pregnant Kee in a barn cites the ending of James's novel, in which a white woman named Julian gives birth in a woodshed in Wychwood Forest in Oxfordshire. Shot through with Christian symbolism—a miraculous birth in humble surroundings and, on the final page, a makeshift baptism—this ending reboots the nation by renewing the white heteropatriarchal family. Julian and Theo are falling in love, so Theo, an Oxford historian, will take up the role of England's first new father in twenty-five years. In James's dystopian world, unlike in Cuarón's adaptation, it's men who are sterile. So the baby born at the end of the novel, the boy whose sex is "like a proclamation," will inherit Theo's name along with that of his biological father, a former priest named Luke (James 1992, 272). He'll likely inherit, too, the power Theo seizes from his despotic cousin, Xan, ruler of Great Britain, when he strips the Coronation ring from Xan's corpse in the final pages of the novel. So James's *The Children of Men* ends by investing Theo with patriarchal and political power, both of which are grounded in his claim to the fruits of Julian's reproductive body. But Cuarón's adaptation takes its barn scene in another

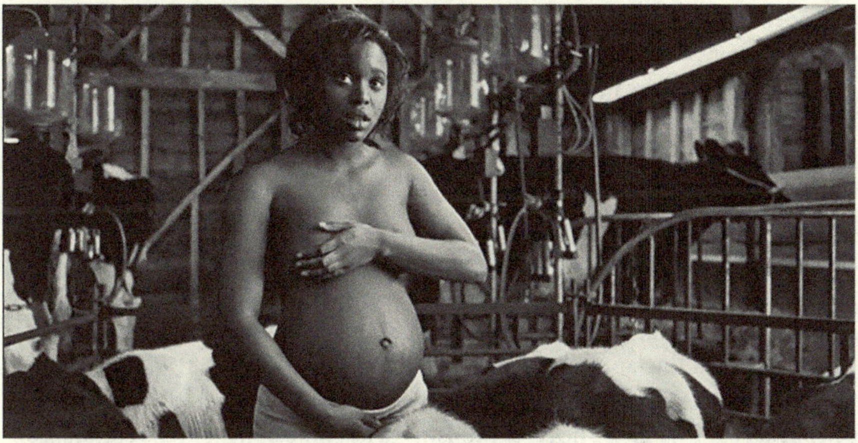

FIGURE 11. Kee reveals her pregnancy to Theo after reflecting on the violence done to the cattle that surround her. Still from *Children of Men* (Universal, 2006).

direction. Instead of a pastoral setting and a white baby boy who "needed no encouragement to suck" (James 1992, 275), *Children* offers a pregnant black woman surrounded by milking machines. As Kee's reflections on cows and "titties" suggest, she, at least, is all too aware of what can happen to living beings valued only for what they carry in their bodies. So what do we make of *Children* as a pointedly unfaithful adaptation, a willful child, perhaps, in relation to its literary parent?[12] And how does the film's mutation of James's reactionary story undo a fantasy of infertility laden with anxieties about the end of whiteness?

Kee's visual alignment with cattle offers a clue about *Children*'s interrogation of a conservative political imaginary animated by fantasies of blackness as an invasive presence that threatens to disintegrate the (white) nation. Standing in the cow pen, Kee is haunted by histories of racist representations of people of color as characterized by "animal-like hyperfertility" (Chaudhary 2009, 97). And the cattle in the background of the scene articulate with the other herd animals seen in the film: piles of smoldering carcasses that dot the British countryside, visually conjuring the 2001 outbreak of foot-and-mouth disease in the United Kingdom. Kee's alignment with animals evokes two strands of a racialized invasion narrative: a reproductive storyline that casts immigrant populations as dangerously fecund dovetails with what Priscilla Wald (2008) calls an "outbreak narrative" that pivots on racialized logics of contagion. Cuarón and his team mobilize these storylines in a cinematic world shaped by its post-9/11 moment of production. From repeated references to "Homeland Security" to the chants of "Allahu Akbar" at the Bexhill uprising, *Children* taps into the racial-generational underpinnings of conservative laments about the decline of Western civilization and the rise, in its place, of an Islamic world perceived as younger and more virile.[13] The figure of the "enemy within" conjured by Melanie Phillips's *Londonistan: How Britain Is Creating a Terror State Within* (2006) underscores how this post-9/11 public discourse reactivates already established narrative coordinates. The Islamic militant builds on a history of postwar "invader" figures that, as Anna Marie Smith shows, tracks back to the "Powellian image of the nation under siege" by black immigrants that laid the foundations for Margaret Thatcher's imagining, in 1978, of a nation "swamped" by outsiders (1994, 26). So *Children*'s take on its post-9/11 moment is also an intervention in James's engagement with Thatcherism. In both historical moments, conservative storytelling summons the declining virility of white Britons to project apocalyptic futures, an exercise in envisioning The End that carries within it the fantasy of a purer rebeginning.

By locating the possibility of national repair in the regeneration of the white patriarchal family, James's novel demonstrates its enmeshment in the cultural conservatism of the 1980s and 1990s. Its reinvestment in the familial roles established by Man's story of humanness—the paternal provider-protector, the good mother, the chosen child—exemplifies the storytelling backlash that I outlined in my introduction. Wynter describes the radical political movements of the 1960s as the "opening phase" of the struggle against Man's overrepresentation (Wynter and McKittrick 2015, 23). With Man's grip on imaginaries of humanness wavering, conservative stories about wayward families and ruined cities emerged to ward off the possible future that flashed into view in the sixties: the end of Man's world. James's *The Children of Men* engages in this storytelling struggle over the meanings—and futures—set in motion by the sixties movements. It locates the beginning of its slowly unfolding apocalypse in 1995, projecting "Year Omega" just three years beyond the novel's publication date. And "the 1990s" emerge in James's narrative as a culmination of the nightmare imaginary crafted by conservatives in the seventies and eighties. In his diary, Theo characterizes the decade as rife with sexual alternatives—"the stroking and anointing," "the non-penetrative sex"—that anticipate the waning of sexual appetites in his childless present (9). Comments such as these prompted Lee Edelman's critique of the novel as presenting a decadent West suffering from a "putative crisis in sexual values" (2004, 11–12). Indeed, the novel taps into the homophobia of Thatcherite discourse, in which the "dangerous queer," like the immigrant, "threatened to invade the nation from the immoral outside" (Smith 1994, 26, 25). This vision of a Britain besieged by enemies both within and without is made explicit by members of the superficially democratic Council of England, who remember the nineties as years of urban crime—when children were "as dangerous as their elders"—and rising European resentment against the "invading hordes" created by open immigration policies (James 1992, 111, 112). And since, as Theo observes, the eighties and nineties are decades in which women are "increasingly critical and intolerant of men" (136), the novel also suggests that the dubious achievements of feminism have made the nation vulnerable. Taken together, these details create a portrait of 1990s Britain as unmoored by the overreaches of feminism, multiculturalism, and queer liberation and burdened, as a result, by the spread of deviance and crime.

The Children of Men presents apparently contrasting responses to these problems in the figures of Xan, who styles himself the "Warden of England," and Theo, whose ascension to fatherhood allows him, in the end, to usurp his cousin. But the closed national space over which Xan presides and the white familial rebeginning Theo represents are situated along a continuum that articulates race, space, and reproduction as the basis of national identity. Attewell argues that the imagined whiteness of the nation animates—and is animated by—a "dream of total reproductive control" facilitated by spatial closure (2014, 37). Xan's Britain is something like its authoritarian counterpart in Cuarón's film: it keeps the outside world at bay through the enactment of an "island solution" that "chart[s] new, insular, geographies of national belonging" (68). The tightly regulated migrant labor system is the exception that reinforces the rule: "Sojourners," with their "dark faces," are imported to support an aging population and then deported to their country of origin when they reach the cutoff age of sixty (James 1992, 83). The crime problems of the 1990s, too, are solved by (imagined) spatial closure. Anyone charged with a crime is sent to the Isle of Man, which, in its abandonment, has devolved into a savage, chaotic place in which only "devils" survive (74). Xan's Britain, then, secures itself against two kinds of racialized contamination by insisting on apartness. The Isle of Man and the social devolution it harbors are, for all intents and purposes, under quarantine. And a ruthless deportation policy wards off the wholesale demographic shift that the Sojourners, were they allowed to stay, would effect. With the transgenerational reproduction of Britishness now impossible, Xan's Council maintains national identity by demarcating a British "inside" through "a never-ending process of filtering, purging, and excising" (Attewell 2014, 49). But while the novel ultimately indicts Xan—and mobilizes a flimsy critique of his policies through the Five Fishes, the activist group of which Julian is a part—the utopian alternative that Theo represents is no less entangled with the fantasy of an "island solution."[14]

A rebeginning anchored by the white patriarchal family form enacts its own filtering and purging of the national imaginary. It pivots on what Alys Weinbaum formulates as "the race/reproduction bind" that undergirds modern notions of political belonging (2004, 5). Ideologies of racism, nationalism, and imperialism, she argues, are premised on the assumptions "that race can be *reproduced*" and, relatedly, that the nation is a reproducible "racial formation" (4, 19, emphasis original). Within the framework of this bind, maternal bodies are figured "as either a repository of racial identity or a racializing force" (17). In the context of nations that imagine themselves as white, white maternal bodies like Julian's seem to materialize a knowable, transparent origin that allows the nation to mythologize itself as racially pure. And black maternal bodies such as Kee's are figured as opaque and therefore suspect. In the postwar British imaginary, specifically, black maternity conjures the uncertain futures that unfold from imperial pasts; from the histories of contact and migration that make postcolonial Britain, to borrow Ashley Dawson's (2007) description, a "mongrel nation." Postwar invasion narratives attempt to suppress the diasporic remixing of British culture and identity by recasting British subjects from the colonies as outsiders. As Attewell shows, these stories of invasion were entwined with a series of legislative changes that, beginning in 1962, redrew the map of Britishness such that "much of what was once imagined as British territory was made over as alien" (2014, 197). And while this reimagining was largely propelled by projections of dystopian futures, the "island solution" it enacts is distinctly utopian. Imaginings of good places and better futures, Attewell observes, tend to tell a "spatial story . . . of apartness, enclosure, and self-sufficiency, promising sequestration from genealogical contamination and disseminatory drift" (38). The separateness of the island enables (or seems to enable) a regaining of reproductive and narrative control—an excision of contaminated, contaminating pasts that ushers in a purer future. So whether or not Theo will reform Xan's policies, the white heteropatriarchal family that emerges at the end of the novel activates the island's promise of a purified rebeginning. It restabilizes a national origin at which Englishness, whiteness, and Christianity intersect.

After all, as the story of Noah and his ark attests, Christian rebeginnings, too, are invested in island spaces. In his essay on the mythological life of the desert island, Gilles Deleuze observes that the place where the ark sets down is "an island or a mountain, or both at once: the island is a mountain under water, and the mountain, an island that is still dry" (2004, 13). The desert island, for Deleuze, is the spatial expression of the principle of rebirth. It's the material that survives catastrophe and serves as a site of rebeginning, a second origin, which means "it gives us the law of repetition" and, in turn, the possibility of difference (13). In other words, desert islands are teeming with transgressive potentialities. For Deleuze, they're spaces of newness and invention. But he's also attentive to how "mythology fails and dies" in most island stories, with inventiveness giving way to the reconstitution of a familiar world (12).[15] This brings me back to the ark and the patriarch at its helm. The Christian iteration of the myth of the flood illuminates how the desert island can morph into an "island solution." Building on Attewell's concept, I suggest that island solutions are animated by a logic of chosenness—or, in Wynter's terms, by a "plan of salvation" that distinguishes the selected from the "dysselected" (2003, 265, 310). Noah and his family are selected by God to survive the apocalyptic cleansing of the earth. This selection guarantees Noah's goodness—his fitness to serve as the patriarchal anchor of a world renewed and given over to Man by God. And renewal will spread out from the island on which the ark lands, making ark and island together "the radiating seed or egg that must be sufficient to re-produce everything" (Deleuze 2004, 13). This chapter has more to say about the island's coupling with what Christina

Sharpe describes as "Noah's saving ship" (2016, 57). For the moment I want to notice how the film, by introducing Kee into James's story, unveils the biopolitical violence of "island solutions" and the Edenic rebeginnings they promise.

As a stateless person whose fertility is evident in her rounded belly, Kee is in the crosshairs of a biopolitical order that sees both reproduction and migration as sites of state control. As Nira Yuval-Davis writes, the boundaries of nations "are constructed in order to sort people into 'us' and 'them' and stretch from generation to generation. As the biological 'producers' of children/people, women are also, therefore, 'bearers of the collective' within these boundaries" (1997, 26).[16] The state propaganda through which Cuarón orients viewers to a childless, dystopian England emphasizes this link. First, an increasingly frenetic montage of global cities in chaos gives way to assertions that "the world has collapsed" and "only Britain soldiers on." The camera pulls back from a shot of Big Ben dissolving into the Union Jack, revealing that the screen viewers have been watching is one among many in the passenger car of a moving train. We hear only the audio track of the next state-sponsored message. After an array of voices claiming connection and kinship—"He's my dentist," "She's my cousin"—we hear the state's corrective: "*They* are illegal immigrants. To hire, feed, or shelter illegal immigrants is a crime." So state propaganda draws a line from global chaos to illegal outsiders to criminalized insiders, and then the camera locates Theo just in time to catch a sign on the side of a boxcar as the train pulls into the station: "Avoiding fertility tests is a crime." These parallel pronouncements establish the power of the state to manage its population, rounding up and deporting refugees on the one hand and routinely inspecting potentially reproductive bodies on the other. So as an expectant mother who's *in* but not *of* the nation, Kee puts pressure on the fault lines in this all-too familiar biopolitical order. The message about illegal immigrants dehumanizes refugees, casting them as "dysselected" by virtue of their belonging to failed nation-states, and, in turn, articulates humanness with Englishness (Wynter 2003, 267). And in the context of this national retrenchment, Dylan's birth heralds a human rebeginning that threatens-promises to reinvent the world.

(II) SOUNDS

Near the end of *Children of Men*, there's a moment that sounds like a pause. Kee has given birth inside the Bexhill Refugee Camp, which is now a scene of uprising. The sights and sounds of the rebellion—and its military suppression—gather in perhaps the film's most notable long take: a shot more than seven minutes in length in which Kee and Theo are separated on their way to the boat and Theo, limping and ducking and dodging, finds her again. As the camera moves with him, witnessing the dying, a soundscape assembles. The long take opens with a discordant swell of strings that waxes and wanes as the shot unfolds. It's joined by

FIGURE 12. Kee, Theo (Clive Owen), and Dylan leave Pierpoint Tower in the midst of a tenuous ceasefire. Still from *Children of Men* (Universal, 2006).

percussion: the rat-a-tat-tat of automatic weapons and the thuds and pings of bullets hitting bodies and buildings. Tanks creak. Dogs bark. Glass shatters. Theo makes his way into a tower block and there, after more than five uninterrupted minutes of war, we hear Dylan crying somewhere above.

The people of the world haven't heard a baby crying, live, in nearly two decades. Suddenly this sound seeps into the chaos and opens a pocket of quiet around it. "Quiet," Tina Campt writes, "is a modality that surrounds and infuses sound with impact and affect, which creates the possibility for it to register as meaningful" (2017, 4). As Dylan's cries broadcast the news of her arrival, a quiet builds, rippling out into the din of war until a ceasefire (temporarily) takes hold around the ruined Pierpoint Tower. This allows Theo, Kee, and the baby to make their way out of the building. And as they do, there are twenty seconds in which, with the exception of distant gunfire, all we hear is Dylan's crying and Kee's and Theo's feet crunching on rubble. Campt elaborates that "quiet must not be conflated with silence"; that it "registers sonically, as a level of intensity that requires focused attention" (6). Quiet surrounds those cries and crunching feet, sounds that announce, respectively, a beginning and its background—or the "histories of labor" that impress themselves on the soundscape in the form of Kee's slow steps (Ahmed 2006, 49). When the film score swells again, these labored steps are audible and so, too, are the soft grunts of a woman forced to move too soon after giving birth. We can hear these sounds because a quiet took hold, lifting them to our ears.

Registering in that quiet intensity—entwined with Dylan's cries and Kee's steps—is an affective reorganization of camp space. At Bexhill, unarmed refugees are caught in the crossfire of a violent confrontation between soldiers and revolutionaries, so the scene is saturated with difficult feelings. But the quiet interlude offers a roomier emotional range: joy mingling with sorrow; awe mixing with terror; rage and horror giving way to wistfulness, even curiosity. This doesn't last. A rocket launcher goes off and the conflict quickly resumes. But those seconds of quiet—an emotionally charged pause—intervene in a struggle over the (near) future in which one side seeks to conserve Britishness to the end while the other side registers as "Islamic alterity" that seems detached from a concrete political vision (Chaudhary 2009, 89). Neither is prepared for the rebeginning of generational time that Dylan portends. In that quiet around her cries and her mother's steps, the future tense vibrates at another frequency, opening a horizon of possibility that, Campt writes, "grammarians refer to as the future real conditional or *that which will have* ***had to*** *happen*" (17, emphasis original).

Kee and Dylan are navigating an impossible time and place, a camp present that effaces their humanness and which, very soon, the British military will raze. So their survival is more than a matter of imagining beyond the now. It demands the activation of "a politics of prefiguration that involves living the future *now*—as imperative rather than subjunctive—as a striving for the future you want to see, right now, in the present" (Campt 2017, 17, emphasis original). Following Campt, I understand Kee's flight into Bexhill and back out as reaching for "a future that hasn't yet happened but must" (17). Her reaching for that future takes shape in the present as transfigurations of space that Katherine McKittrick calls "respatializations," a concept that indexes a legacy of black women contesting captivity and constraint in search of "more humanly workable geographies" (2006, xix, xii). In the next section, then, I explore Kee's undoing of the insular national space that articulates Britishness with the genre of humanness called Man. But first, connected to this undoing is the film's dismantling of the white familial rebeginning that James's novel envisions. Cuarón's film includes a Theo and a Julian and a Luke, but their characterizations and roles are markedly different. No longer the arrogant Oxford historian depicted by James, Theo is a day-drinking bureaucrat with an activist past. His estranged ex-partner, Julian, is known to British authorities as a terrorist for her leadership of the Fishes. Luke (Chiwetel Ejiofor) is a Fish who has his own ideas about the direction the group should take and ultimately kills Julian to make it happen. He's also loaded down, as Brown points out, "with the legacy of black radical revolutionary strategy" that the film sidesteps (2013b, 129). And, of course, the film transfers the role of miraculously expectant mother from Julian to Kee. So attending to the entanglements between these two, in particular, illuminates the storytelling mutations the adaptation induces in its source material. And those entanglements can be traced through the sound design of *Children of Men*.

The story of Julian and Kee plays out aurally rather than visually because, thirty minutes into the film, Julian dies from a bullet to the throat. Following William Whittington, I see Julian as a spectral presence in the film that returns in and through composer John Tavener's orchestral score, which first asserts itself at the scene of her makeshift funeral service. Julian, Theo, Luke, Kee, and her midwife,

Miriam (Pam Ferris), are ambushed while driving to the coast and Julian is shot as they escape attackers who, it turns out, are working with Luke. Miriam and Kee perform an improvised funeral service, the camera traveling the length of Julian's corpse in close-up as the midwife's hands hover over her pelvis, her blood-soaked chest, and finally her face. When Theo walks away from the scene and drops to his knees, sobbing, Julian's body remains in the distant background of the shot as Tavener's "Fragments of a Prayer" overpowers the midwife's chanting. As Whittington describes it, the composition "rises from the bed of the soundtrack to take Julian's place" (2011, 9–10). The film score is anchored in ruined corporeal ground, a wrecked white woman's body shaped by histories both familial and political. Here my reading departs from Whittington's. When "Fragments" rises again in the film's final scene, as Kee announces to a dying Theo that she'll name her baby after the couple's son, the convergence prompts Whittington to argue that the film's ending offers the reunification of "the family of Julian, Theo and child . . . in death" (2011, 12). This interpretation appropriates Kee's maternal labor to remake the white heteropatriarchal family that Cuarón's storytelling actively decenters. But in the final scene, we hear Kee quietly singing a Ghanaian lullaby to comfort her baby, a sound that mixes with the score until the latter recedes, leaving behind a quiet that amplifies Kee's singing. What can we make of this sonic mixing and the two mother figures at its source? How might these overlapping musical waveforms redirect our attention away from the question of Theo's redemption? At stake, for me, is seeing the arrival of the *Tomorrow* not as a deus ex machina but, rather, as the materialization of "intertwining histories of arrival" (Ahmed 2006, 38). It's about how Kee gets to the boat and how the boat gets to Kee. It's about a lullaby mixing with a haunted score, both sounds archiving women's labor and inspiring, for me, a reading of the boat as an indeterminate mesh of desires, contestations, and alliances.

At the level of sound, *Children of Men* generates a complicated, flexible set of articulations among women's labor and activism that belies interpretations of the *Tomorrow* as a symbol of Theo's spiritual redemption. This pattern is established even before Julian becomes a spectral presence haunting the film's orchestral score. Early on, when Theo visits the secluded home of his friends Jasper and Janice Palmer (Philippa Urquhart), the soundtrack invites us to connect Janice and Julian. We see a window taped with old newspaper clippings and antiwar fliers. And we learn from these clippings that Janice is an award-winning photojournalist who documented both the infertility crisis and the state's violent anti-immigrant response. The camera rests briefly on a picture of Janice herself beneath the headline, "MI5 Deny Involvement in Torture of Photojournalist." And there's a family photograph of Theo, Julian, and Dylan that marks Julian's first on-screen appearance. Visually, the emphasis is on the now broken family. But the soundtrack of the scene—a cover of the Rolling Stones' 1967 hit "Ruby Tuesday"—draws attention to the two women, in particular. Bracketing the sexism that runs through the Rolling Stones' larger body of work, "Ruby Tuesday" grapples with the emergence of the "new woman" in postwar Britain, coding this figure in positive terms as an unruly woman on whom no one can "hang a name." She yearns for freedom, warning the narrative persona: "lose your dreams and you will lose your mind."[17] The song figures Janice, even in her silence, as a willful woman whose life tells a story about the work—and cost—of summoning a better world. We're about to find out that this is the shape of Julian's story, too. So later in the film, when Theo, Kee, and Miriam take refuge at the Palmers' on their way to Bexhill, Kee's interactions with Janice reactivate the connection between the two activists so that the one who's absent and the one who's silent both ghost the scene. As Kee sits chatting with Theo and braiding Janice's hair, her actions pull Janice out of the background of the scene, their moment of quiet intimacy a reminder of the different ways the authoritarian state invades the bodies of those it casts as suspect: the dissenting civilian and the reproductive refugee. And behind Janice, who's been tortured into muteness, there's Julian, who's just been shot in the throat. The point is not to flatten out the differences between these women; nor am I positioning Janice and Julian as white savior figures in relation to Kee. Rather, attending to the histories that shape each woman's story makes the boat a collective conjuring, a colonial technology that just might be repurposed for a world, to borrow a phrase from Wynter, "After Man."[18]

Both Kee and Julian are (or were) striving for a more livable world. And their respective struggles illuminate, in different ways, the ideological coordinates of the "mother" figure that makes possible the reproduction of Man's world. For Sharpe, the history of transatlantic slavery has given rise to what she calls "*anagrammatical blackness*," or the ways that blackness both supports and undoes the grammars that order Man's story (2016, 75, emphasis original). "I am thinking," she writes, "of blackness's signifying surplus: the ways that meaning slides, signification slips, when words like *child, girl, mother,* and *boy* abut blackness" (80, emphasis original). In light of a history in which black women's wombs, like the hold of the slave ship, index the passage into unhumanness, Sharpe wonders if "the word *mother* never took hold for Black women in and then out of slavery" (77, emphasis original). As a black woman encountering a ship full of people for whom, in one way or another, both her womb and her child are extremely valuable, Kee might best be understood, following Sharpe, as an "un/mother"—a formulation that is "an index of violability and also potentiality" (77, 75).[19] The tenuousness with which "black maternity" signifies endangers Kee and Dylan. But it opens up, too, the possibility of reinventing "mother" in ways that work against Man's story and the relations it structures. Putting it differently, Kee's fraught relationship to maternity unveils dissonances between everyday practices of bearing and caring for children and what Adrienne Rich has called the "institution of motherhood" (1976, 42). The patriarchal institution that generates black women as "un/mothers" recruits white women into the role of the "good" mother whose labor underpins the patriarchal family form and, in turn, the political and economic systems that organize the nation. It creates "the prescriptions and the conditions," Rich writes, "in which choices are made or blocked" (42). In this context, Julian emerges as what Andrea O'Reilly (2004), building on Rich, calls a "mother outlaw"—a figure that breaks with the institution of motherhood to unlock other ways of being in the world. We learn from Theo's friend Jasper (Michael Caine) that Theo and Julian met at a political rally protesting the war in Iraq well before the infertility crisis began. So the activism that results in Julian's labelling as a "terrorist" preceded her family life. Julian's family took shape—and then fell apart—in the context of her struggle against Man's world, which means her sense of "we" spills over the boundaries of family and nation.

Differently positioned at the margins of motherhood, the alliance of Kee and Julian activates a political project that potentially breathes life into a planetary, species-wide conception of humanness. It's not just that the news of Kee's pregnancy prompts Julian to direct the Fishes' energies toward the Human Project, a move that breaks their deadlock with the British government and (at least temporarily) articulates the group with a transnational collective. The connection between Kee and Julian also puts pressure on the film's uneasy navigation of the legacy—or legacies—of the 1960s. With Julian's death and Luke's emergence as the corrupt new leader of the Fishes, *Children* makes him into Theo's foil. Brown observes that "at the beginning of the film we are allowed to feel the ambivalence between pacifism and militancy, but by the end this conversation has been occluded, and Luke is left carrying the Uzi. In contrast it is Theo, staged as the son and heir of the 1960s Left, who is chosen as the savior, the one to protect the hope of the future" (2013b, 129). With Julian relegated to the narrative background, the film splits the sixties liberation movements—and their unfolding into the 1970s—between two men: Luke becomes the discredited representative of "black or radical anger" from whom Kee must be saved by Theo, representative of "a white liberal left" (Brown 2013b, 128, 127). But behind this splitting, there's Julian, a woman whose activist repertoire included bombings until something went awry—a trauma referred to only as "Liverpool." Together with Luke, then, Julian's presence early in the film fosters what Brown describes as a sense of "the ambivalence between pacifism and militancy." And her history of activism suggests an intersectional approach to state violence that draws on a range of legacies of thought and action that unfolded from the 1960s—an unstable inheritance that can't be neatened into the black radical/white liberal binary the film seems to offer. For Wynter, the sixties are a pivotal moment in the struggle against Man's story because, briefly, different groups with different visions were struggling together. Rinaldo Walcott elaborates that it was a decade in which "the subgenres of humanness—in particular nonwhite, queer, and feminine modes of humanness—were unleashed and pushed against the overrepresentation of Man" (2015, 191). So the cinematic relationship between Julian and Kee might implicate *Children* in a "cultural politics that legitimates political intervention in the name of the racially marked woman" (Chaudhary 2009, 95). But what if Julian's investment in Kee and Kee's investment in Julian also exceed this dynamic? What if they reanimate the multipronged attack on Man's story that made the 1960s so incendiary?[20]

Kee's lullaby is, well, key to such a reading. And its inclusion in the film can be attributed not to Cuarón, but to actress Clare-Hope Ashitey, the British-born child of immigrants from Ghana who taught their daughter the song.[21] Kee's singing of "Kaa fo," or "Don't Cry," is animated by what Paul Gilroy calls a "politics of transfiguration" archived in the forms of cultural expression invented, nurtured, and transmitted in and across the black diaspora (1993, 37). For Gilroy, the politics of transfiguration expresses utopian longing: its countercultural agitation for a better world, he writes, "exists on a lower frequency" that registers the "unsayability" both of legacies of racial terror and of the new desires and relationalities it breathes to life (37). Black musical traditions and inventions are at the center of this counterculture, repeatedly "posing the world as it is against the world as the racially subordinated would like it to be" (36). Kee's singing to Dylan is structured by this tension. Lyrically, both versions of "Kaa fo" are somewhat ominous in light of Kee and Dylan's precarious position at the end of the film. One version stages an imagined conversation with the baby, quieting her after she's been parted from her mother. "Where has your mother gone?," the singer asks, before demanding some of the pawpaw fruit given to the child by her absent mother—a demand the baby explicitly refuses. Another version urges the infant to guard her treasure, warning, "Don't cry and let anyone see in your mouth / There is gold in your mouth."[22] In both cases, "Kaa fo" addresses a child who is or who should be alert to the possibility of dispossession. But Kee's singing also aims to sooth Dylan, to realize, now, the security she seems to promise when she says, on seeing the *Tomorrow*, "We're safe now; we're safe." Singing softly and holding her baby close, Kee works to make her child feel safe—and encrypted in this solace is a note of caution passed down through generations. Kee performs and promises safety even as she begins transmitting to Dylan a critical perspective on the world as it is. From this perspective, the world is neither filled with hope nor filled with doom. Rather, through her lullaby, Kee offers what McKittrick, following Wynter, formulates as "the imperative perspective of black struggle"—a perspective from which the material world comes into view as contested terrain (2006, xi). With Kee's music mingling with the sounds of the Atlantic, the *Tomorrow* arrives as the site of "an unresolved story" (xviii).

(III) SHIPS

The *Tomorrow* reopens the question of humanness in the twilight of Man. Because we can't know in advance what this means, the boat registers an indeterminacy, its possible futures as a ship of science-activism vibrating in the stories of ships and black subjects it inherits. Following McKittrick, I understand ships as both material and metaphorical—as "three-dimensionalities" thick with narrative and open, then, to processes of reimagination and "respatialization" (2006, xx, xix). The boat makes space in which Kee and Dylan might cocreate with others a postapocalyptic story of humanness. And it could be, to return to Wynter, a story for a world "After Man" because the inventions of Man were entangled, from the beginning, with ships and stories of ships. Emphasizing the imbrications of geography and epistemology in Wynter's thinking, McKittrick explains that fifteenth- and sixteenth-century transatlantic voyages ruptured the existing European worldview, which "created an opening through which the conceptions of humanness began to be organized differently" (2006, 124). The disclosure of a planetary distribution of humanness in the aftermath of 1492 shifts Christian European ways of knowing, inciting an epistemological mutation that gives rise to Man. But Man's dispossessing, accumulating, extracting activities foreshorten this mutation, conjuring a hierarchy to restabilize the newly expanded field of humanness: Man over his (exploitable, killable) colonial Others. So the inventions of Man were embroiled in violence, the still-unfolding legacies of which animate the globalized present. But Wynter's work also constructs this figure as the effect of an *unfinished* epistemological "mutation" (1990, 356). Her concept of "demonic grounds," then, locates the "source of an alternative system of meanings" in the silenced story-places typically occupied by women of color (360). Kee and Dylan's now is a space-time vibrating with the possibility of another mutation in the story of humanness—a future, to return to Tina Campt, "that hasn't yet happened but must" (2017, 17).

There are pressing reasons to be wary of the *Tomorrow*. The biopolitical landscape of *Children*'s Britain is a near-future extension of Man's world and its articulation of blackness with subhumanness. Sharpe argues that black subjects live—persist, insist, create—"in the wake" of transatlantic slavery: "to be *in* the wake is to occupy and be occupied by the continuous and changing present of slavery's as yet unresolved unfolding" (2016, 13–14, emphasis original). To be inscribed by "the orthography of the wake" as unhuman is to be marked, too, by the ship, vehicle of the "transubstantiation" by which people became property (20–21, 36). But to observe that Kee waits for a ship and is marked by the ship is not to doom her to a future of violent exploitation. The repetition of the ship opens onto an indeterminate horizon because the transatlantic pasts conjured by the *Tomorrow* are also, in Sharpe's formulation, "Trans*Atlantic" (25). The asterisk operates as a "wildcard" that proliferates meanings, offering a way to think about "the range of trans*formations enacted *on and by* Black bodies" (30, my emphasis). In the wake of the ship and confronted by a ship, Kee and Dylan are haunted by histories of racial terror and their attendant transformations of people into cargo, capital, and credit. To see only hope, in this context, is to elide the history of the Black Atlantic and the critical perspectives it affords. Kee's lullaby evokes the fullness of this inheritance, including "the ship as a location of black subjectivity and human terror, black resistance, and in some cases, black possession" (McKittrick 2006, xi). So to see only precarity, to funnel Dylan's miraculous arrival toward yet another story of black death, is the enactment of what Sharpe calls a "dysgraphic unseeing" (46). What would it mean to see in the repetition of the ship the possibility of difference?

The boat that arrives at the end of *Children of Men* is haunted by the ship stories sedimented in Man's story of humanness, a narrative layer that features men captaining ships and doing God's work. Two of the most enduring of these tales imagine their protagonists—Noah (of the Christian ark) and Columbus (of the *Santa Maria*)—as the patriarchal founders of a purified, postapocalyptic new world. But the worlds they (re)begin inaugurate new differentiations within the category of the human, separating those who are chosen from Others who are exploitable and/or killable. Earlier in this chapter I discussed Noah's ark as an antecedent for the Christian rebeginning projected by James's novel. Sharpe reminds us that the story of "Noah's saving ship" also conjures "the curse upon Canaan," which is popularly understood as marking the descendants of Ham with blackness and condemning them to a life lived in servitude (2016, 57). Wynter, too, attends to this tale. Over the centuries, she argues, interpretations of the narrative of Noah and Ham created a pattern of signification—an articulation of blackness with sin—that prepared the way for the invention of race that occurred in parallel with the inventions of Man. In this context, Wynter writes, Man's Other emerged in "the new concept of the sub-rational Negro, condemned this time by the malediction of Nature rather than by Noah" (2003, 307). Slipping from God to Noah to Nature, the differentiation between the chosen and the cursed infiltrated the story of Man that began to take shape through Columbus's voyages to the New World. Paul Boyer points out that Columbus was "an avid prophecy student" who, late in life, wrote that "'God made me the messenger of the new heaven and the new earth of which he spoke in the Apocalypse of St. John . . . ; and he showed me the spot where to find it'" (qtd. in Boyer 1992, 225). Like the ark coming to rest on a mountaintop-island, the New World takes shape in Columbus's recollection as a utopia erected on land that, according to accepted European geographies, should have been submerged. The ships of Noah and Columbus have brought us back to where this chapter began: to the island as a space of utopian rebeginning. Thought to be "non-navigable, uninhabitable, unlivable, and oceanic," the landmasses of the Western Hemisphere prompted European revisions of the world and the human (McKittrick 2006, 128). And these revisions articulated with an apocalyptic imaginary that promises fresh starts, clean slates, *terra nullius*. A New World.

But ship stories and the new-world imaginaries they animate are rife with countervisions. The question, Wynter insists in her assessment of the "Janus-faced" legacy of 1492, is always "from *which* perspective?" (1995, 14, 6, emphasis original). McKittrick elaborates that, from the "local-cultural" vantage points of Indigenous and black populations, Man's "geographic perspective (his Godly claim to indigenous lands)" comes into view "as mad, irrational, drunk" (2006, 129). And if the ship is essential to this drunken worldview, then the sight lines of "the shipped" cut across Man's geographies, disclosing horrors and unveiling, too, modes of survival that agitate for a world After Man (Sharpe 2016, 25). In her discussion of the *Zong*, the eighteenth-century slave ship from which "132 (or 140 or 142)" Africans were thrown overboard to preserve water and prepare for an insurance claim, Sharpe presents a seeing of transatlantic crossings from the perspectives of "the thrown and jumped" (35, 38). These are vantage points that contest the turning of people into cargo, murder into money. It's a set of perspectives from which the past is now, and not only in the sense that the trafficking of enslaved Africans underwrote the earliest form of a now widespread credit-based economy.[23] The past, Sharpe asserts, is also materially present, now: "the atoms of those people who were thrown overboard are out there in the ocean even today," cycling through the water column in the endless process of "organisms eating organisms" (40). Similarly, in her account of contemporary surveillance practices and their origins in histories of slavery, Simone Browne pauses over the fact "that somewhere along a journey that ends in *The Panopticon; or, The Inspection House* Jeremy Bentham traveled with 'eighteen young Negresses (slaves)'" in the hold of the boat (2015, 32). In this context, she asks, "how might the view from 'under the hatches' be another site from which to conceptualize the operation of power?" (32). The ship is brimming with sight lines from which it emerges as a simultaneously world-making and world-destroying technology—one that's shot through with critical perspectives on Man's emerging worldview.

The locations of "the thrown and jumped" and "under the hatches" attest to the unspeakable human costs of Man's new-world imaginary, unveiling what Paul Gilroy calls the "antinomies of modernity" (1993, 41). These sight lines are encrypted in the thinking, activisms, and aesthetic inventions of the Black Atlantic, grounding black intellectual and cultural production "in a well-developed sense of the complicity of racialised reason and white supremacist terror" (Gilroy 1993, x). In these places where terror and reason, progress and barbarity, are entangled, other new-world views emerge to unsettle Man's separation of humanness into the chosen and the cursed. Aiming to further the epistemological mutation that gave rise to Man, Wynter proposes "a new world view of 1492 from the perspective of the species"—one that attends to both the "interhuman atrocities" and the new human connectedness that unfolded from Columbus's voyages (1995, 8, 14). Nandita Sharma reads Wynter's proposal as "a recognition of the *transversal* character of the Columbian exchange," which invites deviations from Columbus's narrative of chosenness and a reconception, in turn, of a species-wide, planet-wide humanity (2015, 166, emphasis original). For Gilroy, the ship is both the material and the metaphor for thinking this transversality. Ships conjure the Middle Passage and its disastrous wake. But, Gilroy writes, ships were also "something more—a means to conduct political dissent and possibly a distinct mode of cultural production" (1993, 17). Without losing sight of the horrors of the hold, he reminds us that ships were the means by which "ideas and activists" circulated throughout the Atlantic world; that they were "mobile elements that stood for the shifting spaces in between the fixed places that they connected" (4, 16). So ships invite a thinking of space and movement that exceeds the nation—and a thinking of black intellectual and aesthetic cultures as inscribing "a different sense of place" across Man's geographies (McKittrick 2006, x). Perhaps another way of putting this is that the ship not only enables but exceeds the inventions of Man. Its repetition in the form of the *Tomorrow* might renew old horrors. But Kee and Dylan might also (re)activate ways of seeing and knowing that animate new ship stories, orienting the Human Project slantwise across Man's waning world.[24] This is more than an abstract possibility: it's grounded in what Kee has already done to the spaces devised to hold her.

The hold, Sharpe argues, is a formation that begins with but extends beyond the belly of the slave ship. It repeats in the plantation and the prison, the ghetto and the camp. "The holds multiply," Sharpe writes. "And so does resistance to them, the survivance of them" (2016, 73).[25] Kee's journey into Bexhill and out again incites spatial shifts that reveal the porousness of the camp, a space meant to smother the unrecognizable futures unfolding from a migrant population and its simmering rebellion. Like the criminalized Isle of Man in James's novel—and like its real-world counterpart across the Channel, the now-closed refugee camp at Calais—Bexhill is quarantined from the nation that operates it as a dumping ground for migrants. So the camp belongs to a genealogy of "exceptional" spaces that reify the differences underwriting Man's world. McKittrick observes that the colonial fictions of "uninhabitable landmasses" and *terra nullius*—also feminized as "virgin" lands—endure in postcontact processes that organize difference in place (2006, 129). "The colonial enactment of geographic knowledge," she writes, "mapped 'a normal way of life' through measuring different degrees of humanness and attaching different versions of the human to different places" (2013, 6–7). And "the category of 'black woman,'" McKittrick argues, has been crucial to this process: her "seeable presence" is integral to the human/unhuman, masculine/feminine, and habitable/uninhabitable coordinates that underpin Man's "sense of place" (2006, xvii, 40). From the perspective of the state that constructs her as illegal, Kee, a dehumanized refugee who marks out the place where Englishness ends, "belongs" in Bexhill. But she enters the camp surreptitiously—she's smuggled in by a crooked guard—which makes her navigation of the camp an extension of, not an end to, her fugitivity. Kee's negotiation of Bexhill, then, is an instance of the "place-based critiques, or, respatializations" through which black women expose the alterability of the material world (McKittrick 2006, xix). Even outside of what Kee and Dylan do to the soundscape of the camp, there's the fact that the Fishes, chasing Kee in, blow a hole in Bexhill's perimeter. Quarantine fails. Refugees escape, racialized Others and the uprising with which they're associated "leaking" back out into British space. And finally, Kee herself, with Dylan cradled to her chest, flees by boat through Bexhill's sewer system—a subterranean path into open water that belies the spatiotemporal closure on which the camp is premised.

Kee breaches Bexhill's boundaries on her way in and on her way out, reinscribing a space of domination as a site of struggle and, in the process, opening a path to potential rebeginnings. In my introduction, I turned to Hannah Arendt's principle of natality as a complement to Wynter's thinking about Man's overrepresented story. The fact that we're born, Arendt argues, is the ontological basis of the human capacity for action. And action is synonymous with our ability to set new things in motion, to send new storylines rippling out into the origin story that recruits us. I showed, too, that Arendt's thinking about natality can be traced back to her thoughts on terror and camp space in *The Origins of Totalitarianism* (1951). For Arendt, the camp absorbs potential rebeginnings to stabilize the grand narrative of Nature or History, a progressive unfolding toward the perfection of a collective subject she calls "Man" (1951, 466). Bexhill inherits this legacy: a camp space in which the unfit are gathered for culling; a space that separates the cursed from the chosen in the name of securing the future of Man. So against the space-time of the camp, Arendt posits the miracle that "with each new birth, a new beginning is born into the world, a new world has potentially come into being" (1951, 465). Arendt's rooting of action and freedom in birth twists the Nativity story toward a political scene, offering a new angle of approach to the Messianic symbolism that Cuarón inherits from James. The "faith in and hope for the world" that derives from natality, Arendt offers, "found perhaps its most glorious and most succinct expression in the few words with which the Gospels announced their 'glad tidings': 'A child has been born unto us'" (1958, 247). For Arendt, the birth of a child—the arrival of someone new—is an everyday miracle. It's the beginning that sets us up to rebegin, to insert ourselves into a shared world and, in the company of others, spark something unforeseeable. And, seen from the perspective of already-unfolding events, whatever beginning we unleash "breaks into the world as an 'infinite improbability'": from the earth's emergence out of the cosmos to the evolution of the human, "our whole existence rests," she writes, "on a chain of miracles" (1961, 169). In this sense, the miraculous rebeginning that flickers into existence between Kee's little boat and the *Tomorrow* both is and isn't about Dylan. It's about what Kee and Dylan's arrival might set in motion within the Human Project. Much depends, then, on what kinds of scientists—and sciences—they're about to meet.

LAST WORD: SCIENCE

What happens when the ship—and perhaps the island to which it's headed—is a laboratory? Sharpe asks us to remember that the slave ship was a "floating laboratory" where researchers could observe death and disease in a reasonably contained environment (2016, 50). And she goes on to remind us that modern gynecological surgical techniques can be traced to J. Marion Sims, the American physician whose early experiments "were conducted without anesthesia on enslaved women" (50). Sedimented in Man's new-world imaginary, layered into stories of men captaining ships and doing God's work, are histories of black subjects terrorized and violated in the name of an emergent Western science. What's more, the Human Project is rumored to have a base in the Azores, which brings us back to the island. And islands, Attewell observes, have been "conscript[ed] as 'natural' laboratories by a multitude of (especially Western) scientific, economic, and military endeavours, from evolutionary biology to nuclear development" (2014, 47). From a certain point of view, the boundedness of ship and island invites experimentation, offering an illusion of total control that elevates some of us as observers and transmutes others into the observed. The Human Project likely inherits some of these violent legacies of Western science, a knowledge system that "remains haunted by anxieties about the feminine and the primitive" (Harding 2008, 1). But science, too, is contested terrain. From feminist science studies to Indigenous sciences to Afrofuturism, thinkers, cultural producers, and scientists themselves are reimagining Western science from within and without. What if some of these reimaginings inform the work of the Human Project? I say more about scientific futures in the next chapter. So by way of a turn in that direction, let me speculate, briefly, on the possibility of a Human Project shaped by what Michelle Murphy calls a "counter-conduct" (2012, 2).

Writing about feminist engagements with technoscience, Murphy defines a counter-conduct as "an immanent unmaking that is also simultaneously a remaking of another minor, or nonhegemonic formation of conduct that remains conditioned by and entangled with the hegemonic" (2012, 184n3). So it isn't a question of imagining the Human Project and its Azorean base as a "fresh start" uncontaminated by the wider world. After all, islands become "island solutions" in the sense meant by Attewell "only through a never-ending process of filtering, purging, and excising" (2014, 49). She elaborates that for writers located in the Pacific and in the Caribbean, islands are animated by encounters that disturb the drawing of stable boundaries, the fixing of meanings and futures. In other words, as much as islands have been recruited into Man's worldview as sites of purity and control—as "natural" laboratories in which unwanted pasts can be excised—they've also been sites of cultural exchange, creolization, and anti- and decolonial aspiration. A scientific counter-conduct might tap into these legacies, activating counter-readings of Man's story that give rise to new imaginaries of humanness. It's a matter, I propose, of strategically leveraging the apartness of the island to establish critical distance from Man's world and support the kinds of epistemological mutations that Wynter anticipates. In her exploration of "sciences from below," Sandra Harding considers the various relational models proposed in the field of postcolonial science and technology studies that might allow scientific projects based in the global South to take shape on their own terms. Inspired by Egyptian economist Samir Amin, she identifies one of these models as "delinking," a proposed withdrawal from the imperious reach of Western science and its "forag[ing] in other cultures' knowledge systems" (2008, 148, 137). She cautions that this seems practically impossible in a globalized world faced with planetary problems, including climate change, which looms large in my next chapter. But what if delinking is a provisional move? What if, by gaining some separation from a faltering nation-state system, the Human Project can support the flourishing of new scientific—as well as social and political—imaginaries?

At stake here and in the next chapter is both a rethinking of the island as a space of rebeginning and a turn toward scientific imaginaries that contest a Western history of "poking, prodding, and marveling" at black women's bodies in the name of Reason (Brown 2013b, 128). In the visions of apocalypse I study in this book, islands have been sites of quarantine and abandonment or, alternatively, sites of pure rebeginnings for chosen subjects. But in the last chapter, the history of the zombie myth led me to colonial Saint-Domingue and its transformation into Haiti. It was an uprising spurred and supported by a science that Europeans dismissed, at least at first, as "bogus"—by a knowledge of plants and their properties that enabled Vaudou practitioners to challenge Man's claim to the island (Lauro 2015, 58). Whether identifying and cultivating plant-based poisons or growing food for their own sustenance on small plots of land, enslaved Africans and their descendants worked the soil of the New World in ways that ran with and against Man's geographies. In the next chapter I explore this through Wynter's concept of "black metamorphosis," which emphasizes the practical, epistemological, and cultural inventiveness that breathes life into genres of humanness beyond Man. In *Beasts of the Southern Wild* (U.S. 2012), a black child named Hushpuppy who lives on sinking land addresses herself, her story, to "the scientists in the future." In this way, *Beasts* picks up where *Children* leaves off: a child navigates an island delinked from Man's world, a space that's both extremely precarious and animated, at least potentially, by a land-based counter-conduct. From here, she conjures a science invested not just in storytelling, but in *her* story in particular. The scientific horizon to which Hushpuppy addresses herself, I suggest, inspires readings of the Human Project as potentially exceeding Man's imaginaries. Like Kee and Dylan, Hushpuppy lives the grammar of black feminist futurity proposed by Campt: "It is the power to imagine beyond current fact and to envision that which is not, but must be" (2017, 17).

5 • MYTH AND METAMORPHOSIS

Beasts of the Southern Wild

Shortly into Benh Zeitlin's *Beasts of the Southern Wild* (U.S. 2012), six year-old Hushpuppy (Quvenzhané Wallis) accidentally-intentionally sets her house on fire. Startled by the flames and fearing her father's reaction, she takes refuge beneath a cardboard box—still in the burning home—and sketches her story on its insides. Hushpuppy draws a sad little face in thick black lines, asserting in voiceover, "If daddy kill me, I ain't gonna be forgotten. I'm recording my story for the scientists in the future. In a million years, when kids go to school, they gonna know once there was a Hushpuppy and she lived with her daddy in the Bathtub." Outside where the fire rages, the artist's daddy, Wink (Dwight Henry), tears the shack apart looking for his kid. She bolts, drawing both of them out into the gray of an approaching storm, where a furious Wink slaps Hushpuppy and turns away, shame-faced. When she hits him back, Wink collapses, the weather whips up, and the film cuts to Antarctica where the edge of a glacier crumbles into the sea.

For many critics, *Beasts of the Southern Wild* is a post-Katrina southern myth, a fable for the Anthropocene. Nicholas Mirzoeff (2012) argues the film evokes undisciplined ways of seeing that contest the ordering, mastering gaze that drives neoliberal speculations—that it offers, in short, "wild alternatives to governmentality." But a number of black feminist critics, in particular, are wary of the film, seeing in it a romanticization of racialized poverty and the mobilization of tired tropes of primitivism and black familial dysfunction. Christina Sharpe (2013), for instance, wonders about the racial logic of wildness at work in Mirzoeff's analysis. Describing the film as a "romance of precarity," Sharpe argues that readings of Hushpuppy as "inspiring and not tragic" are shaped by a worldview that naturalizes associations between blackness and ferality, poverty, and pathology. Both the film and its celebratory critics, she writes, fail to reckon with the fact that "at least part of the disaster on view here is everyday black life lived in the wake of slavery." We might notice the contours of this unseeing of black life in, for example, *New York Times* film critic A. O. Scott's (2012) proposition that "let's all agree: This movie is a blast of sheer, improbable joy." And it's likely this kind of response that bell hooks (2012) has in mind when she wonders about the viewer who can "look past the traumatic abuse Hushpuppy endures and be mesmerized and entertained" by *Beasts*. Similarly, Jayna Brown (2013a) opens her critique by remarking that those who praise the film's visualization of climate change resistance "don't even seem to notice it as a dystopia" that "evokes the precarity, instability and vulnerability of black life." So Sharpe, hooks, and Brown all argue, in different ways, that *Beasts* puts black characters to work in service of a new American myth that celebrates a too-easy, postracial "we" united against environmental devastation. And they take issue, too, with critics who have cocreated this narrative.

This chapter thinks with these critiques to assemble a reading of the film that sees climate change—and climate change resistance—as entangled in post-1492 new-world dreams and nightmares. In my introduction I described *Undead Ends* as intervening in stories of apocalypse and survival that are anchored by a particular model of humanness that passes itself off as universal. Following Sylvia Wynter, I posited economic Man as the protagonist of neoliberal storytelling. This version of Man, Wynter argues, emerged with the rise of the biological sciences and their conceptualization of the human as a living organism imperiled by natural scarcity. Within this framework, practices of extraction and accumulation are salvific; and freedom is defined as the freedom to compete against others to extract and accumulate at will—and without political interference. Firmly rooted in processes of colonialism and race making, economic Man reifies a way of knowing the world that casts humanness only in Western bourgeois terms—an episteme that enacts "the systemic repression of all other alternative modes of material provisioning" (Wynter and McKittrick 2015, 22). In other words, anthropogenic climate change gathers steam and begins unfolding in parallel with the inventions of Man and the inventions of race. In this context, thinking and responding to environmental crisis requires "a far-reaching transformation of knowledge," including "a new mutation" in our understanding of humanness (Wynter and McKittrick 2015, 24). And if Man's stranglehold on the meaning of humanness depends, as Wynter argues, on the compulsive "'blocking out' of a Black counter-voice," then the epistemological mutation she has in mind necessitates a dismantling of antiblackness and its colonial coordinates (2003, 268). In this chapter, I see *Beasts of the Southern Wild* as an occasion for thinking the coloniality of climate change.

My argument here is not that *Beasts* does this work on its own, nor am I making claims about writer-director Benh Zeitlin's—or cowriter Lucy Alibar's—political leanings. Like the other films I've discussed in this book, all of which vibrate with storytelling possibilities encrypted in uneasy adaptations and unsettled endings, *Beasts* is a protean tale. It morphs through adaptations from life to stage to screen, "a story iterating," as Tavia Nyong'o puts it, "across real and fictive scenarios" with "a protagonist slipping between black and white, male and female bodies" (2015, 254). The film is adapted from Alibar's semiautobiographical play *Juicy and Delicious,* which maps the white writer's childhood experiences with her abusive father onto a father-son story with a queer white boy named Hushpuppy at its center. Alibar and Zeitlin then relocated the story from Georgia to Louisiana, where their desire to work with local actors prompted the "colorblind casting" process that saw Quvenzhané Wallis land the role of Hushpuppy. So the character was revised yet again, this time as a young(er) genderqueer black girl.[1] These revisions of Hushpuppy propel the film into a dialectic in which, as Diana Adesola Mafe argues, it both invokes and interrupts the codes of ethnographic cinema. On the one hand, *Beasts* presents "a mythologized people in their so-called natural habitat"—"noble savages" clinging to lifeways coded as premodern. But on the other hand, Hushpuppy is at the center of the film's storytelling, "functioning interchangeably as voice-over narrator, active screen subject, and returner of the gaze" (2018, 96). What's more, Nyong'o argues that Wallis's version of Hushpuppy can be understood as a "cocreation" because, as production unfolded, the actor herself shaped the character sketched out in the screenplay (2015, 253). This prompts him to propose that Hushpuppy activates what Kara Keeling calls the "black femme function" (2007, 5): the hidden cinematic presence of a figure that attests to histories of surviving-otherwise in a world calibrated to the survival of Man. Between the different iterations of the story and Wallis's involvement in the invention of her character, *Beasts* is a mesh of narrative possibilities—a restless fable.

In this chapter I consider *Beasts of the Southern Wild* as a film that puts pressure on the "problem-space," to borrow a term from David Scott, of anthropogenic climate change (2004, 4). Scott defines a problem-space as a discursive context within which a problem—in this case, human-induced environmental degradation—takes shape according to the kinds of questions we ask about it and the kinds of answers we seek. And "because problems are not timeless and do not have everlasting shapes," the questions and answers that animate a problem-space are historically contingent (Scott 2004, 4). They're conditioned, in part, by the storytelling habits through which we formulate relations between past, present, and future. Given Sharpe's (2013) and Brown's (2013a) critiques of *Beasts* as a "romance of precarity," Scott's thinking about genre is especially illuminating. Romance, he writes, "is a drama of redemption": it enacts "a distinctive rhythm and pacing, a distinctive direction," in which difficult pasts are overcome as history unfolds toward a utopian horizon (Scott 2004, 47, 8). In this context, Hushpuppy is akin, perhaps, to the Boy in *The Road* as seen through the eyes of his papa: a savior holding open the possibility of a better future—or any future at all. It's a lot of baggage for such a small person to carry. And in Hushpuppy's case, in particular, a romantic story arc positions her as redeeming a human "we" without reckoning with a Western legacy of defining humanness in terms that exclude black girls and their daddies. Because the problem-space opened up by some discourses on the Anthropocene tends to assume the human as something "we" all just are.

The Anthropocene is the age in which humans "act as a geological force on the planet, changing its climate for millennia to come" (Chakrabarty 2012, 2). And it offers an occasion to rethink humanness across an(other) expansion in space and time: a species conditioned by a planetary environment that's degrading in response to our own activities. But this leap into geological time and a species-wide perspective can efface the distinction between humanness, and the myriad ways it has and can be practiced, and Man, whose unsustainable world is built on the accumulating, extracting, dispossessing activities that are changing the earth. As a result, many of the questions we ask about climate change—and the answers we seek—are shaped by posthumanisms that dream of transcending both our embodied limitations and the environment from which they arise.[2] Nyong'o describes precisely this problem in his discussion of *Beasts*: "Up until the present time, we are told in one version of this philosophical fable, we have incorrectly centered the human. Now we can, and must, correct that error, if only (paradoxically) to save ourselves. It is in anticipation of such tales that black studies has repeatedly asked: have we ever been human? And if not, what are we being asked to decenter, and through what means?" (2015, 266). One of the challenges for thinking and representing the Anthropocene, then, is to think across timescales; to center, in fact, the histories of colonialism, racial capital, and gendered exploitation through which the genre of humanness called Man has tapped into geological time.[3] What happens if we articulate the advent of the Anthropocene with the inventions of Man? What kinds of questions do we ask about climate change if we understand it as materially entangled in still-unfolding legacies of slavery, colonization, and gender oppression? And how might such questions lead to insights about how to reinvent ourselves as a newly human "we"?

I see *Beasts* as an opportunity to shift the problem-space of climate change—a shift that's activated by disarticulating Hushpuppy from a romantic storyline in which "we" transcend the human as if we're all evenly positioned in relation to this category. So in this chapter, inspired by Hushpuppy's own myth-making, I reassemble *Beasts of the Southern Wild*.

ONCE THERE WAS A HUSHPUPPY WHO MET A GREAT BEAST . . .

Beasts' climax sees Hushpuppy finally face the aurochs: horned, snouted creatures covered in coarse black hair. The aurochs are the extinct wild ancestors of domestic cattle. They emerge from the melting Antarctic ice sheet near the beginning of the film and make their way northward across the Americas to meet Hushpuppy at its end. They dwarf the child they've come to see, but she holds her ground,

FIGURE 13. Hushpuppy (Quvenzhané Wallis) prepares to turn and face the Great Beasts behind her. Still from *Beasts of the Southern Wild* (Cinereach, 2012).

looking the closest one in the eye as it snorts hot air and kneels to a girl who's about to lose her daddy. "You're my friend, kind of," she says to the Great Beast. A reimagining of the four horsemen of the apocalypse, the aurochs arrive as harbingers of the end, forcing Hushpuppy to reckon with the death she knows is coming and all the questions it opens up about what will happen to her. But even as they portend an imminent loss, they embody, too, layers of pastness from the familial to the colonial to the geological. This section explores the aurochs as fleshy returnees who, unexpectedly, crest the filmic horizon *behind* Hushpuppy. Editing and shot composition prepare viewers for a head-on confrontation between the child and the beasts, but they arrive from the back, prompting Hushpuppy to set her jaw and turn around. She's compelled, to borrow Sara Ahmed's phrasing, to "face what is behind [her]" (2006, 142). Here, Ahmed is referring to familial and corporeal inheritances: in her case, "a Muslim name," a "body recognized as 'could be Muslim'" (142). But the larger context of her thinking about backgrounds—which she formulates both as "histories of arrival" and "histories of labor" (38, 49)—invites a scaled-up view of this inheritance, too. What's "behind" Hushpuppy are the layers of happenings that made the Bathtub what it is—happenings that shape and exceed the story the film is telling.

The inspiration for the Bathtub is Isle de Jean Charles, a tiny island connected to the U.S. mainland by a periodically washed-out road. Home to the Biloxi-Chitimacha-Choctaw tribe and members of the United Houma Nation since the early nineteenth century, this sliver of land is disappearing into the Gulf of Mexico, its disintegration spurred by a combination of natural subsidence and human activity. The rerouting of the Mississippi River, the dredging of canals for oil and natural gas pipelines, and the rising sea levels and violent storms associated with climate change all conspire to introduce excess salt into the Terrebonne Basin, transforming rich, biodiverse wetlands into open water.[4] This confluence exemplifies what Rob Nixon calls "slow violence," the "attritional catastrophes" that can displace populations without moving them by stripping away land and resources from beneath their feet (2011, 7). The precarity of Isle de Jean Charles is underscored by the Morganza to the Gulf of Mexico Project, a proposed system of nearly one hundred miles of earthen levees that will ultimately bypass the island.[5] We might see *Beasts* as projecting itself into this near, postlevee future: "They built the wall that cuts us off," Hushpuppy says of "the Dry World." "They think we all gonna drown down here. But we ain't goin' nowhere." A moment later, we see a sign for "Isle de Charles Doucet" on which the name of the island is crossed out in white paint and rewritten as "The Bathtub, pop. 87." On one level, the rewriting of Isle de Jean Charles as Isle de Charles Doucet enacts "a cinematic native removal" (Nyong'o 2015, 264). Indigenous sovereignty "is pushed off the map," Nyong'o writes, a storytelling choice that "renders the resultant wildness recuperable for white fantasies of surrogation, adoption, and transplantation" (264). This superimposition of a fantastical wildness has implications for the film's capacity to depict Wink and his community as cultivating a sustainable, alternative way of living—a problem I consider later in this chapter.

In fact, the history of Isle de Jean Charles features a shifting assemblage of outsiders doing business and making kin at the edge of an emerging United States—a history in which Red and Black Atlantics intersect.[6] The website of the Isle de Jean Charles Band asserts that the island is named for Jean Charles Naquin, a Creole for whom the narrow ridge of land that would become his namesake served as a convenient stopping place when, in the early nineteenth century, he ran goods and supplies for the famed pirate Jean Lafitte. So the island was, first, a way station for smugglers; a place for those seeking to evade the political and economic control through which the United States began securing its territory in the aftermath of the Louisiana Purchase. Sometime in the 1820s, Naquin's son, Jean Marie, married an Indigenous woman named Pauline Verdun (also spelled Verdin). When Jean Marie was, as the Band's website puts it, "disowned by his family for marrying an Indian," the couple settled on the narrow spit of land that his father had come across in the course of his business with Lafitte. Histories of the island also note that the four men who officially purchased Isle de Jean Charles in the late 1870s—one of whom was Jean Marie and Pauline's son, Jean Baptiste Narcisse Naquin—were "often times erroneously reported on early census documents as Mulatto or Negro."[7] The error might reflect the instability of nineteenth-century racial categories, but it's also possible that it obliquely registers the island's entanglement with the legendary Jean Lafitte, the Baratarian privateer. Whether or not he was born in Saint-Domingue, Lafitte was linked to the refugees who fled the Haitian Revolution and settled in Louisiana, many of whom were free people of color and some of whom joined his crew.[8] The historical connection between the Naquins who settled the island and Lafitte's privateers persists in the narrative life of Isle de Jean Charles. There are rumors that some of Lafitte's treasure is buried there. And an article in the June 1940 edition of the *New Orleans Roosevelt Review* claims the island is "peopled by descendants of sailors, Lafitte's buccaneers and Indians."[9]

This narration of the island as simply, passively "peopled" obscures the histories of reproductive labor that index what Wynter calls "demonic grounds," a concept that arises from her reading of the contested island space at the center of Shakespeare's *The Tempest*. "Demonic ground" is Wynter's name for a foreclosed narrative "slot" in the play: the absent presence of a potential mate for Caliban, Prospero's racialized servant, whom Wynter reads as simultaneously Arawak and African (1990, 364). It's a story-place from which a new epistemological mutation might propel humans, collectively, into a future "After Man."[10] The multiplicity of demonic grounds—its encoding of the racialized, colonized presences that Man's story subordinates—resonates in the genealogy of Pauline Verdun, the woman who married Jean Marie Naquin and settled on Isle de Jean Charles. In the will of her father, Alexandre Verdun, Pauline is described as a "free colored woman and child of Marie Gregorie, a savage woman." And while the records on Marie Gregorie (also spelled Gregoire) are scant, one genealogy site includes a note that traces her father's line back to France and claims that her grandfather, Andre Masse Jr., was the son of a Frenchman and an African slave.[11] The point is not to turn to genealogy websites for the "truth" of the island's history as much as it is to underscore the dense mesh of transactions and migrations, oral histories and silences in the record, that comprise the origin story of Isle de Jean Charles. *Beasts*' revision of the island as Isle de Charles Doucet then pulls at this already stretched narrative fabric, rearticulating the real-life Charles name with the fictional Doucet name. And both are eclipsed by "The Bathtub," a designation that exceeds logics of belonging premised on property and paternal inheritance. By putting the Doucet name under erasure, the film registers the colonial history of the island while, at the same time, making space to speculate on the silences in that history: the chain of events behind Wink's French surname and, of course, the maternal lineage stretching backward in time from Hushpuppy's unnamed mama. Wynter's concept of demonic grounds opens up a reading of the Bathtub as *both* Isle de Jean Charles, the "peopling" of which can be traced to Pauline Verdun and her mother before her, *and* Isle de Charles Doucet, from which a worldview shaped by the absent presence of a black maternal lineage opens, through Hushpuppy, onto an uncertain future.

Like the Bathtub, a fictional rendering of a precarious community steeped in Atlantic histories, the aurochs, too, are a cinematic conjuring that troubles the seam where real and imaginary meet. They're introduced in the film by Hushpuppy's teacher, Miss Bathsheba (Gina Montana), who has a tattoo on her outer thigh inspired by the Lascaux Cave Paintings in France. She describes the animal to her young pupils as a "fierce, mean creature that walked the face of the earth back when we all lived in the caves"—a lesson in evolutionary time that Hushpuppy absorbs into her myth-making. As Miss Bathsheba warns her students that "any day now, fabric of the universe is comin' unravelled," Hushpuppy looks from her teacher's tattoo to a poster of the South Pole on the wall of the schoolhouse, the camera zooming in until the image fills the visual field. After cutting to a close-up of Hushpuppy's face, her eyes still intent on the poster, the film jumps to a windswept glacier with an ominous mass at its core. Hushpuppy's gaze directs the movement from the Bathtub to the South Pole, the camera continuing the slow zoom begun in the schoolhouse so that horns, a snout, and even teeth become discernible beneath the ice.[12] Miss Bathsheba's lesson articulates the receding ice with the rising waters that threaten the Bathtub, bringing the Antarctic "there" flooding into Hushpuppy's increasingly waterlogged "here." And Hushpuppy's perspective on the aurochs facilitates the film's break with cinematic realism, unveiling hidden connections across time and space and demanding that we read across disorienting collapses of geographical distance and historical time. For Hushpuppy, "the whole universe depends on everything fitting together just right. If one piece busts, even the smallest piece, the entire universe will get busted." Attentive to the unpredictable entanglements of small- and large-scale systems, Hushpuppy links the catastrophe of global warming to Wink's failing health, which, in turn, she attributes to the angry punch she lands on her daddy's chest when he smacks her for burning down her house.

As a cave-dwelling "then" flows into her watery "now," Hushpuppy repeatedly conjures her absent mama, inscribing a nearer familial past into the collapsing timescales of the Anthropocene. When Wink disappears early in the film—the hospital gown in which he returns providing a clue as to his whereabouts—Hushpuppy draws his outline on the mattress and pillow of her bed, the stark black lines evocative of the cave painting reproduced on Miss Bathsheba's leg. Her mama, called "Marietta" in the screenplay, takes shape in a similar way, her smiling face scribbled in the same black lines on the wall of Hushpuppy's house. A Michael Jordan Chicago Bulls jersey hangs directly beneath it, standing in for her torso. This is the only item Hushpuppy takes from the house when it begins to burn, which means she's clutching it in one hand when she hits Wink in the chest with the other. And here the film begins moving toward a fraught articulation of the absent Marietta with the aurochs that Hushpuppy imagines as reanimated by the unraveling of the universe. When Wink collapses to the ground, a worried Hushpuppy looks skyward as the shot jumps back to the South Pole where the edge of a glacier crumbles into the water. *Beasts* cuts back and forth between these locations three times, holding them together aurally so that, in the thunder that cracks over the Bathtub, Hushpuppy "hears" the sound of ice breaking in Antarctica. Running to the water's edge, she yells, "Mama, I think I broke something!" The film cuts to the crumbling ice shelf once more, the shot focusing, this time, on an iceberg now carrying a still-frozen aurochs through tumultuous waters. Hushpuppy's address to her mama across a great distance—a distance the film defines in its cutting between locations—repeats at the height of the storm itself when, overwhelmed by fear, she again yells for Marietta. At that point the film cuts to a location identified in the screenplay as the Patagonian coast, where a powerful black animal leg, coarse hair slick and wet, makes contact with sucking mud. Alibar and Zeitlin's screenplay confirms the feminization that the editing suggests: the "massive creature" is "testing her limbs after thousands of years of sleep" and "her black eyes" register "something dangerously sad."[13] The aurochs exemplify the riskiness of *Beasts'* investment in wildness, then: the return of the repressed spurred by the Anthropocene is also a feminized, racialized Other—a conjunction with which the film struggles to reckon.[14]

But Hushpuppy's mapping of her crumbling family structure onto violent weather patterns suggests a perspective from which environmental devastation and the colonial, antiblack underpinnings of Man's world both come into focus. What happens to the film's mythologizing of the Anthropocene if we read "the weather" as signaling both the floods and storms associated with climate change and, following Sharpe, "the weather of being in the wake" of transatlantic slavery (2016, 105)? The weather, Sharpe writes, "is the total climate; and that climate is antiblack" (104). Reading Hushpuppy and her family as imperiled by "the weather" in this sense brings into view the forms of world-ending violence that underwrite the story of Man. And at the center of such a reading are the aurochs, returnees that articulate familial and geological pasts and, in the process, lever open all the timescales in between. As the ancestors of domestic cattle, the aurochs conjure the apocalyptic violence through which Europeans extracted value from living beings and ecosystems in the New World: the colonization of Indigenous lands and the for-profit breeding of animals and slaves—cattle, chattel—that gave rise to the earliest forms of capital.[15] Indeed, Nyong'o argues that the aurochs' European origins mean their de-extinction "reenacts the European colonization of the New World in bovine form" (2015, 265). Their return is suggestive, certainly, of a repetition of the settler importation of cattle into the Mississippi Valley in the eighteenth century, which supported simultaneous intensifications of agriculture, Indian removal, and plantation slavery.[16] But if the Anthropocene is, as Nyong'o writes, "the self-reflexive feedback loop of capitalist growth on human environments" (257), then the return of the aurochs might be understood as something like the twist in a Möbius strip—the place where Man's world-destroying violence turns back on the world Man has made. Rendered disposable by this world ("they built the wall that cuts us off"), Hushpuppy yells for her mama, and a "massive creature" with "dangerously sad" eyes emerges through the film's generic seams (Alibar and Zeitlin n.d.). "You're my friend, kind of," Hushpuppy says to the Great Beast—yoked to Man's world by "the weather" and loosed, portending the end, by the weather.

. . . AND THE GREAT BEAST KNEELED TO THE GIRL WHO WOULD BE KING OF THE BATHTUB

When Hushpuppy was born, her daddy took her in his arms and walked her to the doorway of their home. "Breathe some air," he told his newly born child, still marked by her mama's blood. We see this, late in the film, as a flashback that begins with a close-up of a younger, healthier Wink shot from below—from the perspective of the infant he's holding. I want to connect this moment with an earlier scene when, as the storm that will ravage the Bathtub picks up steam, Wink does something that seems futile. Settling Hushpuppy into an empty trunk he calls a boat, assuring her that if the water gets too high they'll "bust through the roof" and "ride away," he slips water wings onto his kid's tiny arms. "I'm your daddy," he asserts as he slides them on, and "it's my job to keep you from dying." This gesture happens in the midst of what Nyong'o describes as "a telling moment of incoherence in the film, when [Wink] refuses to explain why he will not abandon the Bathtub during the storm" (2015, 264). The sense of Wink's connection to this mushy plot of land never really comes together—a problem I consider in the next section of this chapter—which means *Beasts* "cannot avoid presenting this moment as one of dereliction: a dying man ready to abandon his defenseless daughter to her fate" (Nyong'o 2015, 264). Under the pressure of this incoherence, the water wings only seem to highlight Wink's paternal failures. I wonder, though, if the impulse behind this gesture opens up a path for thinking through the incoherence that the film can't resolve. I read the water wings as pointing beyond the filmic imaginary to the form of "wake work" that Sharpe calls "aspiration": the work of "keeping and putting breath back in the Black body in hostile weather" (2016, 113). The first instruction Wink offers his child is to "breathe some air." And for most of the film he prepares Hushpuppy for a future in which she'll be "King of the Bathtub." How are survival and place connected here? And how might Sharpe's concept of aspiration illuminate Wink's teachings?

Hushpuppy's voiceover creates a pattern of meaning in which living beings fight for breath in the environments created, directly or indirectly, by Man's world—or what Hushpuppy calls "the Dry World." And in this construction of the other side of the levee as a space of breath-taking violence, we might discern the sense of Wink's dreaming of a Bathtub-based future for his kid. Our first glimpse of the Dry World is from a distance. Hushpuppy and Wink are drifting near the levee in their makeshift boat: the bed of an old truck buoyed by empty oil drums. A wide shot captures the industrial landscape on the other side of the wall, plumes of smoke rising from an "endless sprawl of oil processing power plants"—"the engine that runs the Northern world" (Alibar and Zeitlin n.d.). Contemplating the sight, Wink asks Hushpuppy, "Ain't that ugly over there? We got the prettiest place on earth." His comments invert the colonial logic of "uninhabitability," a spatial categorization usually deployed to mark out the subhuman spaces at the fringes and in the fissures of Man's world.[17] But for Wink, the Dry World is the impossible place. And Hushpuppy inherits this assessment, elaborating in voiceover that "they only got holidays once a year. They got fish stuck in plastic wrappers. They got their babies stuck in carriages. And chicken on sticks and all that kind of stuff." The Dry World is too sterile, too compartmentalized—a characterization that draws attention to the levee itself. The wall establishes an apartness that allows life to go on after the storm while, in the Bathtub, for "the animals that didn't have a dad to put 'em in a boat, the end of the world already happened. They're all down below tryin' to breathe through water." So Wink blows a hole in the levee—an act in which Hushpuppy accidentally-intentionally becomes a co-conspirator. And their action expresses what Wink knows to be true: the spatial arrangement of the Dry World produces the supposed uninhabitability of the place he's trying to preserve for his kid.

While the Bathtub has become postapocalyptic, mostly submerged terrain, the world beyond also lacks breathing room for Hushpuppies and their daddies. When Wink's bombing of the levee brings the force of the state into the Bathtub, public health officials evacuate its remaining residents to the Open Arms Processing Center—a place that Hushpuppy describes as "a fish tank with no water." If "the whole universe depends on everything fitting together just right," then Man's world has created disastrous imbalances: in the Bathtub, "animals" struggle to "breathe through water" while, in the Dry World, Open Arms is a waterless fish tank. The animals can't breathe and neither can the fishes. And Hushpuppy has gone from being an animal whose daddy kept her afloat to a fish caught in the net of the state and dropped in a place that lacks the basic conditions for her survival. *Beasts* expresses the constraining, smothering force of the Dry World through the invasive interventions that both Wink and Hushpuppy endure at Open Arms. After Wink undergoes an unwanted surgery, he finds himself in a hospital gown, slumped in a wheelchair with an oxygen tube in his nose, as an orderly pushes him through one of the shelter's corridors. Groggily, he catches sight of his kid standing alone in the midst of a room full of playing children. Hushpuppy's wearing a blue dress with puffed sleeves and a delicate white lace collar, her usually big hair combed out and neatly plaited. The lingering shot of a made-over Hushpuppy focuses on her devastated face as she gazes back at her father, articulating her gendered transformation with his invaded body. The linkage is underscored when the scene cuts to an extreme close-up of Wink's surgical scar. A clean white bandage appears to cover wounded black skin, benevolent Man smoothing over the violent, intimate cost of inclusion in an ongoing colonial project.

But the scene at Open Arms is complicated by what Jayna Brown (2013a) diagnoses as the film's inability to envision an "active or sustainable" alternative community. Viewers who question *Beasts*' romanticization of conditions in the Bathtub might be longing to see Hushpuppy and Wink both cared for, their bodies tended to. Putting it differently, if the Bathtub comes across less as a utopian alternative and more as a "bleak, grim and grimy" place full of people whose "self-destructive forms of coping [are] painfully insufficient," then the film's critique of the interventions at Open Arms loses some of its bite (Brown 2013a). Consider Hushpuppy first. Straightened and neatened, she approximates the figure that Michelle Murphy identifies as "the 'Third World girl'" who has, in the era of neoliberal globalization, "become the iconic vessel of human capital" (2017, 117).[18] This racialized, poor feminine figure is understood, Murphy argues, as a good bet for investment because she's responsible and obedient: "her rates of return are dependent on her forecasted compliance with expectations to serve family, to adhere to heterosexual propriety, to study hard, to be optimistic, and hence her ability to be thoroughly 'girled'" (117). The film invites viewers to be leery of this girlification, then, and with good reason. But the sight of a bathed, fully dressed Hushpuppy also highlights the forms of everyday care that seem to be missing from life in the Bathtub. In Wink's case, too, the film interrogates how what happens at Open Arms brings him more in line with the familial roles that order Man's world. As bell hooks points out, the role of "chivalric benevolent patriarch" is one against which black men are constantly measured and usually found wanting (1992, 90). In Wynter's terms, Wink is "dysselected" from the perspective of Man's world (2003, 310), which means the state must stand in as the benevolent patriarch where Wink himself falls disastrously short. Recruited into Man's story as a failed father figure, Wink undergoes a feminizing transformation in the form of too-late medical treatment that leaves him gowned, cut, stitched, and drugged into docility. But here, too, the film runs up against the limits of its imaginary. Because with the exception of Miss Bathsheba's jar of medicinal plant matter, the romanticized "wildness" of the Bathtub doesn't have much to offer Wink by way of alternative medical care. I return to Miss Bathsheba's jar in the next section, where I try to imagine how a more fully realized alternative community in the Bathtub might take shape—and what this could mean for the story *Beasts* is telling.

For now, I'm interested in how the state's "rescuing" of Wink and Hushpuppy from the weather (subsiding land, darkening skies) sucks them further into what Sharpe describes as "a singularity—a weather event or phenomenon likely to occur around a particular time, or date, or set of circumstances" (2016, 106). It's "the singularity," she writes, "of antiblackness" (106). And while the film struggles to come to grips with the ways this singularity is enfolded in the Anthropocene, its "atmospheric density" can be felt in the gendered nature of the interventions carried out at Open Arms (Sharpe 2016, 104). Wynter's work shows that Western modernity articulates humanness with economic viability and that this articulation, in turn, animates a shifting series of gendered figures—a cast of the selected ("the breadwinner") and the dysselected ("the welfare queen"). This is a point explored by scholars in Indigenous, settler colonial, and postcolonial studies, too, who consider how the universalization of the binary sex/gender system has been at the center of Man's world-building.[19] Relatedly, black feminist thought illuminates the dehumanizing legacy of "ungendering" that underpinned the emergence of economic Man—the violent transubstantiations that "unmade" African subjects into fleshy, bodily forms of property as they crossed the Atlantic in the holds of ships (Spillers 1987, 72). In this context, Hushpuppy is in a double bind. Becoming recognizably human entails becoming "thoroughly 'girled'" and reifying, in the process, the colonial coordinates of Man's world (Murphy 2017, 117). But a genderqueer Hushpuppy is haunted by the legacy of ungendering that thinkers like Hortense Spillers and Sharpe have analyzed. In conjunction with the gender-bending casting of Wallis in a role once played by a white boy, this is an insight that might inform bell hooks's (2012) otherwise dismissive description of Hushpuppy as "transgender." I wonder, though, if there's more to Hushpuppy's trans-ing of gender than hooks allows. Does *Beast*'s presentation of a nonbinary Hushpuppy breathe life into forms of kinship and sociality that spill over the wild/civilized binary in which the film is trapped?

For Wink, keeping breath in Hushpuppy's body means holding open the Bathtub as a place apart from the Dry World—and this means recruiting his kid into his plot (of land) as its future King. So his repeated hailing of Hushpuppy as "the man" is oriented toward a future in which she'll live at the unstable edge of Man's world. It's an attempt, however compromised, to give her the tools to survive the changing weather and withstand, in the process, being sucked into the densest parts of "the singularity" (Sharpe 2016, 106). From his "no crying" rule to his command to "show me them guns, man," Wink's fostering of Hushpuppy's genderqueerness comes across, at times, as a vexing devaluation of femininity. But the impulse behind these teachings is more aspirational, a term that Sharpe pointedly disarticulates from its commonsense associations with opportunity and upward mobility. It's about finding a way to "breathe some air," Wink says, in spite of "that deadly *occlusion* that is continually reanimated and called the American Dream" (Sharpe 2016, 109, emphasis original). I'm not suggesting that Wink knows exactly what he's doing. (Who does?) In fact, part of what I see him modeling for Hushpuppy is revolt, a mode of refusal that, as I explored in relation to the *28* films in chapter 3, springs from desires and motivations that aren't fully known to us. Following Dina Georgis, I argued that revolt tears down and tears us away from existing structures and narratives; it "demands change" without assuming what kinds of reinvention are possible in its aftermath—or even if reinvention is possible at all (2013, 109). And alongside this modeling of revolt, Wink gives Hushpuppy an origin story: the tale of a mama who slew a Great Beast, brought a child into the world, and then "swam away" when her love for that child almost undid her. Hushpuppy's inheritance, then, is a narrative with which to piece herself together and the courage to break things—including, perhaps, that story—so that she might assemble the pieces differently.

Wink's revolt against the Dry World can be captured in his injunction to "beast it!," a command that, in its refusal of "civilized" imperatives, fits into the film's valorization of the wild. But reading "beast it!" through the lens of revolt—as breaking with existing structures of power—demands a thinking of wildness in ongoing relation to the civilized world, not as its romanticized outside. It also suggests that wildness, as refusal, might be a condition of possibility of inventing new forms of community and selfhood, but it's not on its own sufficient. Revolt isn't reinvention; it just makes room for the possibility. Consider two different scenes in which Wink and Hushpuppy "beast it!" In the first, Wink loudly interrupts Jean Battiste, a gentle white man, who's teaching Hushpuppy how to shell a crab with a knife. Eying the lesson with disdain, Wink erupts: "No, Hushpuppy! Beast it!" He pounds the table with his fist, smacks Jean's knife away, rips open the crab by hand, and sucks it clean. He then slaps another crab onto the table in front of Hushpuppy and repeats his command. Wink's outburst breaks the scene itself, silencing the boisterous group around (and under) the table. Then, in the quiet and uncertainty created by this break, the room begins to reassemble: everyone joins in encouraging Hushpuppy's efforts, chanting "beast it!" until she successfully replicates Wink's "wild" artistry and cheering her on as she steps up onto the table, flexes her muscles, and lets out a "warrior cry" (Alibar and Zeitlin n.d.). The moment suggests that breaking things can usher in new forms of relationality; the pieces come back together with greater intensity, prompting Wink to yell over the din, "You see what kind of family we got? We got feeling!" But breakages are unguaranteed—especially when they're shaped by uneven relations of power. This becomes apparent when Wink "beasts it" at the levee with a homemade bomb. Wink just knows he can't abide a poststorm world in which, above the levee, "them people go out grocery shoppin' and all that" while life withers in the still-submerged, too-salty Bathtub. So he revolts. And this time his actions propel the community straight into the Dry World's Open Arms.

In this context, it's important that along with his willingness to break things, Wink also offers Hushpuppy a story. His tale breathes life into the absent Marietta, creating for their kid the outline of a mama of mythic proportions. After beasting it with the crab, as Wink settles into a quiet, drunken wistfulness, he tells Hushpuppy the story of her conception. It happened, her daddy says, after Marietta stepped between a sleeping Wink and a fifteen-foot alligator. Zeitlin visualizes the scene from Hushpuppy's perspective, which means that Marietta's face is "always covered, shot from the back, or out of the frame" (Alibar and Zeitlin n.d.). So we see her from the torso down, wearing a pair of white boys' briefs like the ones Hushpuppy wears, as she cocks a shotgun and slays the beast that menaces Wink. "Your mama battered that gator up," Wink says, "and set it to fry. . . . And Hushpuppy popped into the universe maybe four minutes later." Marietta is sexualized by Wink's narrative and by the filming style, which lingers over "her panties, and her long naked legs" both before and after they're splattered with gator gore (Alibar and Zeitlin n.d.). But Hushpuppy is metabolizing this story, recalibrating Wink's fantasy-memory as a hero's tale in which a woman protects the one she loves from a fearsome predator. Fearlessness and protectiveness are at the root of Hushpuppy's existence, the story says. And Wink reinforces this sense that Marietta's love is fierce with the other story he tells his kid. We hear it from Hushpuppy early in the film when, in voiceover, she explains: "Daddy says the first time she looked at me, it made her heart beat so big that she thought it would blow up. That's why she swam away." Whether Marietta left or died is unclear. But the idea of a mama who swam away creates a line for Hushpuppy to follow. It inspires her to swim away from the Bathtub in search of a maternal past, which is how she arrives at a barge called the *Elysian Fields*. It's here, at a catfish shack that doubles as a strip club, that Hushpuppy encounters the pieces of her origin story and considers what to make of them.

Hushpuppy's journey to the Elysian Fields Catfish Shack retraces the line of flight opened up in the film by the figure of the black femme—a figure that exists, Keeling writes, on "the shoreline between the visible and the invisible, the thought and the unthought" (2007, 2).[20] Marietta is a fantasy-memory, a woman without a face who may or may not be alive. She exists at the very edge of what the film can see and think about survival. What Keeling calls the "black femme function" names the cinematic persistence of "kernels of perception that might be capable of supporting alternate forms of sociality"—the "portal through which present (im)possibilities might appear" (5, 9). The fleeting, wavering presence of the black femme disturbs an otherwise immersive viewing experience, potentially making room for viewers to sense the unimaginable within the filmic imaginary. We might sense, in this case, the concrete practices of black survival and invention that *Beasts* can't reckon with, even as it attempts to plot an alternative to capitalist modernity. To make matters more complicated, Nyong'o observes that "the black femme function is dispersed in *Beasts*," distributed across a missing mama, the cook at Elysian Fields who may or may not be her, Miss Bathsheba as an "inconsistent surrogate," and Hushpuppy herself (2015, 254). So Hushpuppy hears a story from her heartbroken daddy about a mama who swam away. It propels her into a cinematic line of flight that immerses her, sensorily, in the origin story Wink offers, complete with a beer-swilling mama figure and frying gator tail sizzling on the cooktop. And there, with the pieces of Hushpuppy's origin story popping in the light above a fry pot, a jaded cook offers her a lesson about disaster and survival that carries with it a potentially radical message about taking care of others.

The cook Hushpuppy meets at Elysian Fields reactivates the story of her arrival into the universe, transforming that story into a lived experience that can inform how Hushpuppy might, in the words of Hannah Arendt, "confirm and take upon [herself] the naked fact of [her] original physical appearance" (1958, 176–177). For Arendt, the beginnings we set in motion on the scene of a shared world derive from the beginnings that we are; from the fact that we appear, naked and new—

FIGURE 14. Hushpuppy meets a cook (Jovan Hathaway) who may or may not be her mama. Still from *Beasts of the Southern Wild* (Cinereach, 2012).

an utterly unique bundle of qualities and talents.[21] Hushpuppy's origin story begins to materialize when a cook (Jovan Hathaway) spontaneously prepares her a meal of fried gator, outlining, as she does, a jaded account of the world premised on being self-sufficient in the wake of disaster. "'Cause yeah, life's some big ol' feast," she says. "But you? You ain't nothin' but a stupid little waitress. One day everything on your plate gonna fall on the floor; ain't nobody gonna be there to pick it up for you. One day it's gonna be all on you.... So smile, girl, 'cause nobody likes a pity-party-having-ass-woman." But the cook's actions belie her tough talk as she engages in the work of scaling, stripping, dredging, and frying the gator tail that Hushpuppy will carry home to a dying Wink. And she promises Hushpuppy that the gator is "magic." So somewhere beyond the forces that might transform Hushpuppy into a "stupid little waitress," there's a "feast." And here, now, she isn't serving but is served. The cook's caregiving exceeds the capitalist apparatus the strip club represents, in which women exchange their emotional and sexual labor for money. A woman is cooking up magic for a little stranger who's arrived in the kitchen where she works, her actions infusing the scene with gestures to a "radical Elsewhere," insisting, in spite of herself, on "the existence of alternatives to existing organizations of social life" (Keeling 2007, 137). This meeting locates "a shared gaze of affirmation between black female characters" at the heart of the film's representation of Hushpuppy's evolving sense of self (Mafe 2018, 116). And later, an experience of being held by the cook, the two of them swaying to slow jazz, nudges Hushpuppy into the only other memory she has of being "lifted": the time when Wink brought his infant to the door of their home and urged her to "breathe some air." Both in this memory and in the present that conjures it, Hushpuppy experiences hands that hold and cook for and feed little bodies—"a social network of hands," to borrow Judith Butler's phrasing, that arises from our material entanglements and shared vulnerabilities (2009, 14). This is the "magic" that Hushpuppy brings back to her daddy, tenderly feeding fried gator to the man who once insisted that "you have to learn how to feed your house." It's a magic that whispers of what the Bathtub could be.

THE GIRL-KING PLOTTED HER NEXT STEPS . . .

Beasts of the Southern Wild ends with Wink's funeral. Hushpuppy meets the aurochs, declares one her "friend, kind of," and then watches over her daddy's death. And when Wink is gone, the Bathtub's survivors gather for a ritual send-off. Hushpuppy sets fire to the boat that will carry her father's body into the Gulf of Mexico and her people speak in unison: "As I stand by the bayou a ship at my side starts her motors and sails for the Gulf. I watch her until she disappears. 'There! She's gone!' Gone where? Gone from my eyes, that's all. She's just as big as when she left me. And somewhere else, other voices are calling out, 'Here she comes!' And that is dying. HERE! SHE! COMES!" Their words give voice to the experience of both the living and the dead: those who watch the "ship" disappear and those on the other side who greet it as one of their own. As Wink's body is consumed by flames, then, the space-time of the Bathtub stretches between two here-and-nows. One is a (passing) present inhabited by the living; and the other—a "here" that's also "somewhere else"—is a future composed of voices from the past. The now of the Bathtub becomes what Avery Gordon describes as a "wavering present" in which the dead charge those who have survived them with a "something-to-be-done" (1997, 168, xvi). And the gendered pronoun "she" zig-zags across this unstable space-time, slipping from the ship it indexes—and the body on board—to a solemn Hushpuppy who watches them float away. This shift, in which Hushpuppy becomes the subject of the statement "here she comes," then carries into the film's final image: a wide tracking shot that rapidly "flies backwards" away from Hushpuppy as she leads her community "forward, into the future" (Alibar and Zeitlin n.d.). The group is walking along the flooded causeway that connects the Bathtub to the mainland. So the "concluding image," Mafe observes, offers "a black female subject on a literal threshold, an in-between space of transition (neither the Bathtub nor the Dry World) where the unknown lies before her" (2018, 119). It gestures to an indeterminate future animated by the coming of the girl-king.

The openness of *Beasts*' final image—its lingering with Hushpuppy in a liminal space—points beyond the more restricted future suggested by the film's romanticization of both precarity and wildness. On one level, *Beasts* seems to map out a path to survival for a species-wide "we." We'll collectively transcend humanness, the film implies, by getting back in touch with our animal selves and our environmental interdependencies—a future modeled on an idealized past

FIGURE 15. Hushpuppy with her people on the threshold between the Dry World and the Bathtub. Still from *Beasts of the Southern Wild* (Cinereach, 2012).

imagined as untamed and somehow more equitable. In this sense, the film taps into an anthropological imaginary that projects a purified, simplified past to serve as the origin story for a revolutionary future—a move that pivots on "the collapse of time into race" (Weinbaum 2004, 127). That is, if salvation lies in the more balanced lifeways associated, in the ethnographic imagination, with premodern societies, then the solution to the "problem-space" of climate change is entangled in the racial logic of developmental time (Scott 2004, 4). The civilized/wild binary at the center of the film sucks it into a nineteenth-century chapter in Man's story, when Western science hierarchically ordered the globe to position Western civilization as the epitome of human development—the point toward which all Others are (or should be) tending.[22] The film inverts this binary, unveiling "civilization" as disastrous and celebrating "wild" alternatives, but leaves intact the underlying logic that aligns racialized peoples with primitivism and animality. As Nyong'o asks, "Even if the film's ambition is to valorize feral human nature, at what price is such transvaluation purchased?" (2015, 251). And are there other storylines bubbling in the Bathtub? If the film's investment in a romanticized, racialized ferality constrains its storytelling potential, then what, exactly, does it stop short of imagining? What might *Beasts* conjure in spite of itself?

I propose the film's posthuman trajectory is haunted by what Katherine McKittrick describes as the "*counterhumanism*" that animates Wynter's work—a way of understanding and doing humanness that derives from a "'gaze from below' emancipatory legacy" (Wynter and McKittrick 2015, 11, emphasis original). The perspective offered by this legacy is one that McKittrick, following Wynter, describes as "the imperative perspective of black struggle"—a way of looking that sees the existing organization of the material world as contingent and contested

(2006, xi). From this perspective, "wildness" comes into view not as the romanticized outside-of-and-prior-to civilization, but as the fearful projection of a speculative gaze that pretends to secure the future, but can't. It emerges from within the logic of capital, a diagnosis to explain away the breakdowns in Man's mechanisms of extraction. We can trace this, as Sarah Franklin does, through the etymological connections between "capital" and "cattle," a history of use that grounds modern capital in practices of breeding animals and slaves "for use or profit" (2007, 53). And if domestication entails fixing Others in place to render them calculable, their futures knowable and therefore profitable, then "the rogue, stray, or 'wild' animal that cannot be tamed" becomes a problem for economic Man (215n10). But, Franklin notes, "such animals are as much products of domestication as their successfully tamed counterparts because it is domestication that makes of their wildness both failure and otherness" (215n10). In other words, Man's dehumanizing narrative posits animality, savagery, and unreason where there is rebellion and revolt. So a nineteenth-century Shawnee prophet, Tenskwatawa, who instructs his people to kill their cattle as a rejection of European domesticity, seemingly confirms the framing of Indigenous peoples as "savage." Similarly, the maroon leader Makandal, who orchestrates the poisonings of planters and their herds on colonial Saint-Domingue, seems to validate the European perspective that Africans are "brutish."[23] *Beasts* invests in wildness without reckoning with these histories, which means the film struggles to envision rebellion as an organized, sustainable set of practices. This struggle, in turn, means it can't quite tell a story in which rebellion goes hand in hand with invention.

For Wynter, rebellion and invention are at the heart of black life in the New World, the intertwined strands of a counterhumanism that she formulates as "black metamorphosis." In an unpublished 935-page manuscript written in the 1970s (and likely into the 1980s), Wynter tells a story of black reinvention in the face of dehumanization. Or, as Scott describes it, this mammoth work presents "her story of how an African becomes a native in the context of New World plantation slavery—the material and metaphysical metamorphosis that *constitutes* the New World black as both an object of power and a subject of creative endeavor" (2016, x, emphasis original). Wynter's thesis concerning the becoming-native of black subjects, or the indigenization of black life in the Americas, makes a provocative contribution to contemporary discussions of the intersections of antiblackness and settler colonialism. A full consideration of the implications of Wynter's use of the language of indigenization is beyond my scope here. Certainly, her thinking of blackness-as-native—like her reading of Shakespeare's Caliban as both African and Arawak—risks complicity with the processes of Indigenous erasure that underwrite settler colonialism as an ongoing structure.[24] But Wynter's work also reaches for an epistemological mutation in which understandings of humanness spring from our "*activities* rather than unchanging biocentric *categories* of being" (McKittrick 2016, 89, emphasis original).

"Black metamorphosis," then, deploys the logic of indigenization to index the rehumanizing reinvention of black life among those who were indigenous to Africa. It names the creative labor of planting oneself in place after being violently, irreparably displaced by Man's production of "alienated realities" on both sides of the Atlantic (McKittrick 2016, 86). And it illuminates, too, modes of survival, sociality, and consciousness that expose the impermanence of Man's world.

Wynter conceptualizes black metamorphosis as both material and narrative, a place-based affirmation of black life that reinvents the human from *within* an economic system and epistemology that "required the impossibility of black humanity" (McKittrick 2016, 82). She attends, as McKittrick explains it, to how "the perspectival economic imperialism of the planet, and attendant racial processes such as plantation slavery, produced the conditions through which the colonized would radically and creatively redefine—*reword*, to be specific—the representative terms of the human" (80–81, emphasis original). Wynter maps this dialectic of dehumanization and redefinition onto the tensions between the plantation and the plot—the provision grounds that the planter class allotted to those they enslaved for the growing of food for their own sustenance. The monoculture plantation system alienated humans from nature, spurring, in Wynter's words, the "large scale beginning" of "that process which has been termed the 'reduction of Man to Labour and of Nature to Land'" (1971, 99). So Wynter locates the plantation at the heart of the unsustainable global capitalist system that spurred anthropogenic climate change, which means enfolded within our destabilizing planetary environment is, to return to Sharpe, "the singularity" (2016, 106). The plantation was a site of both economic extraction and "'social inscription,'" a bothness that Wynter traces by framing "'nigger-breaking'" as a violent "'initiation rite'" that produced the colonizers as human beings and the enslaved as unhuman, nonbeings (qtd. in McKittrick 2016, 82). But the planters' insatiable need for accumulation and profit led to the provision grounds, which were intended to reduce operating costs on the plantation by allowing the enslaved population to sustain itself. The creation of a "plot system" meant to maximize profits became, Wynter argues, "the focus of resistance to the market system and market values" (1971, 99). The plot system opened up the possibility of relationships to the earth that exceeded the imperatives of bourgeois productivity, which, turning on the meaning of "plot" in the context of storytelling, also opened up new story-potentials about life in the New World. The cultivation of crops for survival—with some foods, like the yam, brought to the Caribbean from Africa—allowed for the transplantation and remixing of knowledge, values, and traditions such that the plot became the ground of "a folk culture" (1971, 99).[25] In other words, the same historical processes that produced the plantation system that required black dehumanization also generated a plot system: the living ground of cultural inventions that expressed "'an outlier consciousness that was born from the sustained experience of social marginality'" (Wynter qtd. in McKittrick 2016, 87).

What would it mean to see the Bathtub through this lens—as a space for the cultivation of an "outlier consciousness" that brings the colonial violence of the Dry World into focus? *Beasts* doesn't really get there. As Jayna Brown (2013a) observes in her reading of the Bathtub as "bleak, grim and grimy," it's "no maroon society." As viewers we get only fleeting glimpses of the sustainable alternative the Bathtub could represent. But I attend to these glimpses because they're generated, in large part, by the black femme function dispersed across the film. My focus here is specifically on Hushpuppy's teacher, Miss Bathsheba. One of her lessons articulates survival with community-building practices of environmental repair and caregiving. After the storm, as survivors work together to reinforce the floating schoolhouse, Miss Bathsheba identifies "the most important thing" she can teach her pupils while demonstrating how to calm an overexerted girl named Lizard. It is, she says, a matter of helping her students "learn how to take care of people smaller and sweeter than you are." The context of this lesson points to the deep enmeshment of bodies and environments, the inseparability of remaking the Bathtub and reviving the exhausted child. Survival emerges, here, as a function of "the social network of hands that seek to minimize the unlivability of lives" (Butler 2015, 67). A network of hands comes together, inventing a collective space that reestablishes some kind of public, that "find[s] and produce[s] the public through seizing and reconfiguring the matter of material environments" (Butler 2015, 71). The scene crystallizes a connection between environment and caregiving that makes its first suggestive appearance earlier in the film, when Miss Bathsheba provides Hushpuppy with medicinal plants for her daddy. What the screenplay describes as a "medicine jar" is packed with "herbs and roots" from the teacher's "containers of medicinal oddities"—a characterization that aligns it with the "magic" meal Hushpuppy receives from the cook at Elysian Fields (Alibar and Zeitlin n.d.). That is, without evidence of Miss Bathsheba's growing and foraging and botanical knowledge, the jar slides into a broader pattern in which the community's "sources of survival are utterly mystified by the narrative" (Nyong'o 2015, 264). Lingering in this mystification, though, is a legacy of land-based practices and knowledges, of material and cultural invention that arises from the labor of surviving in a hostile climate.

What *Beasts* can't quite imagine—but what makes itself felt, nonetheless, in that mysterious jar of plant stuff—are a present and future grounded in a tradition that Carolyn Cooper defines as "resistance science" (1995, 4). The Bathtub as envisioned in Zeitlin's film is "no maroon society," I agree (Brown 2013a). But the cinematic line of flight inscribed by the black femme function, the unthought possibilities activated by its dispersal across the film, unfold a *what if?* that runs right off the edge of the story the film is telling. What if the Bathtub was animated by practices, feelings, and ways of knowing associated with marronage? Where could that take Hushpuppy? In chapter 3 I drew on Cooper's definition of marronage as the "tradition of resistance science that establishes an alternative psychic space both within and beyond the boundaries of the enslaving plantation" (1995, 4). In his discussion of "Black Metamorphosis," Greg Thomas sees Wynter as mobilizing a similarly expansive understanding of the concept to narrate a history of black revolt that entails "black intellectual activity; mass cultural resistance (or 'cultures of resistance'); and physical or political movements of liberation" (2016, 74).[26] Marronage as "resistance science" captures the imbrications of consciousness and practice required to summon alternatives in the midst of Man's world. The conjuring of elsewheres and otherwises is about the cultivation of plants and medicines and the building of encampments; it's about armed struggle; it's about Vaudou ceremonies and funeral rites; and it's about music making, storytelling, and the invention of theoretical concepts, too. Resistance science: experiments in physical and psychic space—experiments in living—that "radically expand 'the "outlyer" consciousness of Blacks'" (Wynter qtd. in Thomas 2016, 74). What if *Beasts* told a story in which Wink's connection to the Bathtub was grounded in this tradition? What if his cocreation, with his kid, of a girl-king future came into focus as the expression of what Rinaldo Walcott formulates as "the need to endlessly alter the human beyond Man" (2015, 200)? *Beasts* doesn't imagine beyond Man. At least, not on its own. But the black femme function unzips the story from the inside. And out peeks a Hushpuppy in search of another tale.

. . . AND SHE SET OUT IN THE DIRECTION OF AFTER MAN

Remember: Hushpuppy addresses herself both to viewers and to the "scientists in the future" who, a million years from now, will know her story. She is, in this sense, "the ethnographer of the film" (Mafe 2018, 100). Perhaps the future scientists to whom she addresses herself—her imagined colleagues—have little or nothing to do with a Western legacy of white coats, skull measurements, Drapetomania, and a Great Chain of Being. Maybe they're scientists who spring from the conjurings of Afrofuturists. I take my cue from Kodwo Eshun, who invites a seeing of early twenty-first-century speculative practices from the perspective of "a team of African archaeologists from the future" (2003, 287). Eshun imagines the All-African Archaeological Program sifting through the ruins of one of its museums, a site that archives twentieth- and twenty-first-century black intellectual and cultural production. In these artifacts, the AAAP scientists would see black thinkers, activists, and storytellers assembling countermemories and activating futures—disturbing, in short, the temporal coordinates of a capitalist formation premised on prediction. And these scientists would see through the bad futures projected, now, to authorize economic Man; futures projected in stories that mask Man's role in the making of ruins and cast him as the one who saves us from them. "Imagine the All-African Archaeological Program sweeping the site with their chronometers," Eshun writes. "Imagine the readouts on their portables, indicators pointing to the dangerously high levels of hostile projections. This area shows extreme density of dystopic forecasting, levels that, if accurate, would have rendered the archaeologists' own existence impossible. The AAAP knows better: such statistical delirium reveals the fervid wish dreams of the host market" (291). Eshun's scientists recognize as false, impossible, the "extreme density of dystopic forecasting" that animates the neoliberal now. They can see that projections of stormy weather tend to grow "the singularity" (Sharpe 2016, 106). The singularity—the climate of antiblackness—derives from an exclusionary story of the human that presents Man as "the measuring stick through which all other forms of being are measured" (McKittrick 2015b, 3). But the AAAP knows better.

I think Hushpuppy knows better, too. Early in *Beasts of the Southern Wild*, in voiceover, Hushpuppy imagines a postdisaster future in which "the water's gonna rise up so high there ain't gonna be no Bathtub; just a whole bunch of water." But she and her daddy will stay right where they are, she insists, because "we who the earth is for." Here, just before the film's title flashes onto the screen, *Beasts* walks up to the edge of something it can't quite envision: an expanded understanding of the "we" inaugurated by 1492 and expressed in the subsequent "generalization of the then marginal idea of *propter nos*: the belief that the earth was *for us*" (Sharma 2015, 168, emphasis original). The notion of *propter nos* reflects a shift in the medieval Christian worldview, an opening created by a fifteenth-century treatise that posited that God made the world not for His own glory, but for mankind. For the Renaissance humanists, this premise meant that God "would have had to make [the world/universe] according to rational, nonarbitrary rules that could be knowable by the beings that He had made it for" (Wynter 2003, 278).[27] Enter Copernicus and the rise of the natural sciences. And enter, with them, the figure that Wynter calls Man1: the rational subject, the political subject—the one who will morph over time into economic Man, or Man2. So while the idea of *propter nos* marked a shift in the Christian worldview, it was still, as Nandita Sharma puts it, "a *propter nos* limited by Christendom" (2015, 168). The counterhumanism of Sylvia Wynter aims for a further expansion of the "we" curtailed by the rise of Man—an epistemological mutation, a storytelling innovation, "that can imagine the *propter nos* as one encompassing *all humans as a species*" (Sharma 2015, 169, emphasis original). "We who the earth is for," Hushpuppy says. And her species-wide "we" might extend, too, to the nonhuman animals with whom she shares the Bathtub; to the Great Beast she addresses as her "friend, kind of"; and to the "scientists in the future." Maybe those scientists are as yet undreamed kinds of human, "*some silicon, some carbon, some wet, some dry*" (Eshun 2003, 287, emphasis original). Whoever they are, the story of the Bathtub, its girl-king, and her daddy might be important to them, Hushpuppy knows. It might be part of the tale of how we get to a world—and a "we"—After Man.

EPILOGUE

After Man, or, Death by Story

At the end of Colm McCarthy's *The Girl with All the Gifts* (U.K. 2016), a young black girl named Melanie (Sennia Nanua) starts a fire that changes the world. Adapted from M. R. Carey's 2014 novel of the same name, *The Girl with All the Gifts* tells the story of a near-future Britain ravaged by a fungus that turns humans into flesh-eating monsters called "Hungries." Melanie is a second-generation Hungry. She was found in the ruins of a maternity hospital after she, like the newborns around her, ate her way out of her mother's womb. Melanie doesn't know this when the story begins. She just knows she lives in a concrete cell, eats bowls of worms, and loves attending classes taught by her favorite teacher, Miss Justineau (Gemma Arterton). But as the world continues its unraveling, Melanie begins asking questions about what she is and where she came from. And when she's asked to sacrifice herself to save humanity—to offer her central nervous system as the basis of a cure—she asks maybe the most important question of all: "Why should it be us who die for you?" So Melanie sets a fire that unleashes the next phase in the pathogen's life cycle, making it airborne and inducing, as the film's scientist puts it, "the end of the world . . . Probably."

The Girl with All the Gifts ends with an inversion. The second-generation Hungries who began the story in captivity, menaced by military personnel and surveilled by science, are poised to inherit the earth. And the only human left in the story, Miss Justineau, finds herself trapped in a mobile lab, sealed off from the new environment by an airlock she can never open. Like Richard Matheson's *I Am Legend* (1954), this story ends with a familiar humanness giving way to the "new people of the earth" (170). But while *Legend* turns on the human protagonist's last-minute revision of himself as the new society's boogeyman, *The Girl with All the Gifts* aligns us with the "new people" from the beginning. At the film's opening, before we see anything of Melanie's world, we hear her quietly counting to herself, marking the seconds until she's moved from her cell to the classroom she loves. It's Melanie's perspective, then, that will guide us through this world. This means the first forms of violence we encounter originate with those who are recognizably human: soldiers who enter Melanie's cell with guns drawn; a concrete classroom in which pupils are strapped into wheelchairs; children referred to as "friggin' abortions" by the adults around them. So when Melanie, in defense of Miss Justineau, rips into a soldier's neck and drifts into well-fed bliss, our identification with her might become unsettled. But by then we might be ambivalent about the future of humanity, too, because the cost of our(?) survival is firmly in focus.[1]

Undead Ends began with a story about a Last Man who couldn't reckon with the cost—to others—of his practices of survival. For the Man in *The Road* (U.S. 2009), the only future he can imagine derives from a familial "we" that casts all others as threatening and therefore killable. So *The Road* presents a Last Man who rekindles what I, following Sylvia Wynter, have been calling Man's story of humanness. It's a story that casts as its hero *homo oeconomicus,* or economic Man, the figure who masters natural scarcity through practices of extraction and accumulation and damns those who get in his way. Visions of apocalypse that closely align their Last Man with the worldview, practices, and values of economic Man expose the colonial dimensions of the apocalyptic imaginary: its investment in blank slates, a logic of chosenness, and what Richard Slotkin (1973) calls "regeneration through violence." After *The Road,* though, I looked at a set of films in which the trope of the Last Man begins to fray at the edges, disarticulating in different ways from economic Man and opening, in the process, onto potentially radical rebeginnings. By the end, with *Beasts of the Southern Wild* (U.S. 2012), the Last Man has given way to a black girl-king whose story of survival strains against the limits of Man's grip on the filmic imaginary. Attending to what Kara Keeling calls the "black femme function" (2007, 5), which agitates against *Beasts'* investment in a racialized, romanticized wildness, I wondered, with the film's young protagonist, about a "we" for After Man. Perhaps it's a future collective akin to the one Melanie breathes to life when she asks "Why should it be us who die for you?"

Melanie's "us" is the second-generation Hungrics in whom pathogen and human are symbiotically entwined—a new genre of humanness that thinks, learns, feels, and dreams and seems to be capable, too, of moderating their responses to the smell of uninfected flesh. And that's important. Because Melanie's "we" isn't exclusive to Hungries. She wants the world to fundamentally change so her kind of human can be safe, but that desire carries within it a (perhaps impossible) desire to coexist with the old kind of humans who remain—the ones she ensures are safely behind the airlock before she sets her fire.[2] Melanie, you see, is attached to both worlds, an in-betweenness expressed through her relationship to the human stories she loves; particularly the Greek myths that Miss Justineau has been reading to her class for years. Early in the film, when the teacher invites her pupils to write their own stories, Melanie spins a tale about a beautiful woman in ancient Greece who's menaced by a "friggin' abortion" and rescued by a heroic little girl. Notice the splitting and displacement this story entails.[3] The worst, most monstrous thing Melanie can name is what she and the other kids are called. And even though she doesn't understand why she's called this, she contests the recruitment and conjures instead a "special girl" who wins the love of the woman she admires. This leaves a question mark in the narrative slot reserved for the monster. So later, when the army base is overrun and Melanie sees soldiers hitting her teacher for breaking protocol, her story comes to life—which means the soldiers become "friggin' abortions." The "special girl" intervenes, driven by layers of desire: yearning to be a storybook hero; love for the teacher who's shown her compassion; and a hunger that springs from the fungus coiled around her central nervous system. Through Miss Justineau's storytelling, Melanie has metabolized notions of sacrifice and justice, heroism and monstrosity. And through the invitation to become a storyteller herself, she learns that revision and reinvention are possible. At the end of the film, then, with Miss Justineau sealed behind a glass wall, Melanie recruits her beloved teacher into the role of storyteller for a new generation—and a new genre of the human.

The cinematic adaptation of *The Girl with All the Gifts* includes two noteworthy revisions—casting choices that activate what Sarah Juliet Lauro calls "the 'unlife' of the zombie myth" (2015, 99). Miss Justineau, described in the novel as a woman of color with "dark brown" skin and hair that's "long and black and really crinkly," is cast as a white woman; and Melanie, who in the novel has "skin as white as snow," is cast as a black girl (Carey 2014, 10, 2). As Charles Pulliam-Moore (2017) observes in his meditation on the film's U.S. theatrical release, this "racebending" doesn't impact how the plot unfolds, "but it *does* give the story an added layer of meaning in 2017" (emphasis original). Pulliam-Moore's point of reference is Donald Trump's America, where the new world that Melanie ushers in at the end of the film—one "led by women and people of color"—is utopian from some perspectives and apocalyptic from others. Much depends, as I've been arguing throughout this book, on what we see as ending and who we see as belonging to our "we"—questions that become particularly pressing in the context of zombie apocalypses. As I explored through the *28* films in chapter 3, encrypted in the figure of the zombie are legacies of black dispossession and anticolonial uprising. In the colonies of the Caribbean, the zombie figured both enslavement and revolt, an embodiment of stolen life that whispered, too, of Vaudou epistemologies, botanical weapons, and the revolutionaries they emboldened. But from the perspective of imperial Europe—from Man's perspective—mass revolts of enslaved Africans in the colonies were evidence of black pathology: a terrifying, unreasoning Otherness ushering in bad futures. So American and British appropriations of the zombie that meditate on the end of white nations carry within them a kind of pathogen, a counternarrative that works its way through their storylines, bending them in the direction of After Man. As Melanie says to a dying Sergeant Parks (Paddy Considine) after she sets the fire that changes the world, "It's going to be alright. It's not over. It's just not yours anymore."

I wonder if *The Girl with All the Gifts,* like *Beasts of the Southern Wild,* is a film about climate change. In the last chapter, I drew on the work of Christina Sharpe to reread *Beasts* as an occasion to think about the coloniality of environmental degradation, including how the latter can be linked to ways of practicing humanness that derive from what Sharpe calls "the weather": "antiblackness as total climate" (2016, 21). We might see the fire Melanie starts, then, as changing the weather in more ways than one. She unleashes seeds that will be carried by the winds and devastate uninfected survivors, making the planet inhospitable—uninhabitable—for the human-as-Man. As Hari Ziyad (2017) writes in a review of the film, "Melanie chooses to destroy the world rather than give herself to it," an undoing that opens up the possibility of a future in which she "and the other zombie children are safe." Melanie's insight is that the well-being of kids like her hinges on the end of a world that sees her as a "friggin' abortion"—and the end of a story that can admit only one way of being human, casting all others as "dysselected" and therefore disposable (Wynter 2003, 310). So we might understand Melanie's fire as what Greg Thomas, following Wynter, calls "*Homo*cide"—an "assassination of 'Man'" for the sake of a more capacious sense of humanity (2016, 68, emphasis original). "It's not over," she says. "It's just not yours anymore." From Sergeant Parks's military point of view, this is perhaps a hostile takeover. But from Melanie's perspective, it's the choice of someone who's lived her whole life in a hostile environment and wants something more. Out of her cell, out of restraints, out of her plastic face guard, she feels free where the humans around her feel terror. She sees possibility where they see ruins. She sees a new beginning where they can only imagine rebuilding what was already there.

She sees the end of Man for the sake of the human.

ACKNOWLEDGMENTS

More than a decade ago, a friend thrust a book into my hands and said, "You need this." And as it turns out, I did. Katherine McKittrick's *Demonic Grounds* was full of insights that nestled into my brain, waiting for my thoughts to catch up with them. And it introduced me to the work of Sylvia Wynter, whose thinking about humanness and story is at the center of this book. So in some ways *Undead Ends* began when OmiSoore Dryden introduced me to Katherine who introduced me to Sylvia. I'm fortunate to have had an academic life full of such moments when people have seen me, said yes to me, and then sent me down a rabbit hole. This book has been a labor of love—and not all of that labor is mine.

I want to single out three big-hearted people whose thinking and friendship have enriched my life. Sarah Brophy, my doctoral supervisor, shaped this project in its early stages and continues to be a trusted reader of my work. She's also a loving friend who's shared in most of the ups and downs of my adult life. Nadine Attewell was on my supervisory committee, too, often asking questions that forced me to reckon with assumptions I didn't know I'd made. She still does this—usually over food and scotch. Finally, Dina Georgis helped me through the emotional blocks that, for a time, kept this project from cohering. Her acceptance and protectiveness gave me room to grow. I'm a better thinker, writer, and teacher because of these three people, in particular. But more importantly, they help me feel at home in the world.

There are other scholars whose support and attentiveness have boosted me. Sara Ahmed said yes more times than I can count, repeatedly giving her time and energy to a junior scholar trying to build a career. Katherine McKittrick saw past the dissertation to what this project could be, pointing to a horizon I've been aiming for ever since. And Judith Butler, Tina Campt, Jean Comaroff, Ann Cvetkovich, Avery Gordon, Nat Hurley, Kim Tallbear, and Eve Tuck all listened, laughed, suggested, and just generally made me feel seen and heard. I also want to thank the external reviewers who took the time to read and respond to this project at different stages: Sherryl Vint, James Berger, and two who remained anonymous. Their questions, criticisms, and reading recommendations quite simply made this work better. Similarly, my colleague Michelle Murphy volunteered to read the entire manuscript at a time when I really needed direction. Even for a bona fide speed reader, that's no small thing.

Outside of the people I've already mentioned, there's a long list of colleagues, friends, and mentors who have kept me grounded in this academic life. I've had the privilege of being a student in classes run by Sharon Beckford-Foster, Lily Cho, Julia Creet, Ena Dua, Barbara Godard, Terry Goldie, Marie-Christine

Leps, Bobby Noble, Andrea O'Reilly, and Jonathan Warren—all of whom let me be me. As a graduate student I was mentored and cared for by the dynamic duo of Helen Fielding and Chris Roulston at Western University and, at McMaster, by Amber Dean, Melinda Gough, Janice Hladki, Susie O'Brien, Mary O'Connor, Peter Walmsley, and Lorraine York. Colleagues at the University of Toronto who've offered support (and sometimes hilarity) include Nicole Charles, Chris Johnson, June Larkin, Liz Newbery, Karyn Recollet, Kerry Rittich, Sheila Stewart, Judith Taylor, Alissa Trotz, and Rinaldo Walcott. I've also had the pleasure of sharing a classroom with the loveliest, coolest teaching assistants one could ask for: Nikoli Attai, Angie Fazekas, Zoë Gross, Elisha Lim, Casey Mecija, Kiran Saili, and Aarzoo Singh. Other amazing people who've brought me joy, shared their sadness or mine, and made me feel valued are: Phanuel Antwi, Melissa Carroll, Hannah Dyer, Ailsa Kay Fullwood, Brianna Hersey, Emily Hill, Dan Irving, Cait McKinney, Allyson Mitchell, Dana Mount, Henar Perales, Thy Phu, Imre Szeman, Nora Tataryan, Evan Vipond, and Phebe-Ann Wolframe. I also want to thank, from the bottom of my heart, Elspeth Brown and Eva-Lynn Jagoe for organizing a writing workshop that buoyed me when I'd been knocked flat. I met wonderful people there, including Alexandria Marzano-Lesnevich and Catherine Taylor, gifted writing teachers whose insights and enthusiasm changed my life.

To my undergraduates: there are too many of you to name, but I hope you know how special you are to me. You make me feel humble and hopeful (and old) all at once. Thanks for your respect and curiosity.

I'm deeply grateful to the team at Rutgers that made this book into a real thing: Lisa Banning, my editor, believed in the project when I was still ironing out some pretty big kinks; and Daryl Brower and Westchester Publishing Services' Brian Ostrander walked me through each step of the production process. I couldn't have asked for kinder, more reliable guides through the world of academic publishing.

Outside the university, there's a team of friends, family, and support people who sustain me and remind me of where I come from. Sincerest thanks to Nicola Brown, whose compassion and laughter help me find my way. Love to old friends—people who, for this misfit, were often shelter from the storm: Luci Mok, Meredith Szewchuk, Scott Tanaka, and Brandon Wiedemann. Others who have cheered me on and shared their homes and hearts are Andrika Lawren, Chris Pozzebon, Rachel Robb and Craig Passfield, and Lindsay Stidwill and Deryck Ramcharitar. Jo-Anne and Allan Twamley have provided home cooking, custom shirts, board games, wordplay, and the patient belief that I would, finally, get this thing done. Megan Trimble Pozzebon and Justin Trimble have, in different ways, been fellow travelers through the landscape of pop culture for as long as I've been alive. They keep me (very) humble. Gail and Warren Trimble brought me into the world and inspired this project. Dad, writing it has helped me better understand us. And Mom, you led me to the most important survival skill of all: storytelling. I love you both.

Finally, Jennifer Twamley has shared every step of this journey. Twammers, you're all the things. Between the two of us we have basically no bunker skills, but it's you and me to the end.

NOTES

INTRODUCTION

1. The phrase "military-grade security" comes directly from the website of the Survival Condo project: survivalcondo.com. The description of the "bare-walled room" is included in Evan Osnos's *New Yorker* article "Doomsday Prep for the Super-Rich" (January 2017). The characterization of this locked room as the site of an "adult time-out" comes from Survival Condo Project CEO Larry Hall, who acted as Osnos's tour guide when he visited the site.

2. As both Greg Thomas and Katherine McKittrick observe in their engagements with Wynter's "Black Metamorphosis," an unpublished manuscript that I discuss in chapter 5, Wynter's work critiques the economic reductionism found in some strands of Marxism. "Theoretically," Thomas writes, "she replaces the priority given to the 'ownership of the means of production' with the 'control' of the means of socialization'" (2016, 67). And McKittrick elaborates that Wynter's analysis of the plantation practice of "nigger-breaking" demands a reworking of "Karl Marx's 'factory' hypothesis": "'Nigger-breaking reveals itself as an initiation rite in which the task of social inscription was at least as important as the task of economic extraction. . . . The plantation and the nigger-breaking model of exploitation reveals that the social order of production, in order to function, needs to establish fixed coefficients of social exchange'" (Wynter qtd. in McKittrick 2016, 82). Wynter's thinking about the entanglements of story and political economy is crucial, then, to debates within cultural studies about what Stuart Hall describes as the "ambiguities and uncertainties" of the base/superstructure metaphor inherited from Marx (2016, 74). Importantly, Hall clarifies that "some of the problems are there, at least tendentially, in Marx's texts, while other problems result from the ways in which others have taken those texts, the tendencies they have followed, the interpretations they have institutionalised" (75).

3. For more on Hall's theory of articulation, see his *Cultural Studies 1983* (2016) as well as Jennifer Daryl Slack's "The Theory and Method of Articulation in Cultural Studies" (1996).

4. Since part of the argument of this book is that visions of the end of the world are usually *an* end—the end of Man—rather than The End, I sometimes make that point by dropping the capital letters. I retain the capitalization when I'm referring to a specific discursive formation or imaginary in which "an end" is only legible, from certain points of view, as The End of the world. (So, for example, I might refer to "The End of whiteness" when discussing the apocalyptic imaginaries projected by nations that imagine themselves as white.)

5. I'm endlessly grateful to Katherine McKittrick, whose *Demonic Grounds* (2006) introduced me to the work of Sylvia Wynter and offered me ways of understanding it. McKittrick's more recent edited collection, *Sylvia Wynter: On Being Human as Praxis* (2015a), has also been an invaluable resource.

6. My reference to the "grammars" that order Man's world marks my indebtedness to black feminist scholars including Denise Ferreira da Silva (2015), Christina Sharpe (2016), and Hortense Spillers (1987), who conceptualize blackness, as Sharpe puts it, as both "putting pressure on meaning and that against which meaning is made" (2016, 76). My focus on the dis/ordering presence of black femininities, in particular, within Man's storytelling repertoire is also in conversation with Kara Keeling, who looks at the "black femme function" in cinema (2007, 5), and Kinitra Brooks (2018) and Diana Adesola Mafe (2018), who examine the

pressure that black women characters exert on storytelling conventions in, respectively, the horror genre and speculative visual culture.

7. This is Diana Adesola Mafe's insight, and one that I think with in chapter 3. Mafe is drawing on Carol J. Clover's *Men, Women, and Chain Saws: Gender in the Modern Horror Film* (1992), in which the term "Final Girl" describes the figure left standing at the end of a slasher film.

8. "We were never meant to survive" comes from Lorde's "A Litany for Survival," a poem found in the 1978 collection *The Black Unicorn.*

9. Kathryn T. Gines (2014) and Michael Rothberg (2009) offer important analyses of the racist, Eurocentric assumptions that impact Arendt's thinking. Feminist receptions of her work are also complex and historically varied, due in part to the public/private distinction that Arendt often mobilizes as well as her use of the universal "man," both of which I address in this section. In her introduction to *Feminist Interpretations of Hannah Arendt* (1995), Bonnie Honig usefully points out that interrogations of "the Woman Question in Arendt" may not be as generative as "the Arendt Question in Feminism," which calls for a dynamic encounter with her work that asks "what resources, if any, Arendt has to offer a feminist theory and politics whose constituency is diverse and often fractious" (3). In addition to Honig's edited collection, feminist engagements with Arendt along these lines have proliferated in the last decades. See, for example, Allen (1999), Benhabib (1996), Dietz (2002), and Maslin (2013). My own thinking with Arendt has been most influenced by Adriana Cavarero, whose *Relating Narratives* (2000) focuses on Arendt's ideas about self and story, and Judith Butler, whose *Notes toward a Performative Theory of Assembly* (2015) takes up the promise and limitations of Arendt's conceptualization of public space.

10. I'm drawing here on David Scott's analysis of tragic storytelling and political memory in Arendt's *On Revolution* (1963). As Scott describes it, Arendt's position is that while we may have lost the revolutionary spirit, this "need not lead us into pessimism and paralysis for in the end there are still the consolations of language, the resources of memory, the possibilities of speech and sharing: in a word, storytelling" (2004, 216).

11. Wynter is drawing here on the work of religious studies scholar Norman J. Girardot, one of the many interlocutors from across a range of disciplines with whom she develops her long, richly detailed account of the inventions of Man. I draw primarily on her 2003 essay, "Unsettling the Coloniality of Being/Power/Truth/Freedom," and her extended discussion with McKittrick in the latter's edited 2015 collection on Wynter's work.

12. Like Wynter, Arendt was considering the implications of Darwin's thinking beyond the field of biology. As she saw it, Darwin's theory that "natural movement is not circular but unilinear, [and] moving in an infinitely progressing direction" was part of a larger—and, in Arendt's view, dangerous—intellectual shift in the nineteenth century toward thinking time in terms of development (1951, 463).

13. My characterization of totalitarian time as "processual" derives from Kathrin Braun's (2007) essay on biopolitics in Arendt and Foucault. For more on the temporalities associated with natality, see Vatter (2006) and Thrasher (2016).

14. The removed piece of this quotation specifies that this is a uniquely human development that doesn't apply to "all the other primates." The distinction isn't important to the argument I'm putting forward here. And I suspect that scholars in animal studies might want to press Wynter on this point. As Nandita Sharma observes in an essay on Wynter's notion of the *propter nos*—the world for us—Wynter's call for an expansion in this idea "does not extend to nonhuman life," even if her thinking invites an understanding of human beings as "deeply interconnected with one another and with the environments of which we are a part" (2015, 169).

15. Throughout this book I attend to storytelling strategies that "make room" for the imagination, a formulation inspired by Sara Ahmed's description of her project in *The Promise of*

Happiness (2010): "To kill joy, as many of the texts I cite in the following pages teach us, is to open a life, to make room for life, to make room for possibility, for chance. My aim in this book is to make room" (20). For me, this is connected to Ahmed's insight that "the world 'houses' some bodies more than others" (2010, 12).

16. My use of "lines of flight" is inspired by Kara Keeling's Deleuzian film analysis. As it emerges in Gilles Deleuze and Félix Guattari's *A Thousand Plateaus* (1980), a line of flight refers to a moment and a trajectory in which something passes from the actual into the virtual—a transformative escape. Keeling's *The Witch's Flight* (2007) picks up this idea in relation to the dis/ordering presence of black queer femininity in cinematic worlds.

17. Outside of Edelman and Halberstam, analyses of queer temporalities on which I'm drawing are Ahmed (2006, 2010), Bruhm and Hurley (2004), Dyer (2017), Love (2007), and Stockton (2009, 2016). Claudia Castañeda's *Figurations: Child, Bodies, Worlds* (2002) has also influenced my thinking about children, race, and developmental time.

18. Justin Sully frames "the *last man* story" as a distinct subgenre of postapocalyptic fiction and offers an illuminating account of the trope in a brief discussion of Mary Shelley's 1826 novel *The Last Man* (2016, 102). He highlights that: it's through the Last Man's first-person narrative that we learn what happened to the world; the story he tells is planetary in its scope; and "the genre assumes a capacity to imagine plot and character at the scale of species" (103). My own understanding of the trope is informed by these conventions, though I use the term loosely to shift the emphasis from, literally, "the last man on earth" to the last Man in a Wynterian sense: the protagonist who exemplifies the norms of humanness established by Man's story.

19. I'm thinking here of Hall and his colleagues' observation that the scenes of rebellion and protest associated with the sixties liberation movements represented an "entirely novel *repertoire* of confrontation tactics, theatrical and dramaturgical in inspiration," which meant that, "temporarily, the politics of the street replaced the politics of the convention and the ballot box. Street and community became the sites for a series of politico-cultural happenings" (1978, 237, emphasis original). Revisiting these questions about public assemblies in the wake of events at Tahrir Square in 2011, Butler writes that "when bodies assemble on the street, in the square, or in other forms of public space (including virtual ones) they are exercising a plural and performative right to appear, one that asserts and instates the body in the midst of the political field, and which, in its expressive and signifying function, delivers a bodily demand for a more livable set of economic, social, and political conditions no longer afflicted by induced forms of precarity" (2015, 11).

20. The connection between conservative reactions to the Moynihan Report and their explanation for the Watts Riots is outlined in Lee Rainwater and William L. Yancey's *The Moynihan Report and the Politics of Controversy* (1967). Other sources on the Moynihan Report include James Berger (1999) and Roderick Ferguson (2004), both of whom discuss it in relation to the work of Toni Morrison, and Angela Davis (1972), who addresses the gender politics of the report. And in *Family Values*, Melinda Cooper observes that social theorists in the 1990s were still drawing on Moynihan's diagnosis of black familial dysfunction, depicting the crisis as having "spread to the white middle class, encouraging generations of younger women to forsake the stability of marriage in favor of career-minded narcissism" (2017, 7).

21. Cooper's analysis is shaped by the insight that the history of capitalism "entails the periodic reinvention of the family as an instrument for distributing wealth and income" (17). On the role of gender and the family in the rise of capitalism and in its moments of restructuring, see also Silvia Federici's *Caliban and the Witch* (2004).

22. On the familial coding of neoliberal calls for authoritarian correction, see Butler (2009), Hall (1980), Hall et al. (1978), Mort (2010), and Trimble (2016).

23. On the figure of the demonic or gothic child, see Bohlmann and Moreland (2015), Bruhm (2006), Georgieva (2013), and Hanson (2004).
24. On the British folk horror subgenre, see Young (2010) and Newton (2017).
25. My reference here is to Hall and his colleagues' discussion of a "famous headline" that exemplifies what they call "'the special relationship' which exists between the media in Britain and the United States," and which fueled the moral panic about mugging that erupted in the British media in the early 1970s. As part of a broader pattern of projecting events in the United States as a nightmare future for Britain, one newspaper asked, "'Will Harlem Come to Handsworth?'" (1978, 28).
26. For more on Makandal's postwhite vision for the island that would become Haiti, see Dayan (1995), Fick (1990), Lauro (2015), and Mirzoeff (2011).
27. I'm indebted to Sara Ahmed for her theorization of unveiling as making visible a veil of "shared deceptions" that supports the reproduction of a violently unjust social order (2010, 165). In her analysis of Alfonso Cuarón's *Children of Men*, Ahmed invokes Georg Lukács's image of a "'veil drawn over the nature of bourgeois society,'" musing that "the key might not be so much the distinction between truth and falsity but the role of falsity in the reproduction of truth. . . . The veil is not unveiled to reveal the truth; the veil is revealed, which is a revelation that must be partial and flawed" (2010, 166).
28. Along with McKittrick, black feminists theorizing black women's negotiations of Man's geographies include Simone Browne, whose *Dark Matters* (2015) investigates the antiblack logics of surveillance practices and technologies, and Aimee Meredith Cox, whose sociological study *Shapeshifters* (2015) explores how young black women in postindustrial Detroit tell the stories of their lives. I return to Browne's *Dark Matters* in chapter 3, where I analyze the *28* films' critiques of militarized, surveillance-based rebeginnings.
29. For instance, Juan Carlos Fresnadillo, the Spanish director of *28 Weeks Later* (U.K. 2007), is working with a storyline established by English director Danny Boyle and his screenwriting partner, Alex Garland. And with *Children of Men* (U.K. 2006), Mexican director Alfonso Cuarón offers a pointedly unfaithful adaptation of English novelist P. D. James's 1992 story of global infertility.
30. My reference here is to the subtitle of Wynter's 2003 essay "Unsettling the Coloniality of Being/Power/Truth/Freedom: Towards the Human, After Man, Its Overrepresentation—An Argument." The phrase "After Man" is one that I invoke throughout this book.

CHAPTER 1 TELLING OTHER TALES

1. McCarthy's pared-down writing style entails the nearly complete absence of proper nouns, so the Man, the Woman, and the Boy are all unnamed throughout the novel. And despite their consistent use of an old roadmap, the route traveled by father and son is unspecified. Nevertheless, attending to McCarthy's "roots in Knoxville and the southeast" and his detailed descriptions of dams, mountain gaps, and gorges, Wesley G. Morgan tentatively maps the pair's journey from Kentucky through Tennessee and, most likely, to the South Carolina coast (2008, 46). Hillcoat confirms *The Road*'s location on the eastern seaboard when he visually renders the Man consulting his map.
2. My thinking about the colonial process of "making-killable" is inspired by Eve Tuck and C. Ree's "A Glossary of Haunting," in which they credit Donna Haraway with urging them to consider "making-killable as a way of making-subhuman, of transforming being into masses that can be produced and destroyed, another form of empire's mass production. Making-killable turns people and animals into always already objects ready for violence, genocide, and

slavery" (2013, 649). The notion of making-killable is closely connected, too, to what Sylvia Wynter describes as being "narratively condemned" by Man's story of humanness (1994, 70).

3. McCarthy's July 2007 interview can still be located in the video archives on Oprah.com. In it, the writer shares that his tale of paternal care began to take root at a hotel in El Paso, where he looked out over the city at three o'clock in the morning and "had this image of these fires up on the hill and everything being laid waste and . . . thought a lot about [his] little boy." Hillcoat and Mortensen discuss the importance of their relationships with their own sons as inspiration for the film in "The Making of *The Road*," which was included on the film's DVD release.

4. The apocalypse is described in McCarthy's novel as a "long shear of light and then a series of low concussions" (45).

5. Film critic David L. Pike (2010) designates this as the film's "signature moment," noting that the shot of the interstate disappearing into the tunnel evokes a fear that's "compounded by a visual association with the birth canal from which the boy has, in our minds, just emerged out of a mother whom we have seen fight expelling him into the world with every ounce of her will."

6. Hillcoat's reference to "big cannibal armies"—along with his brief take on the work of fellow Australian director George Miller—can be found in the director's commentary included on DVD and Blu-ray releases of the film.

7. In *Love and Death in the American Novel* (1966), literary critic Leslie Fiedler argues that European gothic storytelling registered the exhilaration and the terror of revolutionary upheaval. Interpreting the haunted castles and abbeys that populate the landscapes of gothic romance, Fiedler writes that "symbols of authority, secular or ecclesiastic, in ruin—memorials to a decaying past—such crumbling edifices project the world of collapsed ego-ideals through which eighteenth-century man was groping his proud and terrified way. If he permitted himself a certain relish in the contemplation of those ruins, this was because they were safely cast down, and he could indulge in nostalgia without risk. If he was terrified of them, dreamed supernatural enemies lurking in their shadows, it was because he suspected that the past, even dead, especially dead, could continue to work harm" (131). Though the (early) American gothic tradition is more politically conservative than its European predecessor, it, too, is shaped by this ambivalence about freedom. For more on the gothic genre and the feelings to which it gives narrative shape, see Bergland (2000), Halberstam (1995), Hoeveler (2010), Khair (2009), Palmer (2012), Punter (1980), and Sedgwick (1985).

8. My reading of *The Road* via the gothic genre resonates with Sarah Dillon's reading of McCarthy's novel as a horror story. Noticing the generic shifts that characterize the conclusion, especially, Dillon observes that either "the novel shifts genres at this moment because the author is seduced by the consolations of fantasy, and/or the novel is self-consciously demonstrating the man's refusal unto the very last to confront the full horror of his situation" (2018, 18). The result, Dillon convincingly shows, is that McCarthy's novel ends with an almost dizzying movement across genres, from horror to fantasy to fairytale to parable.

9. There are only small clues about the family's class background, but flashbacks that offer glimpses of a horse, a piano in the house, and the Man and the Woman at a classical music concert suggest that they were at least comfortably middle class. And when the Man threatens to shoot a member of a road gang in the head, his detailed knowledge of human brain anatomy prompts the intended target to ask if he's a doctor. "I'm not anything," the Man replies.

10. My methodological inspirations here are Avery Gordon and Dina Georgis. Both of these thinkers are attentive to the way that ghosts and/or ghostly feelings, as Gordon puts it, make their "mark by being there and not there at the same time" (1997, 6). Gordon is looking, then, for the shape created by an absence. And Georgis is "reaching for . . . the invisible matter of history" (2013, 10).

11. Wynter borrows the term "descriptive statement" from British anthropologist Gregory Bateson, using it to encompass the complex set of processes through which a particular conception of the human takes on the force of definition and, ultimately, prescription. For a thorough account of the rise and overrepresentation of a Eurocentric descriptive statement of humanness—or the invention(s) of Man—see Wynter (2003).
12. My thinking about entropy, survival, and consumption in *The Road* is inspired in part by A. Samuel Kimball's *The Infanticidal Logic of Evolution and Culture* (2007). Kimball draws on American historian William H. McNeill, who, in his study of civilization and disease, observes that "like all other forms of life, humankind remains inextricably entangled in flows of matter and energy that result from eating and being eaten" (qtd. in Kimball 2007, 39).
13. This description can be found in Hillcoat's commentary on the film's DVD release.
14. For more on the figure of the cannibal in Western imaginaries, see Arens (1979), Bartolovich (1998), Hulme (1998), King (2000), and McClintock (1995).
15. I owe the inspiration for this analysis of subterranean spaces to David Pike's (2010) review of the film, in which he asserts the "interdependence" of the "twinned undergrounds, the only ones in the book." Interestingly, Pike concludes that McCarthy's version of the cellar/bunker relationship is more ethically ambiguous and complex than Hillcoat's—a conclusion that stems, in part, from what I think is a misreading of the cellar scene in the film. (He reads the sound effects and shrieks coming from the house as an indication that the captives are taking revenge on the cannibals, rather than the acoustic evidence of their being hacked apart.)
16. Hillcoat indirectly reinforces this construction of the house as a site of white terror by drawing on sights and sounds associated with Nazism, though these are of course cues that displace the violence of whiteness onto a different space and time. When father and son enter the house through a window, the boy notices a pile of shoes and boots in the living room that visually evokes the Nazi death camps. This connection is enforced when, as the Man and the Boy flee the cellar, one captive grabs at them, pleading for help and explaining that "they're taking us to the smoke house."
17. Morrison does not capitalize "schoolteacher" in *Beloved*, though it's used in the novel as a proper name. This is a practice I follow here.
18. Thanks to James Berger for encouraging me to reflect explicitly on this distinction between the two stories.
19. I borrow the phrase in the section's title from Judith Butler, whose *Notes toward a Performative Theory of Assembly* includes a chapter titled "Precarious Life and the Ethics of Cohabitation." I draw here on Butler's discussion in that chapter of the political philosophy of Hannah Arendt.
20. Williams is perhaps best known for his role as Omar Little, the queer stick-up man in HBO's *The Wire* (2002–2008).
21. My thinking about the Whore of Babylon is indebted to Mary Wilson Carpenter's "Representing Apocalypse: Sexual Politics and the Violence of Revelation" (1995).

CHAPTER 2 ADAPTATIONS AND MUTATIONS

1. For a fuller discussion of Wynter's account of the story of Man, see my introduction.
2. Byrd argues that the "merciless Indian Savage" invoked in the Declaration of Independence, a nightmare projected beyond the frontiers of an emerging nation, is the "paranoid foundation" for the contemporary Islamic terrorist (2011, xxi). Both of these figures, she observes, define civilization by embodying a horror it cannot admit.
3. Olney's "neo-con fantasy" is quoted from Jamie Russell's *Book of the Dead: The Complete History of Zombie Cinema* (2014). Olney goes on to offer a counter-reading of the film as antic-

ipating the Occupy movement that arose after the 2008 financial crisis. Framing *Legend* as a "parable of economic resentment and class warfare under late capitalism," he reads Neville as representing the privileged elite and argues that the film's sympathies lie with the protagonist's more communistic Others (2017, 72). Like Olney, I see the film as more interesting than a "neo-con fantasy," but my focus on race and affect results in a different reading of Neville than the one Olney puts forward.

4. Neville's construction as a military scientist draws on an American history of linking epidemiology to national defense—a linkage that crystallized around fears of biological warfare during the Cold War. See Dahlia Schweitzer's *Going Viral* (2018) for a discussion of this history. Schweitzer looks, for example, at Alexander D. Langmuir, who popularized the term "disease surveillance" to boost funding for the CDC by reimagining its work as a "defense expenditure" (8).

5. Though *Last Man* sticks closest to its source material in many ways (in spite of being filmed in Italy), it does introduce one key change that both *Omega* and *Legend* inherit: its protagonist is a scientist and not, as in the novella, a former plant worker who learns about bacteria by frequenting the local library. This change, and Price's resultant portrayal of something like "scientific objectivity," might be partly to blame for the film's emotionally flat protagonist. A clumsy voiceover notwithstanding, *Last Man* misses all the nuances of Matheson's raging, drunken, grieving, lonely character.

6. The notion of "genres" of humanness arises from Wynter's work. For Wynter, Man is a description of what it means to be human that emerges from a "genre-specific *referent-we*"—a Western bourgeois collective—even as it obscures this specificity to "overrepresent" itself as universal (Wynter and McKittrick 2015, 33, 38, emphasis original). Rinaldo Walcott develops this idea in an essay titled "Genres of Human: Multiculturalism, Cosmo-politics, and the Caribbean Basin" (2015).

7. My thinking about Lisa's negotiation of the postapocalyptic city is indebted to Katherine McKittrick's work on black women's geographies in *Demonic Grounds* (2006). McKittrick writes that "if practices of subjugation are also spatial acts, then the ways in which black women think, write, and negotiate their surroundings are intermingled with place-based critiques, or, respatializations" (xix). Respatialization is a concept that I return to in my analysis of *Children of Men* (U.K. 2006) in chapter 4.

8. Part of the unreality of the Manson trial sprang from the three female defendants—Susan Atkins, Leslie Van Houten, and Patricia Krenwinkel—who sometimes arrived at court singing and other times spoke "in perfect unison" (Bugliosi 1974, 433). At one point, Prosecutor Vincent Bugliosi writes, the three "stood and began chanting something in Latin" after Manson leaped at the judge and was dragged from the court by three deputies (486). Given the repeated association of Manson with the hippie counterculture, it's also worth noting that, according to Bugliosi, "Manson never considered himself a hippie, equating their pacifism with weakness. If the Family members had to have a label, he told his followers, he much preferred calling them 'slippies,' a term which, in the context of their creepy-crawly missions, was not inappropriate" (298). (Members of the Family are known to have broken into private homes to rearrange and steal items, a practice they referred to among themselves as "creepy-crawling" houses.)

9. Alys Weinbaum's analysis of U.S. anxieties about miscegenation and racial purity illuminates the stakes of *Omega*'s envisioning of a benevolent scientist who donates his Anglo-Saxon blood to future generations. After the Civil War, she explains, "the [American] legal apparatus attended to the complicated task of investing white blood with value—rendering whiteness a rare inalienable commodity—and then arresting its circulation in the body politic" (2004, 20). For more on the racial-sexual politics of blood and donation, see Dryden (2015).

10. Having said this, I do want to acknowledge that the relationship between Neville and Lisa—and in particular their onscreen kiss—is a significant representation of interracial intimacy in the history of popular film. As Diana Adesola Mafe points out, Neville and Lisa's "interracial kiss is often cited as a groundbreaking moment in film, much as the 1968 kiss between Uhura and Captain Kirk (William Shatner) is hailed as a groundbreaking moment in television. The fact that both of these moments take place in the speculative genre," she adds, "says something about the potential of this genre to show viewers something new" (2018, 2). I return to Mafe's work in the next three chapters of this book.

11. In addition to Keeling's *The Witch's Flight* (2007), Kimberly Juanita Brown's *The Repeating Body* (2015) addresses the visual life of black revolutionary figures. And for analyses of Black Power in the context of the demonization of communism in the United States, see Boyce Davies (2001, 2003).

12. For an analysis of the questions that emerge from the uncovering of what would become known as the African Burial Ground, see Katherine McKittrick's "Plantation Futures" (2013). And for an account of the 1741 "witch hunt" in Manhattan that resulted in black men being burned at the stake and hanged on suspicion of inciting a slave rebellion, see Jill Lepore's *New York Burning* (2005).

13. There's a connection here, too, to Neville's quoting of Bob Marley: "Light up the darkness." I return to that phrase at the end of this discussion because I see the *Legend* album as holding open within the film the radical future suggested by its discarded ending.

14. Interestingly, one of the studies Browne discusses, which looked at race and gender classifications in the context of facial recognition software, used "actor Will Smith's face as the model of generic black masculinity" (2015, 111). Browne also briefly addresses Smith's role in films like *Enemy of the State* (U.S. 1998) and *I, Robot* (U.S. 2004) that shape popular perceptions of surveillance technologies and practices.

15. My reference here is to Morrison's 1992 collection of essays, *Playing in the Dark*.

16. I want to make a distinction here between Neville's dead wife as she functions in Matheson's novella versus in the 2007 film version of *Legend*. As we saw in the context of both *The Road* and the original *Legend*, the dead wife encrypted in the narrative past activates the survivor's impulse toward mastery precisely because she reminds him that he's already shot through with loss. The 2007 film amplifies this effect by yoking the memory of Neville's wife and child—two characters who are altogether absent in *The Omega Man*—to his constant companion, Sam. In the three-part flashback sequence that depicts Neville rushing his family to a helicopter to be airlifted off the island, we learn that Marley gave him her puppy, Sam, to "protect daddy" just as the door of the chopper was closing. And then we learn the bridges blew too soon, sending another helicopter careening into the one carrying Neville's wife and child. So when Sam is gravely injured by KV-infected dogs in the course of Neville's escape from a mantrap, her wounds reopen old wounds. Back in his laboratory, having made one desperate attempt to save her life, Neville gathers Sam into his arms and slumps to the floor, stroking her head and softly singing Bob Marley's "Three Little Birds" as he waits to see if his latest compound will work. When the serum fails to stop Sam from turning, leading Neville to strangle his only companion in the world, the camera keeps tight to his face, registering how the very act that contains the situation also undoes him. Here *Legend* offers a glimpse of the psychic cost of ending another's story as well as the violence this entails. And when the "Ruth ending" revises Neville's view of the infected and asks us to reevaluate all of his actions, this moment, in particular, appears in a haunting new light.

17. We might compare this to the project of the Man in *The Road*, who sees himself as "carrying the fire" through a hostile land teeming with cannibalistic savages.

18. For a feminist analysis of sex and gender in the context of social contract theory, see Carole Pateman's *The Sexual Contract* (1988). And for an examination of social contract theory in apocalyptic fiction, specifically, see Claire P. Curtis's *Postapocalyptic Fiction and the Social Contract* (2010).

CHAPTER 3 REVOLTING REANIMATIONS

1. My description of this ending as "unimaginable" is inspired by Michel-Rolph Trouillot's description of the Haitian Revolution—an uprising that I consider in this chapter—as "unthinkable" from a European perspective (1995, 73). Trouillot links this unthinkability to the Eurocentric understanding of Man that emerged alongside the invention of "the West" in the sixteenth century. So his argument intersects with Sylvia Wynter's work, discussed throughout this book, on the figure of Man as constraining how we imagine humanness.
2. As Boyle explains in a special feature on the DVD release of *28 Weeks,* the infected are all played by movement artists, their frenetic movements in both films achieved by careful choreography.
3. On the one hand, the postcolonial irony of *Trainspotting* (U.K. 1996) might support an argument that Boyle's work is shot through with suspicion about the greatness of the British Empire. But on the other hand, as Attewell points out, "Danny Boyle's vision for the opening ceremony of the 2012 London Olympics occluded the centrality of empire to many of the events, movements, and institutions it highlighted as having shaped modern Britain" (2014, 200). Jayna Brown sees both tendencies at work in *28 Days,* describing the film as "elegiac, mourning an infected Britain," even as it's "critical of nationalisms and full of self-loathing for Britain's isolationism and rigid class structure" (2013b, 122).
4. I discuss Wynter's work on the inventions of Man at length in my introduction.
5. The experiment alludes to the fictional Ludovico technique imagined in Stanley Kubrick's *A Clockwork Orange* (U.K. 1971), a form of aversion therapy meant to cure a teen psychopath of his violence. It's an allusion that also reworks its source material, which reinforces my claim that the *28* films are exploring and critically responding to conservative storytelling that often links pathologized British youth to dystopian futures.
6. My thinking about circulations of affect is indebted to Sara Ahmed's work on the "world making" force of feelings (2004, 12). Emotions like hate and terror, she writes, "stick" to some bodies more than others—a stickiness effected by "histories of association [that] are reopened in each encounter" between subjects hailed as "ordinary" and those cast as suspect or dangerous (54). So dangerous Others take shape through the discursive circulation of figures that accumulate "affective value" as they circulate precisely because "they do not have a fixed referent" (47).
7. In light of my argument that the *28* zombies visually evoke the street scenes that, beginning in the 1960s, seemed to portend the end of Man's world (see my introduction), it's worth noting that Kristeva's *Revolt, She Said* (2002) fleshes out a concept of revolt based on Kristeva's understanding of the events of May 1968 in France.
8. My thinking about zombies and capitalism is largely inspired by Jean and John Comaroff's 2002 essay "Alien-Nation: Zombies, Immigrants, and Millennial Capitalism." While I don't draw directly on it here, the analysis in this chapter began, really, as an extended reflection on their seemingly straightforward question: "What might zombies have to do with the implosion of neoliberal capitalism at the end of the twentieth century?" (2002, 779). Beyond the Comaroffs, see also Lauro's edited collection, *Zombie Theory: A Reader* (2017).
9. See Orlando Patterson's *Slavery and Social Death* (1982), which examines social death as the outcome of "natal alienation," or "the loss of ties of birth in both ascending and descending generations" (7).

10. See Ian Olney's *Zombie Cinema* (2017) for an interpretation of *White Zombie* as "an indictment not of blackness but of whiteness" (22). On the issue of the zombie master's race, he writes, "While the zombie master portrayed by the European actor Bela Lugosi has been described as creole (or even, inexplicably, as black), his Western garb, elaborate Vandyke beard, and Hungarian-accented English clearly mark him as white" (23).

11. My use of "counter-occupy" is inspired by Lauro's investigation of "the counteroccupation of mythical space" as "an alternative strategy of colonial and postcolonial resistance" (2015, 25).

12. I'm writing about British zombie films but connecting them to an American film history—and I'm discussing the Haitian Revolution, which most directly impacted France. So here I want to reiterate that my reading of British and American apocalypse films via the insights of black feminism calls for an analysis that's transatlantic in scope. As I explained in my introduction, following Paul Gilroy, I take the Atlantic world as "one single, complex unit of analysis" (1993, 15). The ripple effects of the Haitian Revolution were certainly felt in Britain, landing perhaps especially close to home decades later during the Morant Bay rebellion of 1865. And as Greg Thomas writes, glossing the argument of Gerald Horne's *The Counter-Revolution of 1776: Slave Resistance and the Origins of the United States of America* (2014), "African maroonage in the Caribbean effectively ran off many British settlers from the islands, evacuating them into a search for refuge that actually led to the settler-colonial explosion of the U.S. state formation in North America" (2016, 74).

13. On the unthinkability of the Haitian Revolution, see Trouillot (1995). And for the ways in which that revolution challenged Eurocentric understandings of humanness and freedom, see C.L.R. James's *The Black Jacobins* (1938) and David Scott's reading of James's work in *Conscripts of Modernity* (2004). For an argument about the Haitian Revolution's disavowed influence on Hegel's theory of history, see Buck-Morss (2009).

14. I follow Lauro in differentiating "Vaudou," the religion, from the more sensationalized American concept of "voodoo." "Vodun" and "Vodou" are also common spellings used by scholars.

15. For more on the West African origins of the zombie figure and its connection to Vaudou, see Bishop (2008), Dayan (1995), Lauro (2015), and McAlister (2017). And on the topic of second sight, Nicholas Mirzoeff's *The Right to Look* (2011) complements Simone Browne's argument about surveillance and slavery histories. Mirzoeff argues that in the colonial period second sight was the perspectival counter to oversight. And he conceptualizes oversight, a precursor to contemporary surveillance practices, as a regime of colonial power that orders the space of the plantation through a collective gaze that classifies, maps, and polices—one that "compels unwaged labor to generate profit from the land" (52).

16. The "disease" I'm referring to here is Drapetomania, a diagnosis invented by American physician Samuel A. Cartwright in 1851 to account for enslaved people's urges to flee the plantation. For an interesting analysis of Jordan Peele's *Get Out* (U.S. 2017) as a zombie film and a critique of the thinking that informed the invention of Drapetomania, see Sherronda Brown's "'Listen to the Ancestors, Run!'" (2017).

17. Here we might make a connection between the fear of undetected movement incited by the carrier and the history of New York City's lantern laws that I discussed, via Browne, in chapter 2. Without collapsing the two historical moments, it's possible to draw a line from the eighteenth-century ordinances designed to track the nighttime movements of racialized subjects in the city to the nineteenth-century public health discourse that made the invisible carrier suspect. Both are informed by a "racializing surveillance" apparatus designed to protect the supposed sanctity of whiteness (Browne 2015, 16). Additionally, in light of the six months Alice spent on a quarantined island, it's worth nothing that Mallon lived the last years of her life on North Brother Island in the Bronx, where she was quarantined from 1915 to her death in 1938.

18. See also Eve Tuck and C. Ree's "A Glossary of Haunting," which presents the horror story arc as having "the same seduction as math, a solution to the problem set of injustice." They continue, "The crux of the hero's problem often lies in performing that mathematics. Chainsaw the phantom + understand the phantom = a return to the calm of our good present day" (2013, 641).

19. Part of my inspiration here is Jeffery Jerome Cohen's "Monster Culture (Seven Theses)" (1996). Under the heading "The Monster Polices the Borders of the Possible," Cohen observes that monsters mark out the boundaries of where we can go and what we can think, feel, see, and do while still remaining human. "To step outside this official geography," he writes, "is to risk attack by some monstrous border patrol or (worse) to become monstrous oneself" (1996, 12). My thinking about becoming-monster is also influenced by Gilles Deleuze and Félix Guattari's work on becomings in *A Thousand Plateaus* (1980). I'm adapting their ideas very loosely here, but one strand of their argument sees becomings as spurred by the "unnatural participations" (255) that can occur when regulating, classifying, ordering functions are weakened or temporarily suspended.

20. See Clover's *Men, Women, and Chain Saws: Gender in the Modern Horror Film* (1992). And see Mafe (2018) for a detailed, nuanced account of Jim's Final Girl status.

21. The conceit of the Last Man waking up disoriented in a hospital goes back to John Wyndham's *The Day of the Triffids* (1951). It was used again in the 2010 pilot episode of *The Walking Dead*, when the show's protagonist, Rick Grimes, wakes from a coma unaware that the world has fallen apart. Interestingly, Mafe observes that there are "fairy-tale undertones" to "Jim's awakening after a long sleep [that] align him with female characters such as Sleeping Beauty and Snow White" (2018, 26). *28 Days* amplifies the potentially feminizing effects of this narrative strategy by shooting Jim from above, fully nude, emaciated, and pale.

22. My thinking about patriarchal power as structured, in part, by an intergenerational "bargain" is inspired by Pat Barker's First World War novel *Regeneration* (1991). At one point Barker's protagonist, a fictional rendering of the psychiatrist W.H.R. Rivers, meditates on the biblical story of Abraham and Isaac. He sees it as a kind of ur-narrative that delineates the bargain "on which all patriarchal societies are founded. If you, who are young and strong, will obey me, who am old and weak, even to the extent of being prepared to sacrifice your life, then in the course of time you will peacefully inherit, and be able to exact the same obedience from your sons" (149). For a further analysis of gender politics and apocalypticism in Barker's *Regeneration* trilogy, see Trimble (2013).

23. In the context of West's disgusted response to Jones's use of salt, it's worth noting that, in zombie myths, salt is typically understood to have liberatory properties. As Lauro elaborates, "Salt will turn an imprisoned soul against its master in overt rebellion. Therefore, built into this myth was the potential for upheaval, resistance, rebellion, if only the slave came into contact with the right material" (2015, 46).

24. One of the most well-known cases of alleged zombification in Haiti, Felicia Felix-Mentor was discovered, disoriented and naked, in the Artibonite Valley in 1936. In *The Serpent and the Rainbow* (1985), his controversial account of the search for a poison that might explain the zombie phenomenon, ethnobotanist Wade Davis reports that Felix-Mentor had "suddenly taken ill, died, and been buried" twenty-nine years before her reappearance (213). Identified by her brother in 1936, she was taken to a hospital in Gonaïves, which is where Hurston encountered her. Hurston thus opens her chapter on zombies in *Tell My Horse* (1938) with the following lines: "What is the whole truth and nothing else but the truth about zombies? I do

not know, but I know that I saw the broken remnant, relic, or refuse of Felicia Felix-Mentor in a hospital yard" (189).

25. *28 Days* was entirely shot on relatively low-resolution MiniDV cameras, and Boyle's team intensifies the grainy, almost depthless look of digital video when the infected are onscreen. As Boyle explains in an interview, the DV allowed him to alter the frame rate so that "things appear to be speeded up but actually it's real time. So you kind of snatch at fast images, like falling rain or a man running, snatching at them in a slightly unreliable way. The idea is that you can't quite trust your usual sense of judgment about perception, depth, and distance when dealing with the infected" (Hunter 2003). The other advantage of the DV cameras is that they're small and allow for quick setup, which was essential to capturing shots of a deserted London in the brief moments of morning stillness secured by traffic control at such busy sites as Piccadilly Circus, Westminster Bridge, and the Docklands (cf. Bankston 2003).

26. On the pharmacology of zombification, see Davis (1985), Fick (1990), and Lauro (2015).

27. Analyses of debt and guilt as analogous can be found in anthropology, philosophy, and literary studies. See, for example, Friedrich Nietzsche's *On the Genealogy of Morals* (1887), Gilles Deleuze's *Nietzsche and Philosophy* (1983), and Margaret Atwood's lectures in *Payback: Debt and the Shadow Side of Wealth* (2008).

28. As Castañeda, Anne McClintock (1995), and others have shown, the logic of developmentalism writes the parent-child dynamic onto colonial relations, casting Western nations as benevolently ushering global Others into modernity.

29. I make a similar point about *Beasts of the Southern Wild* in chapter 5, where I read Hushpuppy's gender-queerness as generative but haunted, too, by what Hortense Spillers calls the "ungendering" dehumanizations that derive from the Middle Passage (1987, 72).

CHAPTER 4 MATERNAL BACKGROUNDS

1. Žižek's comments about the rootlessness of the *Tomorrow* can be found in "The Possibility of Hope," a special feature included with the film's DVD release.

2. I'm referring in particular to Glissant's *Poetics of Relation* (1990), McKittrick's *Demonic Grounds* (2006), Gilroy's *The Black Atlantic* (1993), and Sharpe's *In the Wake* (2016). Additional texts that inform my understanding of transatlantic modernity are Ian Baucom's *Specters of the Atlantic* (2005), David Scott's *Conscripts of Modernity* (2004), Hortense Spillers's "Mama's Baby, Papa's Maybe" (1987), Alys Weinbaum's *Wayward Reproductions* (2004), and, of course, the writings of Sylvia Wynter. I also want to acknowledge here that my turn to Walter Benjamin at the end of this paragraph is inspired by Gilroy, who uses the passage from which I've quoted as the epigraph for his final chapter in *The Black Atlantic.*

3. Granted, this is in some ways a fair description of my first take on the film in a journal article published in 2009. This chapter builds on those insights but reconsiders the direction in which I originally took them.

4. My description of Kee as "miraculous" is inspired by Hannah Arendt's thinking about natality, which I discuss in my introduction and to which I return near the end of this chapter. In *The Human Condition* (1958), Arendt writes, "The miracle that saves the world, the realm of human affairs, from its normal, 'natural' ruin is ultimately the fact of natality, in which the faculty of action is ontologically rooted. It is, in other words, the birth of new men [*sic*] and the new beginning, the action they are capable of by virtue of being born" (247).

5. Wynter is drawing here on the work of religious studies scholar Norman J. Girardot. The terms "significant ill" and "plan of salvation" come from his *Myth and Meaning in Early Taoism* (1988).

6. My description of Kee as "invented" alludes to the opening lines of Hortense Spillers's classic essay "Mama's Baby, Papa's Maybe" (1987): "Let's face it. I am a marked woman, but not everybody knows my name. 'Peaches' and 'Brown Sugar,' 'Sapphire' and 'Earth Mother,' 'Aunty,' 'Granny,' God's 'Holy Fool,' a 'Miss Ebony First,' or 'Black Woman at the Podium': I describe a locus of confounded identities, a meeting ground of investments and privations in the national treasury of rhetorical wealth. My country needs me, and if I were not here, I would have to be invented" (65). By articulating Spillers's work on an American grammar that generates figurations of black femininity with Wynter's concept of "demonic grounds"—or the suppressed story-places occupied by women of color—I'm emphasizing how Kee is both put to work by and disruptive to the story (or stories) *Children* is telling. On the concept of demonic grounds, see Wynter (1990) and McKittrick (2006).

7. These quotations are again taken from the analysis Žižek presents in "The Possibility of Hope," a special feature included on *Children*'s DVD and Blu-ray releases. For more straightforward examples of readings that emphasize spirituality and redemption, see Brennan (2007), Dargis (2006), and Schwartzman (2009).

8. For further remarks on "donor figures" and white patriarchal benevolence, see my discussion of *The Omega Man* (U.S. 1971) in chapter 2.

9. As film critic James Udden notes, "the longest take in the film is over seven minutes in duration" and occurs in the climactic scenes at the Bexhill refugee camp. But even beyond a handful of extraordinarily long takes such as this, it's worth noting that *Children of Men* has "an average shot length of just over sixteen seconds per, an astonishing figure for a present-day Hollywood feature which sometimes can average less than two seconds per shot" (2009, 31, 29).

10. In this chapter I focus on two white women activists—Julian and Janice Palmer, a former photojournalist tortured into silence—but leave out of the discussion a detailed account of Kee's midwife, Miriam, who's executed by guards on the way into Bexhill. For a smart analysis of Miriam's execution as an instance in which the film's background—in this case, visual references to Abu Ghraib—merges with the foreground, see Chaudhary's "Humanity Adrift" (2009). And for a reading of the colonial undertones of Miriam's role not just as midwife, but as Kee's "spiritual guide," see Mafe (2018, 82).

11. For a more extensive discussion of the articulations among blackness, invasion, and contagion mobilized in Powellism and afterward, see my analysis of the *28* films in chapter 3.

12. I'm thinking here of Sara Ahmed's work in *Willful Subjects* (2014), in which the figure of the willful child—and the force required to bring her in line—illuminates how the "general will" gains power, in part, by receding into the background. The general will, for Ahmed, is the collection of mechanisms through which a social whole organizes its parts in the name of reproducing itself. But when this general will disappears as *will*, "willfulness" becomes available as a charge, an accusation levelled against the "parts that are not willing the preservation of the whole" (20).

13. Rosi Braidotti characterizes the imaginary captured in Samuel P. Huntington's "clash of civilizations" thesis as follows: "It features at centre stage the ruling couple of an allegedly emancipated, ageing and liberated Western world, the emblem of which is the 'soft' and 'feminized' European Union. The EU is opposed to the 'masculine' US partner supervising the war of civilizations through its military power and its supreme contempt of international law. In opposition to them is a more virile, youthful and masculine non-Western world, of which Islamic culture is the standard-bearer" (2006, 46).

14. Over the course of the novel, the difference between Theo and Xan emerges as a function of faith rather than political vision. Theo begins as a self-described "unbeliever" but ends by baptizing Julian's baby himself (James 1992, 59). It's this conversion, not his (reluctant)

involvement in the activism of the Five Fishes, that secures Theo's goodness in relation to Xan's evilness. Indeed, the novel sidesteps the question of what Theo will do with the political power wrapped around his finger in the form of the Coronation ring, sliding our attention from his ring finger to the "thumb wet with his own tears and stained with her blood" that he uses to trace the sign of the cross on the baby's forehead (289). Political activism emerges as something of a red herring in *The Children of Men*, a loose narrative strand that Cuarón's adaptation pulls on as part of its revision of James's story.

15. Deleuze offers as an example Daniel Defoe's *Robinson Crusoe* (1719), in which "the mythical recreation of the world from the deserted island gives way to the reconstitution of everyday bourgeois life from a reserve of capital. Everything is taken from the ship. Nothing is invented" (2004, 12). Deleuze doesn't take this further, but the "reserve of capital" is the ship via which Crusoe was engaged in the buying and selling of enslaved Africans to work his Brazilian plantation. The storytelling fate of the island, it seems, is always entangled with that of the ship. I'll return to this entanglement in the final section of this chapter.

16. Other sources on the roles of maternal bodies in national imaginaries are Collins (2004), Federici (2004), Loomba (1998), McClintock (1995), Roberts (1997), and Weinbaum (2004).

17. In his assessment of attitudes toward women in the Rolling Stones' body of work, Andrew August observes that while "the band produced songs rejecting women's autonomy and celebrating their subordination, they created others endorsing and appreciating free independent women. Though they have been identified as a major cultural force rejecting women's emancipation, the Rolling Stones were ambivalent in confronting the new roles of women in youth culture of the 1960s and 1970s" (2009, 81). August cites "Ruby Tuesday" as a key example of the band's departure from its often sexist messaging.

18. The phrase "After Man" comes from the subtitle of Wynter's 2003 essay. And on the boat as a colonial technology in relation to *Children of Men*, Ahmed refers to Foucault's framing of boats as heterotopic spaces. After quoting Foucault on boats that go "'as far as the colonies in search of the most precious treasures they conceal in their gardens,'" she observes that "we learn from Foucault's description how much the technologies of utopia are also technologies of capital and empire" (Foucault qtd. in Ahmed 2010, 275n25).

19. Here Sharpe is thinking with Hortense Spillers, who sees "the *loss* of gender" as a manifestation of black dispossession in the United States. In this context, she writes, "One treads dangerous ground in suggesting an equation between female gender and mothering; in fact, feminist inquiry/praxis and the actual day-to-day living of numberless American women—black and white—have gone far to break the enthrallment of a female subject-position to the theoretical and actual situation of maternity. . . . Because African-American women experienced uncertainty regarding their infants' lives in the historic situation, gendering, in its coeval reference to African-American women, insinuates an implicit and unresolved puzzle both within current feminist discourse and within those discursive communities that investigate the entire problematics of culture" (1987, 77, 78, emphasis original).

20. My description of the 1960s as "incendiary" is inspired by Sarah Brophy, who offers an account of second-wave feminism that brings "into view coexisting politics and networks, underacknowledged reciprocal influences, and ongoing legacies. I posit," she continues, "that the legacies of 1949–90 are incendiary—desiring, passion-infused, world-transforming. Characterized by their determination to generate powerfully erotic and angry counter-knowledges, thinkers in this period imagined ways of collectively and individually resisting gender and sexual oppression and rethought the very constitution of gender and sexuality" (2017, 93). Brophy's project is thus in conversation with reconsiderations of received narratives of the second wave such as Victoria Hesford's *Feeling Women's Liberation* (2013) and Clare Hemmings's *Why Stories Matter: The Political Grammar of Feminist Theory* (2011).

21. Ashitey shares this in a 2016 interview with *IndieWire*'s David Ehrlich, which was part of a resurgent interest in *Children of Men* on the occasion of the film's ten-year anniversary spurred, in part, by the election of Donald Trump in the United States.
22. Lyrics for the first version of "Kaa Fo" are available on a popular online site called Mama Lisa's World. An English translation of the second version appears in Kofi Agawu's *Representing African Music* (2003).
23. Here Sharpe is thinking with M. NourbeSe Philip's *Zong!* (2008), a poetic dis- and reassembling of the legal decision *Gregson v. Gilbert*, the insurance case connected to the massacre. An extended discussion of that case can also be found in Ian Baucom's *Specters of the Atlantic* (2005).
24. My thinking about "slantwise" orientations derives from Ahmed: "Queer orientations might be those that don't line up, which by seeing the world 'slantwise' allow other objects to come into view" (2006, 107). Ahmed draws, in part, on Foucault, who wrote in "Friendship as a Way of Life" about the homosexual as positioned "slantwise" to, or diagonally across, the social fabric (1981, 138).
25. My thinking here is informed by theorists, along with Sharpe and Wynter, who engage with the "exceptional" spaces of Atlantic modernity, including Baucom (2005), Best and Hartman (2005), Gilroy (1993), McKittrick (2006, 2013), and Wacquant (2001). McKittrick's work in "Plantation Futures" (2013) especially complements Sharpe's argument about the repetitions of the hold. I draw on Sharpe specifically because of the connections she makes between the hold and the womb and because she writes about the now-closed Sangatte refugee camp at Calais, France, which Cuarón clearly had in mind as a model for Bexhill. Opened by the French Red Cross in 1999 and located less than a mile from the entrance to the Channel Tunnel, Sangatte attracted a mix of asylum seekers and people traffickers, and, for three years, served as the launching point for refugees attempting to smuggle themselves into Britain. It was a site of uprising ("riots") in 2001 and 2002.

CHAPTER 5 MYTH AND METAMORPHOSIS

1. For good accounts of the casting and other production-related issues around *Beasts*, see Anders (2012) and Lidz (2012). Regarding the "color-blind casting" process, Nyong'o makes the point that much of what happens to Hushpuppy and Wink, including their apprehension by the state, "should unlock a conversation about race that their color-blind casting as universalized subjects ought not forestall" (2015, 258).
2. "Posthumanism" is by no means a unified term. Sherryl Vint makes a helpful distinction between, on the one hand, a posthumanism driven by a biotech imaginary that fantasizes about existing after or beyond human embodiment and, on the other hand, a posthumanism that's critical of the limitations and exclusions of liberal humanism. While my emphasis in this chapter is on critiquing the assumptions embedded in the former, I'm wary, as is Vint, of the ways these assumptions can inform posthumanism as a scholarly and/or critical discourse as well. In short, there are multiple versions of posthumanism, some of which fail to reckon with the histories of slavery and colonialism that have "excluded certain subjects from . . . definitions of the human" (2007, 11). Later in this chapter, I propose the counterhumanism of Sylvia Wynter as an alternative to this trend in posthumanism. I want to acknowledge, though, that feminists like Vint and Rosi Braidotti (2013) offer posthumanisms that center questions of sexual and racial difference in ways that resonate with what I have in mind. Along these lines, Vint imagines an "ethical posthumanism" that "can embrace multiplicity and partial perspectives, a posthumanism that is not threatened by its others" (189).

3. Dipesh Chakrabarty makes a similar point: "My ultimate proposition in this essay is simple: that the current conjuncture of globalization and global warming leaves us with the challenge of having to think of human agency over multiple and incommensurable scales at once" (2012, 1). This argument forms part of a larger debate around the Anthropocene, history, and humanness—and what all of this means for the future(s) of postcolonial studies. See also Robert Young's "Postcolonial Remains" (2012) along with responses to both Chakrabarty and Young by Simon During, Benita Parry, Ato Quayson, and Robert Stam and Ella Shohat (all appearing in the Spring 2012 issue of *New Literary History*). For a broader set of reflections on the problems of "post-ness," see my cowritten introduction, with Nadine Attewell, to our special issue of *TOPIA* titled "The Work of Return" (2016).

4. My brief description of what's happening to Isle de Jean Charles is drawn from the website of the Isle de Jean Charles Band (http://www.isledejeancharles.com/) as well as the journalism of Dan Barry (2006) and John McQuaid and Mark Schleifstein (2002).

5. A brief description of the incomplete Morganza to the Gulf of Mexico Project can be found on the website of the U.S. Army Corps of Engineers: http://www.mvn.usace.army.mil/About/Projects/Morganza-to-the-Gulf/. An account of this project and its planned bypassing of Isle de Jean Charles can be found in Dan Barry's "In Louisiana, a Sinking Island Wars with Water and the Government" (2006). Barry's article includes an interview with a representative of the Terrebonne Levee and Conservation District who, in a telling slip, explains that "for the cost" of including the island in the new levee system, "you could buy the island *and all the residents* tenfold" (my emphasis).

6. My thinking about "making kin" is inspired by Kim Tallbear, who argues that "blood talk" for Indigenous peoples isn't reducible to biological essentialism or nationalism. In a July 2016 episode of *The Henceforward* podcast, Tallbear offers, "I think that we need to also look at Indigenous peoples more fluidly as kin groups that are very dynamic and change over time and space. And I think what the nation does as an entity or an idea is that it sort of reinforces this notion of stasis, of purity.... But when you have a fluid kin group, you have the ability to incorporate others into your kin group" (Tuck and Tallbear 2016). On the Red Atlantic as a unit of analysis akin to the Black Atlantic, see Jace Weaver (2014).

7. This detail about the "erroneous" racial designations no longer exists on the website of the Isle de Jean Charles Band, but it can still be found on an older version of their history included on a website for the documentary film *Can't Stop the Water* (U.S. 2013): www.cantstopthewater.com/the-island/.

8. As Nathalie Dessens explains in her history of the Saint-Dominguan migration to Louisiana, "Whether or not Pierre and Jean Lafitte were refugees is highly disputed among historians. Until recently, biographies specified that they were born at Port-au-Prince in 1779 and 1782. Some sources even stress their role in transporting Saint-Dominguan refugees to America. Despite the evidence advanced by others that they had been born in France, there seems to be little doubt that they had, at least, come by way of Saint-Domingue" (2007, 82). See also Bell (1997).

9. The *New Orleans Roosevelt Review* was a monthly magazine, published by the Roosevelt Hotel, the archive of which is held in the New Orleans Public Library system. For more on Jean Lafitte's role in the defeat of the British at the Battle of New Orleans, see Bell (1997), Sugden (1979), and Vogel (2000).

10. The phrase "After Man" comes from the subtitle of Wynter's 2003 essay. And see note 24 in this chapter for sources that illuminate the tensions inherent in Wynter's reading of Caliban as simultaneously Arawak and African.

11. The will of Pauline Verdun's father, Alexandre Verdun, is available online through Our Family History, an interactive genealogy website: http://danielscheer.com/family/getperson

.php?personID=I99&tree=Scheer. Information about Marie Gregoire exists on the same site: http://danielscheer.com/family/getperson.php?personID=I100&tree=Scheer.

12. Mafe writes that "Cinematographer Ben Richardson . . . describes the camera's perspective as an extension of Hushpuppy: 'I tried to just be Hushpuppy's sense, if not literally her eyes'" (2018, 94). For Mafe—and for me—this is key to a reading of the film as disturbing rather than reproducing "the ethnographic spectacle" (96).

13. An undated screenplay for *Beasts of the Southern Wild* is available on the Internet Movie Script Database (IMSDb): http://www.imsdb.com/scripts/Beasts-of-the-Southern-Wild.html.

14. See Mafe for a complementary reading of the aurochs as evocative of "the monstrous-feminine" and, as such, "an important counterforce" to Wink's paternal power (2018, 108).

15. Sarah Franklin considers the entanglements of cattle and capital in *Dolly Mixtures* (2007). I return to this point later in this chapter.

16. My understanding of this history comes from Christopher Morris's (cheekily titled) "How to Prepare Buffalo, and Other Things the French Taught Indians about Nature" (2005).

17. On the colonial logic of "uninhabitability," see McKittrick (2006, 2013). This is something I take up in more detail in my discussion of camp space in chapter 4.

18. Hushpuppy is (tenuously) American, but she's also a poor and racialized subject whose home can be understood as part of what Wynter has called the "damned archipelagoes of the Poor," which is also "the archipelago of [Man's] modes of Human Otherness" (2003, 317, 321). It's in this context that I read her as a "Third World girl" figure.

19. On the sex/gender binary as a mechanism of colonial power, see, for example, Loomba (1998), Lugones (2007), Maile, Tuck, and Morrill (2013), McClintock (1995), and Morgensen (2011).

20. Hushpuppy's visit to Elysian Fields follows the basic outline of the "hero's journey" as described by Joseph Campbell (1949): a call to adventure (the sense that mama is out there, on the watery horizon), help along the way (a grizzled tugboat captain), challenges and temptations (a cook who invites her to stay), revelation and rebirth (the memory of being lifted by Wink on the day she was born), and the return of a transformed hero who carries a boon for the community (magic gator and a readiness to reckon with the loss of her daddy). I turn to Keeling's work to unravel the neatness of this circular structure, attending, instead, to the way Hushpuppy's journey opens onto the limits of the filmic imaginary. The black femme function, Keeling writes, "rips the cinematic open from the inside" (2007, 137).

21. I discuss the Arendtian principle of natality in detail in my introduction.

22. My understanding of the racialization of developmental time is informed by Castañeda (2002), Fabian (1983), McClintock (1995), and Weinbaum (2004).

23. On Tenskwatawa, see Hutchings, who argues that many Indigenous leaders during the Romantic period "turned the rejection of European domesticity into a full-fledged program of political resistance"—one that was meant to restore a precontact sense of Indigenous identity along with the organisms and lifeworlds that were devastated by European conquest (2009, 63–64). In other words, for some Indigenous political and spiritual leaders, the European figuration of Indigenous peoples as "wild savages living beyond the pale of civilization" lent itself to a rhetorical strategy that unsettled Western value systems and, in turn, the practices and institutions anchored by them (64). For a further discussion of the maroon leader Makandal, see chapter 3 in this book.

24. My description of settler colonialism as a "structure" refers to Patrick Wolfe's assertion that "settler colonialism is a structure, not an event" (2006, 387). For discussions of the potential problems of conflating racialization and colonization, especially with respect to Shakespeare's Caliban, see Byrd (2011), Jackson (2012), and Newton (2013).

25. See also DeLoughrey (2011) on this history.

26. Greg Thomas offers an illuminating discussion of the conceptual, geographical, and disciplinary distinctions between "maroonage" and "marronage." "Apparently," he writes, "what gets called *maroon*age has become much less bounded than what gets called *marron*age. 'Black Metamorphosis' may spell it 'marronage,' but the text does not respect these boundaries, either conceptually or geographically" (2016, 72).

27. The fifteenth-century treatise to which Wynter refers is Pico Della Mirandola's *Oration on the Dignity of Man,* an excerpt from which she includes as one of the lengthy "guide-quotes" that opens her 2003 essay.

EPILOGUE

1. The plight of Melanie and the other children in the military bunker at the beginning of the film is reminiscent of Ursula Le Guin's short story "The Ones Who Walk Away from Omelas" (1973), in which the well-being of a seemingly utopian city hinges on the unabating misery of a single child locked in a windowless room.

2. Melanie leaves both Miss Justineau and Sergeant Parks unconscious in the airlock when she heads out to start her fire. She's unaware that Sergeant Parks wakes up and goes looking for her, which leads to his death.

3. Drawing on the work of Anne McClintock, I've focused at different points in this book on the "splitting and displacement" through which Man disavows his violence by projecting it onto a monstrous Other (1995, 27). I see Melanie as doing something psychically similar from the perspective of the Other: she splits herself away from the monster she's been scripted as, reinventing herself as a "special girl" and displacing the "friggin' abortion" into a new narrative slot.

REFERENCES

Agawu, Kofi. 2003. *Representing African Music: Postcolonial Notes, Queries, Positions*. New York: Routledge.

Ahmed, Sara. 2004. *The Cultural Politics of Emotion*. New York: Routledge.

———. 2006. *Queer Phenomenology: Orientations, Objects, Others*. Durham, NC: Duke University Press.

———. 2010. *The Promise of Happiness*. Durham, NC: Duke University Press.

———. 2014. *Willful Subjects*. Durham, NC: Duke University Press.

Aldiss, Brian. 1973. *Billion Year Spree: The True History of Science Fiction*. London: Weidenfeld and Nicolson.

Alibar, Lucy, and Benh Zeitlin. N.d. "Beasts of the Southern Wild." Internet Movie Script Database. www.imsdb.com/scripts/Beasts-of-the-Southern-Wild.html.

Allen, Amy. 1999. "Solidarity after Identity Politics: Hannah Arendt and the Power of Feminist Theory." *Philosophy and Social Criticism* 25, no. 1 (January): 97–118. doi:10.1177/019145379902500105.

Anders, Charlie Jane. 2012. "The Making of a Modern Fable: Inside *Beasts of the Southern Wild*." *io9*, July 3. https://io9.gizmodo.com/5923309/the-making-of-a-modern-fable-secrets-of-beasts-of-the-southern-wilds.

Arendt, Hannah. (1951) 1994. *The Origins of Totalitarianism*. New York: Harcourt.

———. (1958) 1998. *The Human Condition*. Chicago: University of Chicago Press.

———. (1961) 1993. *Between Past and Future: Eight Exercises in Political Thought*. New York: Penguin.

———. (1963) 2006. *On Revolution*. New York: Penguin.

Arens, William. 1979. *The Man-Eating Myth: Anthropology and Anthropophagy*. New York: Oxford University Press.

Attewell, Nadine. 2014. *Better Britons: Reproduction, National Identity, and the Afterlife of Empire*. Toronto: University of Toronto Press.

Attewell, Nadine, and S. Trimble. 2016. "Introduction: The Work of Return." *TOPIA: Canadian Journal of Cultural Studies* 35 (Spring): 7–25.

Atwood, Margaret. 2008. *Payback: Debt and the Shadow Side of Wealth*. London: Bloomsbury.

August, Andrew. 2009. "Gender and 1960s Youth Culture: The Rolling Stones and the New Woman." *Contemporary British History* 23, no. 1: 79–100. doi:10.1080/13619460801990104.

Bankston, Douglas. 2003. "All the Rage: Anthony Dod Mantle, DFF Injects the Apocalyptic *28 Days Later* with a Strain of Digital Video." *American Cinematographer* 84, no. 7 (July): 82–90.

Barker, Pat. 1991. *Regeneration*. New York: Penguin.

Barry, Dan. 2006. "In Louisiana, a Sinking Island Wars with Water and the Government." *New York Times*, June 19. www.nytimes.com/2006/06/19/us/19road.html.

Bartolovich, Crystal. 1998. "Consumerism, or the Cultural Logic of Late Cannibalism." In *Cannibalism and the Colonial World*, edited by Francis Barker, Peter Hulme, and Margaret Iversen, 204–237. Cambridge: Cambridge University Press.

Baucom, Ian. 2005. *Specters of the Atlantic: Finance Capital, Slavery, and the Philosophy of History*. Durham, NC: Duke University Press.

Bell, Caryn Cossé. 1997. *Revolution, Romanticism, and the Afro-Creole Protest Tradition in Louisiana, 1718–1868*. Baton Rouge: Louisiana State University Press.

Benhabib, Seyla. 1996. *The Reluctant Modernism of Hannah Arendt*. Thousand Oaks: Sage Publications.

Benjamin, Walter. (1968) 1986. *Illuminations*. Edited by Hannah Arendt. New York: Schocken Books.

Berger, James. 1999. *After the End: Representations of Post-Apocalypse*. Minneapolis: University of Minnesota Press.

Bergland, Renee. 2000. *The National Uncanny: Indian Ghosts and American Subjects*. Hanover, NH: University of New England Press.

Best, Stephen, and Saidiya Hartman. 2005. "Fugitive Justice." *Representations* 92, no. 1 (Fall): 1–15. www.jstor.org/stable/10.1525/rep.2005.92.1.1.

Bishop, Kyle. 2008. "The Sub-Subaltern Monster: Imperialist Hegemony and the Cinematic Voodoo Zombie." *Journal of American Culture* 31, no. 2 (June): 141–152. doi:10.1111/j.1542-734X.2008.00668.x.

Bohlmann, Markus P. J., and Sean Moreland, eds. 2015. *Monstrous Children and Childish Monsters: Essays on Cinema's Holy Terrors*. Jefferson, NC: McFarland.

Boyce Davies, Carole. 2001. "Deportable Subjects: U.S. Immigration Laws and the Criminalization of Communism." *South Atlantic Quarterly* 100, no. 4 (Fall): 949–966.

———. 2003. "Claudia Jones: Anti-imperialist, Black Feminist Politics." In *Decolonizing the Academy: African Diaspora Studies*, edited by Carole Boyce Davies et al., 45–60. Trenton, NJ: Africa World Press.

Boyer, Paul. 1992. *When Time Shall Be No More: Prophecy Belief in Modern American Culture*. Cambridge, MA: Harvard University Press.

Braidotti, Rosi. 2006. *Transpositions: On Nomadic Ethics*. Cambridge: Polity Press.

———. 2013. *The Posthuman*. Cambridge: Polity Press.

Braun, Kathrin. 2007. "Biopolitics and Temporality in Arendt and Foucault." *Time & Society* 16, no. 1 (March): 5–23. doi:10.1177/0961463X07074099.

Brennan, Matt. 2007. "What a Waste: The Apocalyptic Prophecies of T.S. Eliot and Alfonso Cuaron." *Bright Lights Film Journal* 57 (August). http://brightlightsfilm.com/waste-apocalyptic-prophecies-t-s-eliot-alfonso-cuaron/#.WwyBcMi1s6U.

Brooks, Kinitra. 2018. *Searching for Sycorax: Black Women's Hauntings of Contemporary Horror*. New Brunswick, NJ: Rutgers University Press.

Brophy, Sarah. 2017. "Paris–Boston–Berkeley–The Mexico/Texas Borderlands 1949–1990; or, Gender and Sexuality." In *A Companion to Critical and Cultural Theory*, edited by Imre Szeman, Sarah Blacker, and Justin Sully, 91–113. Hoboken, NJ: Wiley-Blackwell.

Brown, Jayna. 2013a. "*Beasts of the Southern Wild*—The Romance of Precarity II." *SocialText Online*, September 27. https://socialtextjournal.org/beasts-of-the-southern-wild-the-romance-of-precarity-ii/.

———. 2013b. "The Human Project: Utopia, Dystopia, and the Black Heroine in *28 Days Later* and *Children of Men*." *Transition* 110: 120–135.

Brown, Kimberly Juanita. 2015. *The Repeating Body: Slavery's Visual Resonance in the Contemporary*. Durham, NC: Duke University Press.

Brown, Sherronda. 2017. "'Listen to the Ancestors, Run!' *Get Out*, Zombification, and Pathologizing Escape from the Plantation." *Racebaitr*, March 7. http://racebaitr.com/2017/03/07/listen-ancestors-run-get-zombification-pathologizing-escape-plantation/#.

Browne, Simone. 2015. *Dark Matters: On the Surveillance of Blackness*. Durham, NC: Duke University Press.

Bruhm, Steven. 2006. "Nightmare on *Sesame Street*: or, The Self-Possessed Child." *Gothic Studies* 8, no. 2 (November): 99–113.

Bruhm, Steven, and Natasha Hurley, eds. 2004. *Curiouser: On the Queerness of Children*. Minneapolis: University of Minnesota Press.

Buck-Morss, Susan. 2009. *Hegel, Haiti, and Universal History*. Pittsburgh: University of Pittsburgh Press.

Bugliosi, Vincent, with Curt Gentry. (1974) 1994. *Helter Skelter: The True Story of the Manson Murders*. New York: Norton.

Butler, Judith. 2009. *Frames of War: When Is Life Grievable?* London: Verso.

———. 2015. *Notes toward a Performative Theory of Assembly*. Cambridge, MA: Harvard University Press.

Byrd, Jodi A. 2011. *The Transit of Empire: Indigenous Critiques of Colonialism*. Minneapolis: University of Minnesota Press.

Campbell, Joseph. (1949) 2004. *The Hero with a Thousand Faces*. Princeton, NJ: Princeton University Press.

Campt, Tina. 2017. *Listening to Images*. Durham, NC: Duke University Press.

Carey, M. R. 2014. *The Girl with All the Gifts*. London: Orbit Books.

Carpenter, Mary Wilson. 1995. "Representing Apocalypse: Sexual Politics and the Violence of Revelation." In *Postmodern Apocalypse: Theory and Cultural Practice at the End*, edited by Richard Dellamora, 107–135. Philadelphia: University of Pennsylvania Press.

Castañeda, Claudia. 2002. *Figurations: Child, Bodies, Worlds*. Durham, NC: Duke University Press.

Cavarero, Adriana. 2000. *Relating Narratives: Storytelling and Selfhood*. Translated by Paul A. Kottman. London: Routledge.

Chakrabarty, Dipesh. 2009. "The Climate of History: Four Theses." *Critical Inquiry* 35, no. 2 (Winter): 197–222. doi:10.1086/596640.

———. 2012. "Postcolonial Studies and the Challenge of Climate Change." *New Literary History* 43, no. 1 (Winter): 1–18. doi:10.1353/nlh.2012.0007.

Chaudhary, Zahid. 2009. "Humanity Adrift: Race, Materiality, and Allegory in Alfonso Cuarón's *Children of Men*." *Camera Obscura* 24, no. 3: 73–109. doi:10.1215/02705346-2009-010.

Chu, Patricia. 2006. *Race, Nationalism and the State in British and American Modernism*. Cambridge: Cambridge University Press.

Clover, Carol J. 1992. *Men, Women, and Chain Saws: Gender in the Modern Horror Film*. Princeton, NJ: Princeton University Press.

Cohen, Jeffery Jerome. 1996. "Monster Culture (Seven Theses)." In *Monster Theory: Reading Culture*, edited by Jeffery Jerome Cohen, 3–25. Minneapolis: University of Minnesota Press.

Collins, Patricia Hill. 2004. *Black Sexual Politics: African Americans, Gender, and the New Racism*. New York: Routledge.

Comaroff, Jean, and John Comaroff. 2002. "Alien-Nation: Zombies, Immigrants, and Millennial Capitalism." *South Atlantic Quarterly* 101, no. 4 (Fall): 779–805.

Cooper, Carolyn. 1995. *Noises in the Blood: Orality, Gender, and the "Vulgar" Body of Jamaican Popular Culture*. Durham, NC: Duke University Press.

Cooper, Melinda. 2017. *Family Values: Between Neoliberalism and the New Social Conservatism*. Brooklyn: Zone Books.

Cox, Aimee Meredith. 2015. *Shapeshifters: Black Girls and the Choreography of Citizenship*. Durham, NC: Duke University Press.

Creed, Barbara. 1993. *The Monstrous-Feminine: Film, Feminism, Psychoanalysis*. London: Routledge.

Curtis, Claire P. 2010. *Postapocalyptic Fiction and the Social Contract: We'll Not Go Home Again.* Lanham, MD: Lexington Books.

Dargis, Manohla. 2006. "Apocalypse Now, but in the Wasteland a Child Is Given." *New York Times,* December 25. www.nytimes.com/2006/12/25/movies/apocalypse-now-but-in-the-wasteland-a-child-is-given.html.

da Silva, Denise Ferreira. 2015. "Hacking the Subject: Black Feminism, Refusal, and the Limits of Critique." Lecture at Barnard College. Filmed October 22. Video, 1:07:03. www.youtube.com/watch?v=T3B5Gh2JSQg.

Davis, Angela. 1972. "Reflections on the Black Woman's Role in the Community of Slaves." *Massachusetts Review* 13, nos. 1–2: 81–100. www.jstor.org/stable/25088201.

Davis, Mike. 2002. *Dead Cities and Other Tales.* New York: New Press.

Davis, Wade. 1985. *The Serpent and the Rainbow: A Harvard Scientist's Astonishing Journey into the Secret Societies of Haitian Voodoo, Zombis, and Magic.* New York: Simon & Schuster.

Dawson, Ashley. 2007. *Mongrel Nation: Diasporic Culture and the Making of Postcolonial Britain.* Ann Arbor: University of Michigan Press.

Dayan, Joan. 1995. *Haiti, History, and the Gods.* Berkeley: University of California Press.

Deleuze, Gilles. 1983. *Nietzsche and Philosophy.* Translated by Hugh Tomlinson. New York: Columbia University Press.

———. 2004. "Desert Islands." In *Desert Islands and Other Texts: 1953–1974,* translated by Michael Taormina, 9–14. New York: Semiotext(e).

Deleuze, Gilles, and Félix Guattari. (1980) 1987. *A Thousand Plateaus: Capitalism and Schizophrenia.* Translated by Brian Massumi. Minneapolis: University of Minnesota Press.

DeLoughrey, Elizabeth. 2011. "Yam, Roots, and Rot: Allegories of the Provision Grounds." *Small Axe* 15, no. 1 (March): 58–75. doi:10.1215/07990537-1189530.

Dessens, Nathalie. 2007. *From Saint-Domingue to New Orleans: Migrations and Influences.* Gainesville: University Press of Florida.

Dietz, Mary G. 2002. *Turning Operations: Feminism, Arendt, and Politics.* New York: Routledge.

Dillon, Sarah. 2018. "The Horror of the Anthropocene." *C21 Literature: Journal of 21st-century Writings* 6, no. 1: 1–25. doi:10.16995/c21.38.

Douglass, Frederick. (1845) 2004. *Narrative of the Life of Frederick Douglass, an American Slave.* New York: Modern Library.

Dryden, OmiSoore. 2015. "'A Queer Too Far': Blackness, 'Gay Blood,' and Transgressive Possibilities." In *Disrupting Queer Inclusion: Canadian Homonationalisms and the Politics of Belonging,* edited by OmiSoore Dryden and Suzanne Lenon, 116–132. Vancouver: UBC Press.

Du Bois, W.E.B. (1903) 2005. *The Souls of Black Folk.* New York: Simon & Schuster.

During, Simon. 2012. "Empire's Present." *New Literary History* 43, no. 2 (Spring): 331–340.

Dyer, Hannah. 2017. "Queer Futurity and Childhood Innocence: Beyond the Injury of Development." *Global Studies of Childhood* 7, no. 3: 290–302. doi:10.1177/2043610616671056.

Edelman, Lee. 2004. *No Future: Queer Theory and the Death Drive.* Durham, NC: Duke University Press.

Ehrlich, David. 2016. "'Children of Men' Turns 10: Finding Hope in Dystopia for the Age of President Trump." *IndieWire,* November 16. www.indiewire.com/2016/11/children-of-men-10-years-clare-hope-ashitey-interview-president-trump-1201746204/.

Eshun, Kodwo. 2003. "Further Considerations on Afrofuturism." *CR: The New Centennial Review* 3, no. 2 (Summer): 287–302. doi:10.1353/ncr.2003.0021.

Fabian, Johannes. (1983) 2002. *Time and the Other: How Anthropology Makes Its Object.* New York: Columbia University Press.

Federici, Silvia. 2004. *Caliban and the Witch: Women, the Body and Primitive Accumulation.* Brooklyn: Autonomedia.

Ferguson, Roderick A. 2004. *Aberrations in Black: Toward a Queer of Color Critique.* Minneapolis: University of Minnesota Press.

Fick, Carolyn E. 1990. *The Making of Haiti: The Saint Domingue Revolution from Below.* Knoxville: University of Tennessee Press.

Fiedler, Leslie. 1966. *Love and Death in the American Novel.* New York: Stein and Day.

Foucault, Michel. (1981) 1997. "Friendship as a Way of Life." In *Ethics: Subjectivity and Truth: Essential Works of Foucault, 1954–1984,* edited by Paul Rabinow, 135–140. Translated by Robert Hurley et al. New York: New Press.

———. 1984. "Nietzsche, Genealogy, History." In *The Foucault Reader,* edited by Paul Rabinow, 76–100. New York: Pantheon.

———. 2008. *The Birth of Biopolitics: Lectures at the Collège de France, 1978–79.* Edited by Michael Senellart. Translated by Graham Burchell. New York: Palgrave Macmillan.

Franklin, Sarah. 2007. *Dolly Mixtures: The Remaking of Genealogy.* Durham, NC: Duke University Press.

Georgieva, Margarita. 2013. *The Gothic Child.* New York: Palgrave Macmillan.

Georgis, Dina. 2013. *The Better Story: Queer Affects from the Middle East.* Albany: State University of New York Press.

Gilroy, Paul. 1993. *The Black Atlantic: Modernity and Double Consciousness.* Cambridge, MA: Harvard University Press.

Gines, Kathryn T. 2014. *Hannah Arendt and the Negro Question.* Bloomington: Indiana University Press.

Girardot, Norman J. 1988. *Myth and Meaning in Early Taoism.* Berkeley: University of California Press.

Glissant, Édouard. (1990) 1997. *Poetics of Relation.* Translated by Betsy Wing. Ann Arbor: University of Michigan Press.

Gordon, Avery. (1997) 2008. *Ghostly Matters: Haunting and the Sociological Imagination.* Minneapolis: University of Minnesota Press.

Halberstam, Jack. 1995. *Skin Shows: Gothic Horror and the Technology of Monsters.* Durham, NC: Duke University Press.

———. 2005. *In a Queer Time and Place: Transgender Bodies, Subcultural Lives.* New York: New York University Press.

Hall, Stuart. 1980. "Reformism and the Legalization of Consent." In *Permissiveness and Control: The Fate of Sixties Legislation,* edited by the National Deviancy Conference, 1–43. London: Macmillan.

———. 1981. "The Whites of Their Eyes: Racist Ideologies and the Media." In *Silver Linings: Some Strategies for the Eighties,* edited by George Bridges and Rosalind Brunt, 28–52. London: Lawrence and Wishart.

———. 2016. *Cultural Studies 1983: A Theoretical History.* Edited by Jennifer Daryl Slack and Lawrence Grossberg. Durham, NC: Duke University Press.

Hall, Stuart, Chas Critcher, Tony Jefferson, John Clarke, and Brian Roberts. (1978) 2013. *Policing the Crisis: Mugging, the State, and Law and Order.* London: Palgrave Macmillan.

Hall, Stuart, Doreen Massey, and Michael Rustin. 2013. "After Neoliberalism: Analyzing the Present." Framing statement for *After Neoliberalism? The Killburn Manifesto,* edited by Stuart Hall, Doreen Massey, and Michael Rustin, 3–19. *Soundings: A Journal of Politics and Culture.* www.lwbooks.co.uk/soundings/kilburn-manifesto.

Hanson, Ellis. 2004. "Knowing Children: Desire and Interpretation in *The Exorcist*." In *Curiouser: On the Queerness of Children*, edited by Steven Bruhm and Natasha Hurley, 107–136. Minneapolis: University of Minnesota Press.

Harding, Sandra. 2008. *Sciences from Below: Feminisms, Postcolonialities, and Modernities*. Durham, NC: Duke University Press.

Hartman, Saidiya. 1997. *Scenes of Subjection: Terror, Slavery, and Self-Making in Nineteenth-Century America*. New York: Oxford University Press.

Harvey, David. 2005. *A Brief History of Neoliberalism*. Oxford: Oxford University Press.

———. 2007. "Neoliberalism as Creative Destruction." *Annals of the American Academy of Political and Social Science* 610 (March): 22–44.

Hemmings, Clare. 2011. *Why Stories Matter: The Political Grammar of Feminist Theory*. Durham, NC: Duke University Press.

Hesford, Victoria. 2013. *Feeling Women's Liberation*. Durham, NC: Duke University Press.

Hoeveler, Diane Long. 2010. *Gothic Riffs: Secularizing the Uncanny in the European Imaginary, 1780–1820*. Columbus: Ohio State University Press.

Honig, Bonnie, ed. 1995. *Feminist Interpretations of Hannah Arendt*. University Park: Pennsylvania State University Press.

hooks, bell. (1992) 2015. *Black Looks: Race and Representation*. New York: Routledge.

———. 2012. "No Love in the Wild." *NewBlackMan (in Exile)*, September 5. www.newblackmaninexile.net/2012/09/bell-hooks-no-love-in-wild.html.

Hulme, Peter. 1998. "Introduction: The Cannibal Scene." In *Cannibalism and the Colonial World*, edited by Francis Barker, Peter Hulme, and Margaret Iversen, 1–38. Cambridge: Cambridge University Press.

Hunter, Sandy. (2003) 2017. "28 Days Later: An Interview with Danny Boyle (2003)." *Scraps from the Loft*, June 5. http://scrapsfromtheloft.com/2017/06/05/28-days-later-an-interview-with-danny-boyle-2003/.

Huntington, Samuel P. 1996. *The Clash of Civilizations and the Remaking of World Order*. New York: Simon & Schuster.

Hurston, Zora Neale. (1938) 2009. *Tell My Horse: Voodoo and Life in Haiti and Jamaica*. New York: Harper Perennial.

Hutchings, Kevin. 2009. *Romantic Ecologies and Colonial Cultures in the British Atlantic World, 1770–1850*. Montreal: McGill-Queen's University Press.

Ingebretson, Edward J. 2001. *At Stake: Monsters and the Rhetoric of Fear in Public Culture*. Chicago: University of Chicago Press.

Jackson, Shona N. 2012. *Creole Indigeneity: Between Myth and Nation in the Caribbean*. Minnesota: University of Minnesota Press.

James, C.L.R. (1938) 2001. *The Black Jacobins: Toussaint L'Ouverture and the San Domingo Revolution*. London: Penguin.

James, P. D. (1992) 2005. *The Children of Men*. Toronto: Vintage.

Keeling, Kara. 2007. *The Witch's Flight: The Cinematic, the Black Femme, and the Image of Common Sense*. Durham, NC: Duke University Press.

Khair, Tabish. 2009. *The Gothic, Postcolonialism and Otherness: Ghosts from Elsewhere*. New York: Palgrave Macmillan.

Kilgour, Maggie. 1990. *From Communion to Cannibalism: An Anatomy of Metaphors of Incorporation*. Princeton, NJ: Princeton University Press.

Kimball, A. Samuel. 2007. *The Infanticidal Logic of Evolution and Culture*. Newark: University of Delaware Press.

King, C. Richard. 2000. "The (Mis)uses of Cannibalism in Contemporary Cultural Critique." *Diacritics* 30, no. 1 (Spring): 106–123. www.jstor.org/stable/1566438.

King James Bible. The Pure Cambridge Edition. 1900. http://Bibleprotector.com.

Klein, Naomi. 2007. *The Shock Doctrine: The Rise of Disaster Capitalism*. Toronto: Knopf.

Kristeva, Julia. 1982. *Powers of Horror: An Essay on Abjection*. Translated by Leon S. Roudiez. New York: Columbia University Press.

———. 2002. *Revolt, She Said*. Translated by Brian O'Keeffe. Los Angeles: Semiotext(e).

Lauro, Sarah Juliet. 2015. *The Transatlantic Zombie: Slavery, Rebellion, and Living Death*. New Brunswick, NJ: Rutgers University Press.

———, ed. 2017. *Zombie Theory: A Reader*. Minneapolis: University of Minnesota Press.

Le Guin, Ursula. (1973) 2004. "The Ones Who Walk Away from Omelas." In *The Wind's Twelve Quarters: Stories*, 275–284. New York: Perennial.

Lepore, Jill. 2005. *New York Burning: Liberty, Slavery, and Conspiracy in Eighteenth-Century Manhattan*. New York: Random House.

Lidz, Franz. 2012. "How Benh Zeitlin Made *Beasts of the Southern Wild*." *Smithsonian Magazine*. December. www.smithsonianmag.com/arts-culture/how-benh-zeitlin-made-beasts-of-the-southern-wild-135132724/.

Loomba, Ania. 1998. *Colonialism/Postcolonialism*. New York: Routledge.

Lorde, Audre. (1978) 1995. *The Black Unicorn: Poems*. New York: Norton.

Love, Heather. 2007. *Feeling Backward: Loss and the Politics of Queer History*. Cambridge, MA: Harvard University Press.

Lugones, Maria. 2007. "Heterosexualism and the Colonial/Modern Gender System." *Hypatia* 22, no. 1 (Winter): 186–209. www.jstor.org/stable/4640051.

Mafe, Diana Adesola. 2018. *Where No Black Woman Has Gone Before: Subversive Portrayals in Speculative Film and TV*. Austin: University of Texas Press.

Maile, Arvin, Eve Tuck, and Angie Morrill. 2013. "Decolonizing Feminism: Challenging Connections between Settler Colonialism and Heteropatriarchy." *Feminist Formations* 25, no. 1 (Spring): 8–34. doi:10.1353/ff.2013.0006.

Marks, Kathleen. 2002. *Toni Morrison's* Beloved *and the Apotropaic Imagination*. Columbia: University of Missouri Press.

Maslin, Kimberly. 2013. "The Gender-Neutral Feminism of Hannah Arendt." *Hypatia* 28, no. 3 (Summer): 585–601. doi:10.1111/j.1527-2001.2012.01288.x.

Matheson, Richard. (1954) 1995. *I Am Legend*. New York: Orb.

May, Elaine Tyler. (1988) 1999. *Homeward Bound: American Families in the Cold War Era*. New York: Basic Books.

McAlister, Elizabeth. 2017. "Slaves, Cannibals, and Infected Hyper-Whites: The Race and Religion of Zombies." In *Zombie Theory: A Reader*, edited by Sarah Juliet Lauro, 63–84. Minneapolis: University of Minnesota Press.

McCarthy, Cormac. 2006. *The Road*. New York: Knopf.

———. 2007. Interview with Oprah Winfrey. *Oprah.com*. Posted July 17. Video, 05:50. www.oprah.com/oprahsbookclub/Oprahs-Exclusive-Interview-with-Cormac-McCarthy-Video.

McClintock, Anne. 1995. *Imperial Leather: Race, Gender and Sexuality in the Colonial Contest*. New York: Routledge.

McKittrick, Katherine. 2006. *Demonic Grounds: Black Women and the Cartographies of Struggle*. Minneapolis: University of Minnesota Press.

———. 2013. "Plantation Futures." *Small Axe* 17, no. 3 (November): 1–15. doi:10.1215/07990537-2378892.

———, ed. 2015a. *Sylvia Wynter: On Being Human as Praxis*. Durham, NC: Duke University Press.

———. 2015b. "Yours in the Intellectual Struggle: Sylvia Wynter and the Realization of the Living." In *Sylvia Wynter: On Being Human as Praxis*, edited by Katherine McKittrick, 1–8. Durham, NC: Duke University Press.

———. 2016. "Rebellion/Invention/Groove." *Small Axe* 49 (March): 79–91. doi:10.1215/07990537-3481558.

McQuaid, John, and Mark Schleifstein. 2002. "Washing Away." Five-part series for the *New Orleans Times-Picayune*, June 23–27. http://topics.nola.com/tag/washing%20away/.

Mirzoeff, Nicholas. 2011. *The Right to Look: A Counterhistory of Visuality*. Durham, NC: Duke University Press.

———. 2012. "Becoming Wild." *Occupy 2012*. September 30. www.nicholasmirzoeff.com/O2012/2012/09/30/becoming-wild/.

Morgan, Wesley G. 2008. "The Route and Roots of *The Road*." *Cormac McCarthy Journal* 6 (Autumn): 39–47. www.jstor.org/stable/42909380.

Morgensen, Scott. 2011. *Spaces Between Us: Queer Settler Colonialism and Indigenous Decolonization*. Minneapolis: University of Minnesota Press.

Morris, Christopher. 2005. "How to Prepare Buffalo, and Other Things the French Taught Indians about Nature." In *French Colonial Louisiana and the Atlantic World*, edited by Bradley G. Bond, 22–42. Baton Rouge: Louisiana State University Press.

Morrison, Toni. (1987) 2000. *Beloved*. New York: Penguin.

———. 1992. *Playing in the Dark: Whiteness and the Literary Imagination*. Cambridge, MA: Harvard University Press.

Mort, Frank. 2010. *Capital Affairs: London and the Making of the Permissive Society*. New Haven, CT: Yale University Press.

Murphy, Michelle. 2012. *Seizing the Means of Reproduction: Entanglements of Feminism, Health, and Technoscience*. Durham, NC: Duke University Press.

———. 2017. *The Economization of Life*. Durham, NC: Duke University Press.

Newton, Melanie. 2013. "Returns to a Native Land: Indigeneity and Decolonization in the Anglophone Caribbean." *Small Axe* 17, no. 2 (July): 108–122. doi:10.1215/07990537-2323346.

Newton, Michael. 2017. "Cults, Human Sacrifice, and Pagan Sex: How Folk Horror Is Flowering Again in Brexit Britain." *Guardian*, April 30. www.theguardian.com/film/2017/apr/30/folk-horror-cults-sacrifice-pagan-sex-kill-list.

Ngai, Sianne. 2005. *Ugly Feelings*. Cambridge, MA: Harvard University Press.

Nietzsche, Friedrich. (1887) 1969. *On the Genealogy of Morals*. Edited and translated by Walter Kaufmann. New York: Vintage.

Nixon, Rob. 2011. *Slow Violence and the Environmentalism of the Poor*. Cambridge, MA: Harvard University Press.

Nyong'o, Tavia. 2015. "Little Monsters: Race, Sovereignty, and Queer Inhumanism in *Beasts of the Southern Wild*." *GLQ* 21, nos. 2–3: 249–272. doi:10.1215/10642684-2843335.

Olney, Ian. 2017. *Zombie Cinema*. New Brunswick, NJ: Rutgers University Press.

O'Reilly, Andrea. 2004. *Mother Outlaws: Theories and Practices of Empowered Mothering*. Toronto: Women's Press.

Osnos, Evan. 2017. "Doomsday Prep for the Super-Rich." *New Yorker*, January 30. www.newyorker.com/magazine/2017/01/30/doomsday-prep-for-the-super-rich.

Palmer, Paulina. 2012. *The Queer Uncanny: New Perspectives on the Gothic*. Cardiff: University of Wales Press.

Parry, Benita. 2012. "What Is Left in Postcolonial Studies?" *New Literary History* 43, no. 2 (Spring): 341–358. doi:10.1353/nlh.2012.0019.

Pateman, Carole. 1988. *The Sexual Contract*. Stanford, CA: Stanford University Press.

Patterson, Orlando. 1982. *Slavery and Social Death: A Comparative Study*. Cambridge, MA: Harvard University Press.

Penhall, Joe, adapter. 2009. *The Road*, by Cormac McCarthy. www.cinefile.biz/script/road.pdf.

Philip, M. NourbeSe. 2008. *Zong! As Told to the Author by Setaey Adamu Boateng*. Toronto: Mercury Press.

Phillips, Melanie. 2006. *Londonistan: How Britain Is Creating a Terror State Within*. London: Gibson Square.

Pike, David L. 2010. "Goin' Down the Road Feeling Bad." *Bright Lights Film Journal*, January 31. http://brightlightsfilm.com/goin-down-the-road-feeling-bad-john-hillcoats-the-road/#.VfH-MHtedU8.

Pulliam-Moore, Charles. 2017. "*The Girl with All the Gifts*' Racebending Means So Much More in Trump's America." *io9*, March 6. https://io9.gizmodo.com/the-girl-with-all-the-gifts-racebending-means-so-much-m-1792786423.

Punter, David. 1980. *The Literature of Terror: A History of Gothic Fictions from 1765 to the Present Day*. London: Longman.

Quayson, Ato. 2012. "The Sighs of History: Postcolonial Debris and the Question of (Literary) History." *New Literary History* 43, no. 2 (Spring): 359–370. doi:10.1353/nlh.2012.0021.

Rainwater, Lee, and William L. Yancey. 1967. *The Moynihan Report and the Politics of Controversy*. Cambridge, MA: MIT Press.

Razack, Sherene H. 2015. *Dying from Improvement: Inquests and Inquiries into Indigenous Deaths in Custody*. Toronto: University of Toronto Press.

Rich, Adrienne. (1976) 1995. *Of Woman Born: Motherhood as Experience and Institution*. New York: Norton.

Roberts, Dorothy. 1997. *Killing the Black Body: Race, Reproduction, and the Meaning of Liberty*. New York: Pantheon.

Rothberg, Michael. 2009. *Multidirectional Memory: Remembering the Holocaust in the Age of Decolonization*. Stanford, CA: Stanford University Press.

Schwartzman, Sarah. 2009. "*Children of Men* and a Plural Messianism." *Journal of Religion and Film* 13, no. 1 (April). Available at https://digitalcommons.unomaha.edu/jrf/vol13/iss1/1/.

Schweitzer, Dahlia. 2018. *Going Viral: Zombies, Viruses, and the End of the World*. New Brunswick, NJ: Rutgers University Press.

Scott, A. O. 2012. "She's the Man of This Swamp." *New York Times*, June 26. www.nytimes.com/2012/06/27/movies/beasts-of-the-southern-wild-directed-by-benh-zeitlin.html.

Scott, David. 2004. *Conscripts of Modernity: The Tragedy of Colonial Enlightenment*. Durham, NC: Duke University Press.

———. 2016. "Sylvia Wynter's Agonistic Intimations." *Small Axe* 49 (March): vii–x. doi:10.1215/07990537-3481390.

Seabrook, William. (1929) 2016. *The Magic Island*. Mineola, NY: Dover.

Sedgwick, Eve Kosofsky. 1985. *Between Men: English Literature and Male Homosocial Desire*. New York: Columbia University Press.

Sharma, Nandita. 2015. "Strategic Anti-essentialism: Decolonizing Decolonization." In *Sylvia Wynter: On Being Human as Praxis*, edited by Katherine McKittrick, 164–182. Durham, NC: Duke University Press.

Sharpe, Christina. 2013. "Beasts of the Southern Wild—The Romance of Precarity I." *Social Text*, September 27. http://socialtextjournal.org/beasts-of-the-southern-wild-the-romance-of-precarity-i/.

———. 2016. *In the Wake: On Blackness and Being*. Durham, NC: Duke University Press.

Slack, Jennifer Daryl. 1996. "The Theory and Method of Articulation in Cultural Studies." In *Stuart Hall: Critical Dialogues in Cultural Studies*, edited by David Morley and Kuan-Hsing Chen, 113–130. New York: Routledge.

Slotkin, Richard. 1973. *Regeneration through Violence: The Mythology of the American Frontier, 1600–1860*. Middletown, CT: Wesleyan University Press.

———. (1992) 1998. *Gunfighter Nation: The Myth of the Frontier in Twentieth-Century America*. Norman: University of Oklahoma Press.

Smith, Anna Marie. 1994. *New Right Discourse on Race and Sexuality: Britain, 1968–1990*. Cambridge: Cambridge University Press.

Spillers, Hortense. 1987. "Mama's Baby, Papa's Maybe: An American Grammar Book." *Diacritics* 17, no. 2 (Summer): 65–81. doi:10.2307/464747.

Stam, Robert, and Ella Shohat. 2012. "Whence and Whither Postcolonial Theory?" *New Literary History* 43, no. 2 (Spring): 371–390. doi:10.1353/nlh.2012.0010.

Stockton, Kathryn Bond. 2009. *The Queer Child, or Growing Sideways in the Twentieth Century*. Durham, NC: Duke University Press.

———. 2016. "The Queer Child Now and Its Paradoxical Global Effects." *GLQ* 22, no. 4: 505–539. doi:10.1215/10642684-3603186.

Sugden, John. 1979. "Jean Lafitte and the British Offer of 1814." *Louisiana History* 20, no. 2 (Spring): 159–167. www.jstor.org/stable/4231887.

Sully, Justin. 2016. "On the Cultural Projection of Population Crisis: The Case of *The Omega Man*." *Criticism* 58, no. 1 (Winter): 87–113. doi:10.13110/criticism.58.1.0087.

Thomas, Greg. 2006. "*Proud Flesh* Inter/Views: Sylvia Wynter." *ProudFlesh: New Afrikan Journal of Culture, Politics and Consciousness*, no. 4. www.africaknowledgeproject.org/index.php/proudflesh/article/view/202.

———. 2016. "*Marronnons*/Let's Maroon: Sylvia Wynter's 'Black Metamorphosis' as a Species of Maroonage." *Small Axe* 49 (March): 62–78. doi:10.1215/07990537-3481546.

Thrasher, Laura J. 2016. "Still Moving Images: Natality, Art, and the Temporal Structure of Inheritance." In "The Work of Return," edited by Nadine Attewell and S. Trimble. *TOPIA: Canadian Journal of Cultural Studies* 35 (Spring): 47–63.

Trimble, S. 2013. "'The Unreturning Army That Was Youth': Social Reproduction and Apocalypse in Pat Barker's *Regeneration* Trilogy." *Contemporary Women's Writing* 7, no. 1 (March): 73–91. doi:10.1093/cww/vpq022.

———. 2016. "There Goes the Neighbour Hood: On Feral Children and Alien Invaders." In "The Work of Return," edited by Nadine Attewell and S. Trimble. *TOPIA: Canadian Journal of Cultural Studies* 35 (Spring): 65–85.

Trouillot, Michel-Rolph. 1995. *Silencing the Past: Power and the Production of History*. Boston: Beacon.

Tuck, Eve, and C. Ree. 2013. "A Glossary of Haunting." In *Handbook of Autoethnography*, edited by Stacey Holman Jones et al., 639–658. Walnut Creek, CA: Left Coast Press.

Tuck, Eve, and Kim Tallbear. 2016. "Red and Black DNA, Blood, Kinship and Organizing." *The Henceforward*, episode 4, July 25. Podcast, 30:41. www.thehenceforward.com/episodes/2016/7/25/episode-3-red-and-black-dna-blood-kinship-and-organizing-with-kim-tallbear.

Udden, James. 2009. "Child of the Long Take: Alfonso Cuaron's Film Aesthetics in the Shadow of Globalization." *Style* 43, no. 1 (Spring): 26–44. http://cupola.gettysburg.edu/idsfac/16.

Vatter, Miguel. 2006. "Natality and Biopolitics in Hannah Arendt." *Revista de Ciencia Politica* 26, no. 2: 137–159. 10.4067/S0718-090X2006000200008.

Vint, Sherryl. 2007. *Bodies of Tomorrow: Technology, Subjectivity, Science Fiction*. Toronto: University of Toronto Press.

Vogel, Robert C. 2000. "Jean Laffite, The Baratarians, and the Battle of New Orleans: A Reappraisal." *Louisiana History* 41, no. 3 (Summer): 261–276. www.jstor.org/stable/4233673.

Wacquant, Loïc. 2001. "Deadly Symbiosis: When Ghetto and Prison Meet and Mesh." *Punishment & Society* 3, no. 1: 95–134.

Walcott, Rinaldo. 2015. "Genres of Human: Multiculturalism, Cosmo-politics, and the Caribbean Basin." In *Sylvia Wynter: On Being Human as Praxis*, edited by Katherine McKittrick, 183–202. Durham, NC: Duke University Press.

Wald, Priscilla. 2008. *Contagious: Cultures, Carriers, and the Outbreak Narrative*. Durham, NC: Duke University Press.

Weaver, Jace. 2014. *The Red Atlantic: American Indigenes and the Making of the Modern World, 1000–1927*. Chapel Hill: University of North Carolina Press.

Weinbaum, Alys Eve. 2004. *Wayward Reproductions: Genealogies of Race and Nation in Transatlantic Modern Thought*. Durham, NC: Duke University Press.

Whittington, William. 2011. "Sound Design for a *Found* Future: Alfonso Cuarón's *Children of Men*." *New Review of Film and Television Studies* 9, no. 1 (March): 3–14. doi:10.1080/17400309.2011.521714.

Wolfe, Patrick. 2006. "Settler Colonialism and the Elimination of the Native." *Journal of Genocide Research* 8, no. 4 (December): 387–409. doi:10.1080=14623520601056240.

Wynter, Sylvia. 1971. "Novel and History, Plot and Plantation." *Savacou* 5 (June): 95–102.

———. 1990. "Afterword: Beyond Miranda's Meanings: Un/Silencing the 'Demonic Ground' of Caliban's 'Woman.'" In *Out of the Kumbla: Caribbean Women and Literature*, edited by Carole Boyce Davies and Elaine Savory Fido, 355–372. Trenton, NJ: Africa World Press.

———. 1994. "'No Humans Involved': An Open Letter to My Colleagues." *Forum N.H.I.: Knowledge for the 21st Century* 1, no. 1 (Fall): 42–70.

———. 1995. "1492: A New World View." In *Race, Discourse, and the Origin of the Americas: A New World View*, edited by Vera Lawrence and Rex Nettleford, 5–57. Washington, DC: Smithsonian Institution Press.

———. 2003. "Unsettling the Coloniality of Being/Power/Truth/Freedom: Towards the Human, After Man, Its Overrepresentation—An Argument." *CR: The New Centennial Review* 3, no. 3 (Fall): 257–337. doi:10.1353/ncr.2004.0015.

Wynter, Sylvia, and Katherine McKittrick. 2015. "Unparalleled Catastrophe for Our Species? or, To Give Humanness a Different Future: Conversations." In *Sylvia Wynter: On Being Human as Praxis*, edited by Katherine McKittrick, 9–89. Durham, NC: Duke University Press.

Young, Rob. 2010. "The Pattern under the Plough." In "The Films of Old, Weird Britain," edited by Nick James. *Sight & Sound: The International Film Magazine* 20, no. 8 (August): 16–22.

Young, Robert. 2012. "Postcolonial Remains." *New Literary History* 43, no. 1 (Winter): 19–42. doi:10.1353/nlh.2012.0009.

Yuval-Davis, Nira. 1997. *Gender and Nation*. London: SAGE.

Ziyad, Hari. 2017. "'The Girl with All the Gifts' and Black Girls Destroying the World to Save Themselves." *Black Youth Project*, July 19. http://blackyouthproject.com/girl-gifts-black-girls-destroying-world-save/.

FILMS

Beasts of the Southern Wild. 2012. Directed by Benh Zeitlin. Cinereach.

Blood on Satan's Claw. 1971. Directed by Piers Haggard. Tigon British/Chilton Films.

A Boy and His Dog. 1975. Directed by L. Q. Jones. LQ/JAF.

Children of Men. 2006. Directed by Alfonso Cuarón. Universal.

A Clockwork Orange. 1971. Directed by Stanley Kubrick. Warner Brothers.

Day of the Triffids. 1963. Directed by Steve Sekely and Freddie Francis (uncredited). Allied Artists.

The Girl with All the Gifts. 2016. Directed by Colm McCarthy. Poison Chef.

I Am Legend. 2007. Directed by Francis Lawrence. Warner Brothers.

The Last Man on Earth. 1964. Directed by Ubaldo Ragona and Sidney Salkow. Associated Producers (API).

Last Woman on Earth. 1960. Directed by Roger Corman.

Mad Max. 1979. Directed by George Miller. Kennedy Miller Productions.

Night of the Living Dead. 1968. Directed by George A. Romero. Image Ten.

The Omega Man. 1971. Directed by Boris Sagal. Walter Seltzer Productions.

The Road. 2009. Directed by John Hillcoat. Dimension Films.

28 Days Later. 2002. Directed by Danny Boyle. DNA Films.

28 Weeks Later. 2007. Directed by Juan Carlos Fresnadillo. Fox Atomic.

Village of the Damned. 1960. Directed by Wolf Rilla. Metro-Goldwyn-Mayer British Studios.

White Zombie. 1932. Directed by Victor Halperin. Victor & Edward Halperin Productions.

The World, the Flesh, and the Devil. 1959. Directed by Ranald MacDougall. HarBel Productions.

INDEX

ABOUT THE AUTHOR

S. TRIMBLE teaches at the University of Toronto. Her essays have appeared in *The Review of Education, Pedagogy, and Cultural Studies* (2010), *Science Fiction Film and Television* (2011), *Contemporary Women's Writing* (2013), and *TOPIA* (2016). An essay on haunted houses will appear in Allyson Mitchell and Cait McKinney's edited collection *Inside Killjoy's Kastle* (2019). And Trimble coedited, with Nadine Attewell, a special issue of *TOPIA* titled "The Work of Return" (2016).